ANCIENT SICILY

ANCIENT SICILY

M. I. FINLEY

*Master of Darwin College
and Professor of Ancient History
in the University of Cambridge*

A REVISED EDITION

1979
CHATTO & WINDUS
LONDON

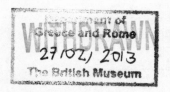
27090

Published by
Chatto & Windus Ltd
40 William IV Street
London, WC2N 4DF

*

Clarke, Irwin & Co. Ltd
Toronto

First published 1968
This revised edition 1979

British Library Cataloguing
in Publication Data
Finley, Moses I.
Ancient Sicily. – Revised ed.
1. Sicily – History
I. Title   II. Mack Smith, Denis
945.8   DG866
ISBN 0–7011–2463–6
© M. I. Finley 1968, 1979

Printed in Great Britain by
REDWOOD BURN LIMITED
Trowbridge & Esher

To
† Hugo Jones
and
Tony Andrewes

CONTENTS

FIGURES

MAPS

ILLUSTRATIONS

PREFACE

This book was originally published in 1968 as the first of a three-volume comprehensive history of Sicily, on the initiative of my friend and colleague Denis Mack Smith, who himself wrote the medieval and modern volumes. Although there are major themes, important demographic, political and cultural patterns, that recur throughout Sicilian history, ancient Sicily is a self-contained subject. That is first because the Arab conquest, with which the book closes, created a fundamental divide; and second because in antiquity Sicily was heavily and continually involved in the histories of Greece, Carthage, Rome and Byzantium in a way that was perhaps unique among the individual regions of the Mediterranean world.

The present version is more than a corrected reprint, it is a new edition. One change has been the introduction of source references. Although full account had been taken in the first edition of both the original sources and the vast modern scholarship on the subject, reference to the ancient literary sources was restricted to a rather general statement in the bibliographical section at the end of the book. Many readers have asked for more specific citation, and I have now provided it, though within limits so as not to overburden the text with minutiae that could interest only the specialist. The book was written in the first instance for the educated general reader; it offers a personal analysis, for which I take professional responsibility, not a flat summary of received ideas or a succession of scholarly controversies, many unresolved and probably not capable of resolution.

The stress in the text on archaeological evidence is made necessary by the extreme paucity of documentary evidence for long periods of time, not only in what is conventionally known as the prehistoric period but even in such later eras as the centuries of Greek colonization or the centuries of Roman rule. Within the past three decades the older pioneering efforts of Paolo Orsi and a few disciples have at last evolved into a programme of systematic archaeological exploration of the island. Now Sicilian archaeology is in floodtide, so much so that in places my book, the first attempt by a historian to evaluate and employ the new evidence synoptically, has become out of date. I have therefore revised the early chapters more than the later ones, and I must express thanks to my pupil and now colleague, Mr. Philip Lomas of King's College, Cambridge, for his advice.

I also take this opportunity to repeat from the original publication the acknowledgement of my indebtedness to friends and colleagues who were generous with their assistance: Dr. Dinu Adamesteanu, Professor A. Andrewes, Professor L. Bernabo Breà, Professor P. A. Brunt, J. A. Crook, Professor Keith Hopkins, the late Professor A. H. M. Jones, Dr. C. M. Kraay, Professor E. Lepore, Dr. G. Manganaro, Dr. P. Orlandini, Professor Stuart Piggott, J. G. Pollard, General Professor Giulio Schmiedt, J. Stevenson, Professor V. Tusa, Professor G. Vallet; and to my wife, for whom the publication of this volume in English in 1968 was what the Greeks called a *seisachtheia*.

Cambridge
August 1978

A NOTE ON PROPER NAMES

No effort has been made to be rigidly consistent in Anglicizing Greek proper names, whether of persons or of places. Where modern place-names are noticeably different from the ancient, or where they were changed in the course of ancient Sicilian history, I have given the equivalents at the first occurrence and again in the index. On the whole I have preferred the ancient names, but not always.

CHRONOLOGICAL TABLE

Prehistoric

c. 10,000 B.C.	Cave paintings in Levanzo
c. 3000	First peasant communities Use of copper
c. 1800	Beginning of Bronze Age
	c. 1600–1400 "Late Minoan" Crete
c. 1200(?)	Sicels arrive from Italy
	c. 1200 End of Mycenaean Age in Greece

Archaic (Greek)

c. 750–*c.* 580 GREEK (and PHOENICIAN) COLONIZATION
Zancle-Naxos-Syracuse-Leontini-Catania-Megara

c. 700 Motya

c. 688 Gela

c. 650 Himera

c. 630 Selinus

c. 600 Kamarina

c. 580 Akragas   Raid by Cnidians under Pentathlus

c. 570–555 Phalaris tyrant in Akragas

c. 530 Defeat of Phocaeans off Corsica

Classical (Greek)

505–466 FIRST AGE OF TYRANTS

505–491 Cleander and Hippocrates in Gela

499–494 Ionian revolt against Persia

491–485 Gelon in Gela

490–479 Persian Wars

488–472 Theron in Akragas

485–478 Gelon in Syracuse

483 Theron captures Himera

480 Carthage invades, defeated at Himera

476–467 Hiero (I)

466–405 DEMOCRATIC INTERLUDE

c. 452 Revolt of Ducetius begins

440 Death of Ducetius

431–404 Peloponnesian War

427–4 War between Syracuse and Leontini
424 Congress at Gela

415–3 Athenian invasion

410–405 Carthaginian invasion
409 Himera destroyed

xiii

Classical (Greek)

405–367 DIONYSIUS I
   398–6   First war with Carthage
           397 Fall of Motya
   388–7   Plato visits Syracuse

367–344 DIONYSIUS II
                           359–336 Philip II of
                                     Macedon
   354   Dion rules Syracuse and is
             assassinated
   346/5   Carthaginian invasion

344–c. 337 TIMOLEON
   c. 340   Defeat of Carthaginians at
              Crimisus R.

Hellenistic

                          336–323 Alexander the
                                     Great

317–289 AGATHOCLES
   311   Carthaginian invasion of Sicily
   310–306 North Africa invaded
   c. 305   Assumes royal title
 282   Gela destroyed by Phintias of Akragas
 c. 280   Carthaginian invasion
 278–6   Pyrrhus in Sicily
                          272   Rome captures
                                      Tarentum
 269   Hiero II becomes king of Syracuse

264–241 FIRST PUNIC WAR
   261   Romans capture Akragas
   250   Selinus destroyed

Republican (Roman)

 238   Rome seizes Sardinia

218–201 SECOND PUNIC WAR
   215   Death of Hiero II
   212   Rome captures Syracuse
 c. 139–132 First slave revolt
 131   *Lex Rupilia*
 c. 104–100 Second slave revolt
 73–71   Governorship of Verres   73–71   Slave revolt in
                                                  Italy under
 44–36   Sextus Pompey in Sicily   Spartacus
                                      31   Battle of Actium

Imperial (Roman)		
		A.D. 14 Death of Augustus
		117–138 Hadrian emperor
		193–211 Septimius Severus
		284–305 Diocletian
	c. 303/4 Martyrdom of S. Lucia and S. Euplus	
		306–337 Constantine
		313 Edict of Toleration
		325 Council of Nicaea
		429 Vandals capture North Africa
	440 First Vandal raid	440–461 Pope Leo I
		451 Council of Chalcedon
	468–476 Vandal control of Sicily	
	476–535 Ostrogoth rule	476–493 Odoacer
		492–496 Pope Gelasius I
		493–526 Theoderic
		527–565 Justinian

Byzantine		
	535 Belisarius captures Sicily	
		590–604 Pope Gregory the Great
		610–641 Heraclius
	651/2 First Arab raid	
	663–8 Emperor Constans II in Syracuse	
		687–701 Pope Sergius I
		689 Arabs capture Carthage
	c. 692 Sicily becomes Byzantine theme	717–741 Leo III the Iconoclast
	c. 726 Emperor confiscates papal patrimony	741–775 Constantine V
	c. 751 Sicilian church attached to Patriarchate	751 Lombards capture Ravenna
	781–2 Revolt of Elpidius	
	827 Revolt of Euphemius—Arab invasion	
	831 Fall of Palermo	
	878 Fall of Syracuse	

PART 1

Prehistoric and Archaic Sicily

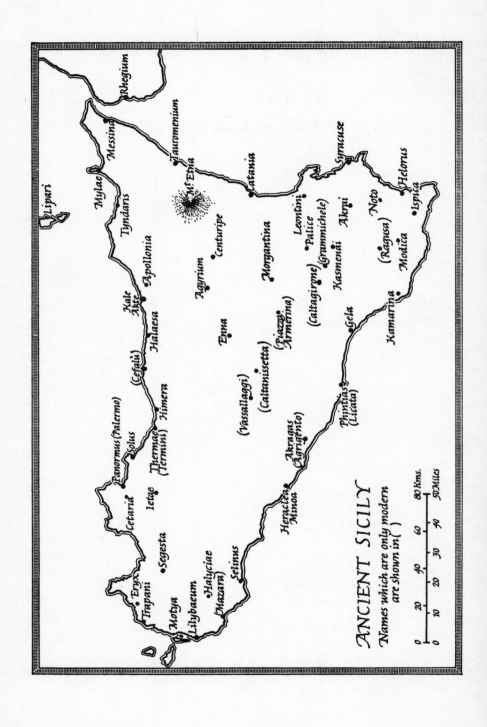

ANCIENT SICILY

Names which are only modern
are shown in ( )

Lipari

Rhegium

Messina

Mylae

Tyndaris

Apollonia

Kale
Akte

Halaesa

(Cefalù)

Panormus (Palermo)

Solus

Ietae

Thermae
(Termini) Himera

Cetaria

Segesta

Eryx

Trapani

Motya

Lilybaeum

(Mazara)

Halyciae

Selinus

Heraclea
Minoa

Akragas
(Agrigento)

Vassallaggi

Enna

(Caltanissetta)

Tauromenium

Mt. Etna

Centuripe

Agyrium

Catania

Morgantina

Piazza
Armerina

Leontini

(Caltagirone) Palice

Grammichele

Kasmenai

Akrai

Phintias
(Licata)

Gela

Kamarina

Syracuse

Helorus

Ispica

Noto

(Ragusa)

Modica

0   20   40   60   80 Kms.

0   10   20   30   40   50 Miles

Chapter 1

THE BEGINNINGS

Sicily is an island. Few islands have played a greater, or even comparable, role in history over long spans of time, and no other which is so small. Sicily is just under 25,000 square kilometres in area, less than a third the size of Ireland and less than one fourth of Cuba. But Sicily is a Mediterranean island, the biggest of those that have rightly been called "continents in miniature"[1] and which have, ever since the Bronze Age, been heavily involved in the larger affairs of Europe, North Africa and Western Asia.

Sicily is easily accessible by sea on all sides, has a variegated and fertile terrain, and an unparalleled location. At the northeast, the straits of Messina separating her from Italy narrow to a mere three kilometres at one point; in the west, the shortest distance from Africa is about 160 kilometres. The island has therefore been both a gateway and a crossroads, on the one hand dividing the eastern and western Mediterranean, on the other hand linking Europe and Africa as a stepping-stone. Cultural connections with the other regions in the Mediterranean basin can be traced back into the Old Stone Age, and when more advanced civilizations diffused westward from older centres in the east, Sicily inevitably became a meeting-place and sometimes a battleground. Her size and fertility were sufficient to raise her far above the level of the trading-post or naval station and to attract migrants and conquerors seeking a new homeland (not just a colonial dependency). Yet Sicily was not big enough to be a serious threat to neighbours in Europe or Africa, nor to retain independence against a power such as Rome in antiquity, or Spain or Italy in more modern history.

This halfway position, in both location and scale, fixed the *leitmotifs* of Sicilian history. Sicily could not long live undisturbed, except in those periods when she was securely in the possession of a strong external power. The list of migrants and

[1] Fernand Braudel, *La Méditerranée et le monde méditerranéen à l'époque de Philippe II* (2nd ed., 2 vols., Paris 1966) I 136. English translation by S. Reynolds, (2 vols., London 1972) I 148.

3

invaders in the course of ancient, medieval and modern history is considerable: unnamed prehistoric peoples, then Sicans, Elymians, Sicels, Greeks, Carthaginians, Romans and others from Italy, mercenaries and slaves from the whole Mediterranean basin, Jews, Vandals, Saracens, Normans, Spaniards and a sprinkling of others. A few, like the Vandals, merely swept through leaving no traces behind. Most stayed, however, for long periods or for all time, contributing in different ways to a continuous process of biological and cultural fusion. Today Sicily is Italian, though, as in so much of Italy, the local dialect retains deposits of earlier languages spoken on the island, the population is racially very mixed, and the cities are filled with architecture of nearly every age and style, sometimes, as in the Duomo at Syracuse (Plate 5), combined within a single building in a most remarkable way.

From the end of the third century B.C., when the Romans reduced the whole of the island to a province, foreign domination was the rule, save for relatively brief periods of independence in the Middle Ages. That meant rule to the material advantage of the foreign power at the expense of the Sicilians, through rents, taxes and plain looting. This parasitical interest inevitably (though slowly and intermittently) did great harm to the countryside and to the people. Not to all the people though, for the traditional way of ruling Sicily has been through the agency of local magnates—both 'natives' and newcomers—who shared rather handsomely in the profits in return for their services in exercising the administrative and police powers.

Despite the long history of maladministration, neglect and parasitic exploitation, Sicily today still has a considerable agricultural yield and the acreage under cultivation is large. But the productive rate for cereals is apparently no greater, and possibly even slightly less, than under the Romans, despite chemical fertilizers, seed selection and other modern technical advances. In ancient times such fertility, a consequence of the island's geology (a limestone base with heavy coatings of lava) and climate, was altogether extraordinary. "As for the goodness of the land," wrote the Greek geographer Strabo (6.2.7) who died after A.D. 20, "why should I speak of it when it is talked about by everyone?" What Strabo and his contemporaries had particularly in mind was wheat, the chief element in the diet,

4

and then wine, olives and fruits. Ancient Sicily was also a country of forests—oak, chestnut, pine and fir—especially in the mountainous regions stretching from Mount Etna west and south to Agrigento. Today no more than 5 per cent is wooded, in some provinces very much less, a basic transformation in the ecology brought about relatively recently, with deleterious effects, above all on the water supply. Since 1800 alone, the average annual rainfall at Catania, in the centre of the greatest and most fertile of all Sicilian plains, has apparently dropped some 30 per cent. Many of the island's springs have disappeared and not one river is any longer navigable.

These few comparisons are necessary not only to underscore the point that contemporary Sicily is in some ways a different island from what it had been for most of its history—different in its very look as well as in the kind of life it makes possible for most of its inhabitants—but also to explain how a region which we immediately associate with emigration in large numbers, was during so many centuries a magnet drawing migrants and invaders to itself.

The earliest migrants came by sea, for the geologists assure us that there has never been a land bridge between Sicily and either Italy or North Africa, and they came in the Advanced Palaeolithic period, perhaps before 20,000 B.C. Evidence of Old Stone Age habitation, in caves and rock shelters, is concentrated in three areas on the north coast (around Termini Imerese, Palermo and Trapani) and in the southeastern triangle, but that geographic distribution may reflect nothing more than the current state of exploration and excavation. Their stone tools link them with the cultures of central and western Europe and so does their art, in particular the engravings on cave walls (found since the Second World War) on the tiny island of Levanzo off Trapani (then still part of the land mass) and in Monte Pellegrino at Palermo. The naturalistic animal and human figures from Levanzo, mostly in profile and in excellent perspective, are in the same tradition as the cave drawings and paintings of the Rhone valley and of central and southern Spain. The Monte Pellegrino art, on the other hand, with a far higher proportion of human figures grouped in an unusual and complicated composition (Plate 1), seems to be more recent and to be linked perhaps with the later art of southern Spain. One radiocarbon date near 10,000 B.C. (9,694±110) has been reported for Levanzo but the chronology as a whole is still obscure, as is the historical development within Sicily during the long Palaeolithic era. A major impediment to study is the almost complete absence of burial finds and skeletal remains: so far only one group has been discovered, in the San Teodoro cave on the coast about halfway between Palermo and Messina.

Palaeolithic life seems to have gone on for thousands of years with little disturbance from outside. When the break came it revolutionized the island, radically changing the character of its culture and stimulating a very considerable growth and dispersal of the population. The ultimate source of the changes lay in the eastern Aegean, specifically in northern Greece and earlier perhaps still further east, in Asia Minor and Syria. That new migrants were involved seems likely, though if so—and caution is needed whenever a migration is suggested on purely cultural evidence—their numbers were probably small and they were soon biologically fused with their predecessors on the island.

What happened in Sicily, probably not long after 5000 B.C., was part of a slow transformation in the central Mediterranean region generally, that is, the emergence of peasant communities, still dependent on stone tools which they manufactured by much finer techniques, but having at their disposal the new arts of agriculture, domestication of animals, and pottery. Our earliest evidence in this region comes from potsherds alone, first from vessels with decorations impressed on the clay before firing, and later from painted pottery, both revealing an affinity with the products from Sesklo and Dimini in northern Greece that is much too close to be coincidental. Two unpainted specimens from Liguria can be dated to the period 4600–4200 B.C. and they are the oldest so far discovered in the central Mediterranean. In Sicily the earliest genuine Neolithic culture seems to be the one now conventionally known as Stentinello, after the village of that name near Syracuse where it was first identified, and where the settlement aspect is marked out by a rock-cut ditch surrounding an oval area approximately 210 × 180 metres.

It does not necessarily follow, as one might assume, that the

6

Stentinello culture, which was largely restricted to eastern Sicily and the region of Mount Etna, was brought to the island directly from the nearest land mass, namely, Italy. Both on the volcanic Aeolian islands above the north-eastern corner of Sicily (the boat sails from Milazzo), of which Lipari was, and still is, the most important, and on the Maltese islands less than 100 km below the south-eastern tip, the earliest settlements show close kinship to the Stentinello culture. In neither Lipari nor Malta is there evidence of a Palaeolithic base from which the new culture could have arisen or of a less developed Neolithic stage. The Neolithic culture seems to have begun there on an advanced level symbolized by the fortified village and the complexity of the decoration on the pottery.

Then, by about 3000 B.C., two new features appear more or less simultaneously in southern Italy and Sicily: metallurgy (the use of copper) and the rock-cut chamber-tomb. Previously graves were either shallow ditches or so-called 'cist-graves', box-like enclosures dug in the ground and usually lined with pebbles or stones. These were now replaced by chambers cut into rock, often with a sort of ante-chamber, the two together forming a structure not unlike the Sicilian peasant oven (so that some archaeologists actually call them 'oven-shaped tombs', *tombe a forno*). The famous Mycenaean bee-hive tombs are only a spectacular elaboration of the type, while the megaliths of western Europe are a transfer of the idea to a burial-chamber above the ground. The *tombe a forno* became ubiquitous in Sicily and remained the standard burial-chamber, with little significant architectural variation, until the more or less complete Hellenization of the pre-Greek population in the course of the fifth century B.C. The one notable change that did occur, perhaps by 2500 B.C., was the introduction of multiple burials within a single chamber, a new practice the significance of which is by no means clear. It probably reflects nothing more than a considerable growth in population, as does the continuing proliferation of inhabited sites all over the island (no longer concentrated on the eastern rim), a process that can be observed archaeologically for the next 1000 years or so.

On the Maltese islands the megaliths also took the form of a spectacular and unique group of monumental stone temples, the earliest known to the world. The largest, on the island of

Gozo, has a façade that may have reached 16 metres in height and a great court measuring 23 metres from apse to apse. There is no possible external source of inspiration (or any sequel) for these structures, which may date well back into the third millennium B.C. No better warning could be imagined against the old, and still not uncommon, tendency to seek a diffusionist explanation for every important cultural innovation. On the other hand, there can be little doubt that the introduction of metallurgy into this region was a borrowing either from the northern Balkans or from the Aegean.

The Copper Age, it must be understood, was one in which stone and bone were still the predominant hard materials (in Malta effectively the only ones). The age of metals really began with bronze, and in Sicily that was probably not before about 1800 B.C. Prior to that still another influence from a new quarter made itself felt, somehow linked with an extraordinarily widespread disturbance and movement of peoples noticeable all the way from western Asia across Europe to the Atlantic. On the western flank there was a complicated series of migrations, absorption and re-migration, originating in the Iberian peninsula, of people skilled in working copper and gold and identifiable by a characteristic kind of pottery known as 'bell beakers'. Their impact led to various hybrid cultures as they merged with local populations. Sicily seems to have received them or their influence (it is impossible to tell which) in the later, 'reflux' stage, either from the Iberian peninsula itself or by way of southern France and Sardinia. Apart from the appearance of bell beakers on the island, there seem to have been no startling changes, but there is an interesting, and at present unanswerable, question, tied to the hypothesis that all this migration and re-migration was responsible, among other things, for introducing dialects of the Indo-European family of languages into western Europe for the first time. What, in fact, were the languages spoken in Sicily immediately before and after 2000 B.C.?

According to the Greeks, when they first began to settle in Sicily in the eighth century B.C., they found three different peoples there, the Sicels in the eastern half, the Sicans in the west, and the Elymians in the northwest. Surviving Greek accounts (and there are no other) about these people and their

8

origins are confused and contradictory. The oldest, by the historian Thucydides writing at the end of the fifth century B.C., who took it from Antiochus of Syracuse, author of a history of Sicily from earliest times to 424 B.C., is worth quoting nearly in full (6.2.1–5):

> The most ancient people said to have inhabited a part of the region are the Cyclopes and the Laestrygones, but I cannot say what their race was nor where they came from nor where they went to. . . . The first to have settled there afterwards, it seems, were the Sicans. To believe them, they were even earlier since they claim to be autochthonous, but the truth is that they were Iberians, driven out by the Ligurians from [the shores of] the Sicanus River. It was from them that the island was then called Sicania, having formerly been known as Trinacria, and they still inhabit western Sicily.
>
> When Troy was captured, some Trojans, having escaped from the Achaeans in boats, reached Sicily, settled as neighbours of the Sicans, and took the name of Elymians in common, their cities being Eryx [now Erice] and Segesta. They were joined by some Phocians, [Greeks] who, leaving Troy, were driven by storms, first to Libya and then to Sicily.
>
> As for the Sicels, they crossed over to Sicily from Italy where they were living, fleeing the Oscans. . . . There are still Sicels in Italy, which received the name Italy from one of the Sicel kings, Italus. Arriving in Sicily in force, they defeated the Sicans in battle, drove them to the south and west of the island, and gave it the name of Sicily instead of Sicania. . . . From their arrival it was nearly 300 years before the Greeks came to Sicily.

That is what a learned Sicilian Greek believed about the island's prehistory, and it is approximately worthless. The inclusion of the mythical Cyclopes and Laestrygones is proof enough (the obvious scepticism of Thucydides about them merely reflects the views of a tiny 'enlightened' minority). The link with Troy is characteristic of much Greek legendary history, and from them it reached the Romans, who at a relatively late date proceeded to bring Aeneas from Troy to found Rome. The Sicels are a problem on their own, to which we shall return. The chronology is desperately foreshortened (as in all Greek legend), revealing no appreciation whatever of the long antiquity of Sicilian culture or of its complicated evolution. Even the different names of the island are retrospective, Trinacria reflecting the image of Sicily as a triangle with headlands at each point, never abandoned by ancient geographers.

In sum, the tradition helps not at all in identifying the pre-Greek peoples or their languages. We must admit that we know nothing about the Sican language. Of Elymian we have brief, usually fragmentary, texts on 200 potsherds of the late sixth and fifth centuries B.C. found in Segesta, and some inscriptions on coins from Segesta and Eryx. These are written in Greek characters. However, the language is clearly not Greek, but, it appears with increasing probability, an Indo-European dialect (which Sicel certainly was) of the Italic group.[1]

The beginning of the Bronze Age in Sicily is not marked by any real break in the archaeological record. The culture of the Copper Age, characterized by distinct regional variations, now acquired an improved metallurgical technique, the great importance of which was not to become fully evident for another 300 years or so. It was in the Aeolian islands rather than in Sicily that the consequences were first apparent. Lipari owed its initial importance and prosperity chiefly to one resource, a hard volcanic glass called obsidian, superior to flint for certain purposes. There is massive evidence of a large-scale obsidian industry, the products of which travelled widely. Then came a very considerable decline, the effect presumably of the new metallurgy and perhaps also of an upsurge in obsidian production on the Aegean island of Melos, another well endowed source of that material. The discovery of bronze brought a revival of prosperity, not only on Lipari but also on several of the other islands in the Aeolian cluster. There is no obvious reason why this should have happened. The production of obsidian had stopped completely. Probably the explanation is that these islands lay on the route by which metals were shipped from west to east. From 1600 at the latest, the Aeolian villages were receiving considerable quantities of goods from the Greek mainland and islands, and the trade had an unbroken continuity until the last decades of the thirteenth century B.C.

Eventually pottery from the Greek mainland and islands also found its way to Sicily along with other goods and cultural

[1] M. Lejeune, "Observations sur l'épigraphie élyme", *Revue des études latines* 47 (1970) 133–83.

influences, on weaponry for example. However, few of the finds can be dated before about 1400 B.C.; they are heavily concentrated in the cemeteries scattered along the east coast, from one of which, Thapsos north of Syracuse, the archaeologists' label 'Thapsos culture' derives. Only sporadic examples have been found elsewhere, and both their number and their variety are very much smaller than in the Aeolian islands. Apparently Sicily, lacking mineral resources, was of much less interest to her more advanced eastern neighbours than were the strategically located tiny islands to the northeast. Given Sicily's far greater size and larger population, this inference reinforces the suggestion that the Aeolian cluster owed their closer relations with Greece primarily to their position on a main sailing route. And in Sicily, too, there was a decline, if not a total cessation, of eastern imports just before 1200 B.C.

Once again the story is bedevilled by later Greek legend.[1] The fabled master-craftsman and inventor Daedalus, virtually a prisoner in Crete, escaped by making waxen wings and flying off. That was the famous occasion when his impetuous son Icarus flew too near the sun, which melted the wings, causing him to fall into the sea and drown. The more disciplined Daedalus kept close to the earth, occasionally cooled his wings by dipping them in the sea, and reached western Sicily, where he was much honoured by King Kokalos of the Sicans, for whom he constructed many engineering marvels. In time Minos, the Cretan king, took a naval force, landed on the southwestern coast of Sicily and demanded the surrender of Daedalus. Kokalos tricked Minos, invited him to a feast, and had him drowned while being bathed. The Cretan force buried their king in a great mausoleum and then, finding all retreat cut off, settled permanently in Sicily. A thousand years later, in the 480s, Theron, tyrant of Akragas, rediscovered Minos' bones and sent them home to Crete.

Scholars have made repeated attempts to discover in this legend a kernel of historic truth, a reminiscence of an unsuccessful attempt by Cnossus, in its great period about 1500 B.C., to establish a settlement in Sicily. One difficulty, however, is that the tale is incompatible with the archaeological record. Not only does it take place at the wrong end of the island, where

[1] See Diodorus 4.77.8–79.7.

traces of influence from the eastern Mediterranean at this time are very scarce and second-rate, but it contradicts the archaeological picture as a whole. All the Bronze Age objects so far found in southern Italy, the Aeolian islands and Sicily are either imports from the mainland of Greece and the Aegean islands (especially Rhodes and Cyprus) or local ware based on prototypes from these areas. Not a single identifiably Cretan ('Minoan') import is known. It is therefore hard to see why the Daedalus tale should be given any more credence than another, which had Heracles, on his grand tour of the west, swim the straits of Messina and then wander about in Sicily, again in all the wrong places (Diodorus 4.23–24). Or, for that matter, why it should have greater standing than the myth of Aeolus, keeper of the winds, and his father-in-law Liparus, from whom the Aeolian islands got their names. We know there were contacts between Sicily and the Aegean at this period. Nothing is added, except confusion and error, by insisting on a 'memory' many centuries later or by trying to draw retrospective inferences from place-names, such as Minoa, an unimportant settlement, probably of the sixth century B.C., on the coast between Agrigento and Selinunte. The Greeks were old hands at linking current activities with distant legendary and mythological figures, and these Sicilian tales could have originated at any time down to the sixth century. They can be shown to have been still further embellished and modified long after that, too, in adaptation to new political developments on the island.

The half-century ending about 1200 B.C. was again an age of widespread movement and disturbance all the way from Asia Minor to the western Mediterranean. That was when Troy and the mainland Greek power-centres were destroyed, and when changes of the greatest significance for the future were taking place in Italy. The immediate impact on Sicily was disastrous as she caught a whiplash of destruction from Italy. The Aeolian islands caught it worse: the evidence of destruction by fire speaks clearly, and the smaller islands were apparently abandoned more or less permanently. Only in Lipari did life go on; for the next 400 years Lipari was linked with Italy in a way that had never been the case before. New pottery styles match those of Apulia; a new kind of wooden house, of which many foundations remain, is central Italian, also known from, among other places, the Palatine Hill and the Old Forum in Rome; above all, the burial practice changes radically to cremation, and by 1050 or 1000 there appear the 'urnfields' which were characteristic of the whole of central and much of western Europe.

Similar cultural traits appear at the nearest point in Sicily, in Milazzo, but nowhere else on the island (apart from rare and scattered exceptions). And that brings us back to the mystery of the Sicels. This ought to be the moment of their entry into Sicily from Italy, and an intrusive hand-made pottery attests the introduction of an alien population. Villages in the coastal plains in the district around Syracuse were abandoned and the people moved to the greater security of the hills, where they lived in relatively large concentrations to judge from the vastness of their cemeteries (at Pantalica and elsewhere). But they continued to bury their dead in rock-cut chamber-tombs, not in urnfields, and most of their still traditional pottery and their implements bear no resemblance to the ware from Italy and Lipari. Such connections as can be traced are still with the eastern ·Mediterranean at first, and then with the west. For 400 or 500 years Sicilian cultural history appears to be very complex and varied, but the lines of development were unaffected by what was happening in Italy. Lipari was again destroyed about 850 B.C., for reasons we do not know, and remained uninhabited until a Greek settlement was established there after 600. But Sicily went its own way until the eighth century, when the Greeks began to migrate to the island and brought it finally into the historical age.

How much did this long period of prehistory contribute to historical Sicily, in particular to Sicilian culture under the Greeks? Obviously there was a physical contribution, so to speak, in the sense that much land had been cleared and brought under cultivation. And the Greek settlers found wives among the natives, and also a labour force. Other than that, however, the lasting effects of the pre-Greek populations would not seem to have been very significant. Even in religion the impact appears to have been mostly topographical. The Greeks, like their predecessors, maintained cults of the dark subterranean powers, associated with such natural phenomena as mountain grottoes and hot springs, not surprising in an island dominated by the highest volcano in Europe, Mount Etna, which is never completely dormant.[1] One instance of continuity is particularly noteworthy, the cult of the Palici, whom the Greeks converted into sons of Zeus, at a place, now uninhabited, about 40 km west of Catania just off the main inland road to Caltagirone.[2] In the crater of an extinct volcano there is a small lake in which the water bubbles and gives forth gaseous vapours, hence its present name, Laghetto di Naftia. If a considerable number of Greek and Roman writers are to be believed, the water was once much more active, with two geyser-like jets constantly in evidence. This water had miraculous powers: it could judge right from wrong, the gods promptly punishing anyone who swore a false oath there, some say with death, others with blindness. In the mid-fifth century B.C. a certain Ducetius, aiming at a Greek-style tyranny, claimed to be heading a Sicel 'liberation' movement, and he secured the blessing of the Palici. Three hundred years later they were still on the side of the oppressed, this time in support of a major slave revolt.

[1] If there is little reference in this volume to serious eruptions of Mount Etna, that is because not more than 12 or 14 are attested for the whole of antiquity, only one of which, in 122 B.C., was heavily destructive. Earthquakes, even more surprisingly, are virtually unrecorded.

[2] For what follows, see Diodorus 11.88.6–90.2; 36.3.3; 36.7.1.

Chapter 2

THE COMING OF THE GREEKS

The Greek colonization of Sicily was an impressive operation and rather a mysterious one. The word 'colonization', conventional among historians to describe what happened, is actually misleading insofar as it suggests the establishment of subject communities overseas, as in North America in the sixteenth, seventeenth and eighteenth centuries, or in Australia in the nineteenth. The westward emigration from Greece was an organized movement, to be sure, equipped, armed and planned by various 'mother-cities'. The effect, however, and, so far as we can tell, the intention were from the outset not to colonize but to encourage (and sometimes to compel) men to move out permanently to new and independent communities of their own. Details are lacking. Although the Greeks had become literate by this time, having borrowed and improved the Phoenician alphabet, they did not yet employ the new art to keep historical records. In consequence, their own traditions about the opening up of Sicily and the west, preserved in Greek writers of later centuries, are very unsatisfactory, a combination of myth and heroic legend rather than history. One reasonably sober example, the accepted story of the foundation of Syracuse as repeated by the geographer Strabo (6.2.4), reads like this:

Archias, sailing from Corinth, founded Syracuse about the same time that Naxos and Megara [also in Sicily] were established. They say that when Myscellus and Archias went to Delphi to consult the oracle, the god asked whether they preferred wealth or health. Archias chose wealth and Myscellus health, and the oracle then assigned Syracuse to the former to found and Croton [in southern Italy] to the latter. . . . On his way to Sicily, Archias left a part of the expedition to settle the island now called Corcyra [modern Corfu]. . . . The latter expelled the Liburni who occupied it and established a settlement. Archias, continuing on his journey, met some Dorians . . . who had separated from the settlers of Megara; he took them with him and together they founded Syracuse.

15

This stress on a few individuals and their quarrels is characteristic of most of the traditions, as is the advisory role of the Delphic oracle. There is little reference to the deeper social reasons which drove so many Greeks, time and again, to go off on a most hazardous and uncertain adventure. There is nothing about how the new settlements were organized, their size or their early history, apart from scattered references to internal conflicts and wars among them. Nor is the question seriously posed as to how much knowledge any particular group had of the territory to which it was heading, or how it obtained its information. We need not credit the Delphic oracle with too much practical wisdom. "The oracle assigned them Syracuse to found"—that oft-repeated formula is a later fiction, at least in most cases, designed to provide sanction after the fact. And this question of knowledge is the great puzzle in the story.

Greeks were sailing in the Aegean Sea with some regularity, having even established a trading-post or two in northern Syria by about 800 B.C., and we must suppose that an occasional ship also entered the western Mediterranean. Otherwise the earliest of the westward migrations would have been unthinkable. Explorers precede settlers, and in this period the 'explorers' were presumably merchants, shading off into pirates, seeking metals, above all, in central Italy and Spain. They may have been Greeks or Phoenicians or both. Despite the unanimous Greek tradition that the Phoenicians had preceded them in the west (even to the wildly inaccurate assertion that there were Phoenician outposts in Tunisia and Spain as early as 1200 B.C.), there is no clear archaeological evidence of either a Greek or a Phoenician presence in the western Mediterranean much before 750 B.C., and then the two peoples began to leave traces in the record at about the same time. It is hard to find evidence earlier than the settlements themselves, but that is not very surprising. Nor is it puzzling that our earliest Greek literature, the poems attributed to Homer and Hesiod, which were almost certainly composed in the early colonization age, are vague, confused and inaccurate about Sicily, Italy and the surrounding seas. In the *Odyssey* the west is still a land of monsters and wonders (and even Thucydides, as we have seen, repeated the tradition of fabled inhabitants in Sicily). No one could have drawn a map of Sicily or of the Italian mainland. But then, common European beliefs about the Atlantic Ocean and the Americas in the seventeenth century were not much better.

What mattered was that there was enough knowledge for the specific practical objectives. Archaeology has confirmed the ancient tradition that the first Greek settlement was on the island of Ischia, but a mainland community was soon set up as well at Cumae, north of Naples, both probably by 750 B.C. These were not, geographically speaking, either the nearest or the most obvious places to choose, unless access to Italian metal deposits was one aim, if not the only one; this explanation is supported by the indication that the most active Greeks in these first moves were Euboeans, the islanders who had already taken leadership in the Levantine trade, also with metals as the prime objective. Not many years went by before there were two further settlements on the sailing route, at Zancle (later Messina) in Sicily and then at Rhegium (now Reggio) in Italy, the most strategic points on the straits of Messina. Neither Messina nor Reggio is situated in notably fertile territory; in this respect, as in their deliberate siting on the sea-route, they constitute an exception among the colonies in both Sicily and southern Italy (the latter conventionally referred to, collectively, as Magna Graecia, the Latin translation of the Greek *Megalē Hellas*).

Sicily lacks metals, and there is no other reason why purely trading ventures from Greece should have been calling there with any regularity. The colonization of the island was otherwise motivated, by a desire to make a new life on the land. Not even Syracuse was an exception, despite its magnificent harbours (Figure 1). In the eighth century, and for a long time to come, the Greek habit was to beach their ships. That is why they were able to plant two of their most successful Sicilian settlements on the south coast, where there are good beaches but no harbours worthy of the name. One was at Gela, lying on a small plateau by the sea, the other at Akragas (called Agrigentum by the Romans, Girgenti from the Arabic period until recently, and now Agrigento), which is some three kilometres from the sea and never had a proper harbour in antiquity, though at its apogee it exported large quantities of fruit and

17

agricultural products by sea, chiefly to North Africa. Syracuse, too, drew its wealth largely from its soil, hence its ruling aristocracy were known as the *Gamoroi*, which means literally 'those who divided the land'. Once established, of course, these colonies had their commercial activities as well, but that is a different matter. Unlike a trading-post, they were chiefly concerned to further their own interests rather than those of the motherland. Hence the Euboean colonies and Gela were as willing to import Corinthian pottery as was Corinthian Syracuse.

The early merchant-explorers, in sum, found the sea-lanes and spied out the land, to be followed by a genuine emigration. In the second half of the eighth century there were three foundations in the great Catanian plain and its northern extension east of Mount Etna: first a relatively unimportant one at Naxos, a headland below Taormina which is the first landfall a ship would reach by the prevailing current coming from the east round the 'instep and toe' of Italy; then Leontini, nine kilometres in from the coast, at the southern edge of the plain; and last Catania (Katane in Greek) itself. In the same period, Syracuse was established as well as Zancle and Megara Hyblaea, this last a rather unhappy and not very successful colony on a poorish site less than twenty kilometres north of Syracuse. Finally, in 688, according to the traditional date, the first colonizing wave in Sicily from overseas was completed with the foundation of Gela. We have no figures for the early population, though no doubt each colony originally numbered its households only in the hundreds, most of the women presumably natives, since it is hardly likely that an adequate number (if any) were brought from Greece. Each new foundation had an acknowledged 'mother-city', which provided the leader of the expedition and did the planning, but there was nothing exclusive about the operation, and men joined in from other Greek communities at the start as well as in such later recruiting as may have occurred. The official founders of the four most northern colonies were Chalcidians from Euboea, of Megara Hyblaea men from Megara, of Syracuse Corinthians, and of Gela a combined Rhodian-Cretan group.

Intensive archaeological study in the present century has shown not only that the successful colonies grew rapidly and

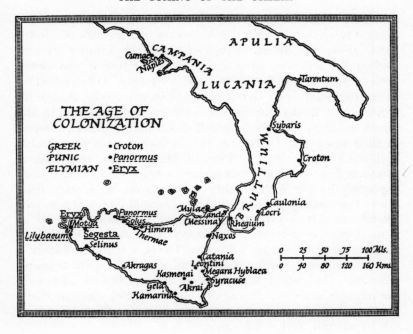

THE AGE OF
COLONIZATION

GREEK   • Croton
PUNIC   • Panormus
ELYMIAN • Eryx

flourished, but also that they differed significantly in their relations with the Sicels. Both at Naxos and at Leontini there is evidence that the first Greek migrants and the Sicels lived side by side for a time, the latter being pushed out only gradually. At Leontini, for example, the Greeks first occupied the Colle S. Mauro, while the Sicels maintained their old settlement on the adjoining Colle Metapiccola. Not till half a century later did the Greeks take over the latter, too, extending their original fortification walls to encompass Metapiccola and the intervening valley, and making the valley the centre of their public life. The Sicels now disappear from the archaeological record there, whether absorbed or expelled we cannot say.

Outside the immediate zone of the Greek settlements, peaceful and useful relations continued with the Sicels of the interior so long as the Chalcidian colonies remained independent communities, which means until Syracuse became the dominant power in eastern Sicily at the beginning of the fifth century B.C. Greek goods were moved inland through several natural routes—following the Alcantara valley north of Mount Etna, along the Simeto River or along the smaller streams feeding the southern part of the plain. At first it was Greek pottery which was both imitated and imported (including vases from mainland Greek cities), but eventually the architecture and finally the graves were radically altered to the Greek manner, and religious influences manifested themselves in their sculpture. In return, the Sicilian Greeks presumably took out timber from the slopes of Mount Etna, and pastoral products from the highlands further west, some of which were exported, by the fifth century at the latest, to Greece itself where they were highly rated. An occasional Greek also moved inland, usually a craftsman. Only at Grammichele and at Serra Orlando (ancient Morgantina) near Aidone does there seem to have grown up an actual Greek settlement within a Sicel community, from about the middle of the sixth century. Grammichele is about fifteen kilometres east of Caltagirone on the modern road from Syracuse, but the Greek element there, judging from the archaeological remains, was Chalcidian and not Syracusan, and at Morgantina too.

The upshot of this Chalcidian activity was that by 500 B.C. the whole Sicel area as far as Enna seems to have become Hellenized. That statement must be qualified by a warning; we can judge solely from material remains, lacking any information about their ideas and beliefs, their social customs or their politics. And it is certain that Hellenization did not immediately destroy their self-consciousness as Sicels or their desire to remain free from overlordship by the original Greek settlements. Otherwise the claim of Ducetius to be leading a Sicel revolt in the middle of the fifth century B.C. would be unintelligible, as would, later in the same century, the explicit assertion by Thucydides (6.88.3–4) that the Sicel communities assisted the Athenians when they invaded the island in 415 and attacked Syracuse.

At Syracuse the pattern of relations had been different from the Chalcidian all along. The colonists began by conquering and subjugating the Sicels of their district, reducing them to a servile status (except, presumably, for those women the Greeks took as wives, at least in the first generation or two). Herodotus

and later Greek writers record a special name—*Kyllyrioi*—
for these subjects, whom they classified as slaves, but they provide neither details nor any clear indication of the fate of this
system in subsequent times. The position of the Kyllyrioi may
have been analogous to that of the Spartan helots (also classed
as slaves in a general sense). If so, they lacked freedom of
movement or occupation and, in effect, they worked in-
voluntarily for the Syracusan citizenry; but, unlike the more
familiar chattel slaves, they could not be sold or removed
from the land they tilled and they retained their own family
and community life, a 'national' existence, one could almost say.

Within a century of its foundation, Syracuse established
three strong-points: in the interior at Akrai (now Palazzolo
Acreide) about halfway on the road to Grammichele, then a
few kilometres further west at Kasmenai (at Monte Casale), and
on the coast at Helorus below the present Noto Marina. That
these were military-strategic points and not independent communities is fairly certain, and the only possible reason for them
at so early a date is a continual and serious struggle with the
Sicels outside the immediate territory of Syracuse. In these
districts the Sicels who were not reduced to the status of
Kyllyrioi were apparently pushed into a sort of 'reservation' in
the southeastern corner, centring about modern Ragusa,
Modica and Ispica.

There is no satisfactory explanation for the difference in
behaviour between the Chalcidian communities on the one
hand and Syracuse on the other. The Geloans, it should be
added, followed the latter pattern. They found the coastal
plain virtually unpopulated, and in the years following their
settlement they drove the Sicels out of the ring of hills to the
north and occupied various sites as strong-points, at Butera, for
example. Because the Corinthians, Cretans and Rhodians, the
main elements in Syracuse and Gela, brought to Sicily the
Dorian Greek dialect, whereas the northern colonists, apart
from Megara Hyblaea, belonged to the Ionian-speaking wing,
some historians have suggested a basic temperamental difference as the root-cause. They point further to the propaganda
which we find in some fifth-century writers, when Greek
Sicily was deeply divided, calling upon Dorians to support
Dorians and Ionians to support Ionians. But the propaganda

was never wholly successful, and it is anyway not helpful in explaining a phenomenon two or more centuries earlier, at a time when, at home, there was little other than dialect to distinguish Corinthians or Rhodians from Chalcidians. Furthermore, when about 600 B.C. Syracuse did set up a genuinely new independent community, Kamarina on the south coast some 115 km away (due south of modern Comiso), she soon found herself at war with the latter, who sought and won the support of the Sicels of the Ragusa region. That they were willing to help Kamarina is explained by the fact that this Syracusan offshoot, like the Chalcidians, seems to have maintained peaceful relations with the natives. Kamarina was presumably the place from which some Greeks went to settle among the Sicels at Ragusa in an enclave not unlike that at Grammichele and of about the same date. Yet the inhabitants of Kamarina were as Dorian as the Syracusans and the Geloans.

The irrelevance of the supposed racial factor is further driven home by still another foundation, in which Chalcidians cooperated with Dorians. About 650 a group from Zancle joined with refugees from Syracuse, sailed along the north coast, and settled at Himera, an easily defended site with a restricted hinterland but good anchorage. At the same time or perhaps two decades later (the date depends on complicated archaeological arguments), Selinus was founded from Megara Hyblaea, probably with reinforcements from the original Megara in Greece. This, too, was not the most obvious choice on the south coast, for it lacks a harbour or even good shelter and it has a marshy river delta. However, unlike Himera, Selinus possessed fertile lands and quickly became a flourishing city, perhaps partly through trade with Carthage. Finally, in 580, if we accept the traditional date, Akragas on the south coast, some 100 km east of Selinus, was established by Geloans and Rhodians, to become, in the long run, Syracuse's only real rival on the island in wealth and power.

Akragas completes the story of Greek colonization in the strict sense, but it is far from the end of the settlement history. The number of cities at the time the island passed into Roman hands in the third century B.C. was many times greater than those so far mentioned. Some, such as Tauromenium (Taormina) or Agyrium, the native cities of the ancient Sicilian historians Timaeus and Diodorus respectively, were Sicel towns that had been dragged into the Greek power struggles of the fourth century B.C., when tyrants forcibly depopulated and repopulated almost at will. Other Sicel towns of the interior managed to escape that fate, became Hellenized without any noticeable Greek influx, and in due course slipped into the catalogue of Greek cities quietly, so to speak. A good example is Centuripe, a few kilometres east of Agyrium on the Catania-Palermo road, about which the literary tradition has virtually nothing to say, but which blossomed at the end of the Greek period as an important ceramic centre, specializing in terracotta figurines, and which remained well-favoured and prosperous under the Romans.

The establishment of Himera, Selinus and Akragas brought the Greeks into the Sican and Elymian districts and marked their furthest westward movement, along with Thermae (modern Termini Imerese), about 15 km west of Himera, where there was a settlement from just before 400 B.C., and Mazara, about halfway between Selinus and Marsala, where the Selinuntines for a time maintained a trading-post, presumably for their African commerce. The Sicans, who were apparently thinner on the ground than the Sicels, seem also to have been more resistant to Hellenization, the Elymians still more. Hence the development in the interior west of Enna is not comparable in scale and rapidity to the Hellenization of the eastern regions. Admittedly Greek goods from Gela made their way into Sican territory quite early: to the northeast as far as Caltagirone, on the border of the Syracusan and Chalcidian spheres, north to Piazza Armerina, and, above all, up the Salso valley from Licata on the coast to the Caltanissetta district. In the sixth century many Sican sites were transformed and fortified, taking on a clearly Greek aspect. However, in their new look they seem to have been garrison-points rather than new Greek cities, and even in Roman times they remained insignificant in contrast with the eastern part of the interior.

In the Elymian territory the puzzling exception was Segesta, where, as has already been noted, the Greek script was adopted though the native language remained in use, and where the shell of a Doric temple was built in the late fifth century that still stands as one of the greatest of surviving Greek temple-remains. The people of Segesta had even become so Greek, or at least so un-barbarian, in Greek eyes that a formal agreement was eventually made with Selinus accepting intermarriage among their respective citizens as legitimate (Thucydides 6.6.2). This last is particularly significant. Such arrangements were by no means universal even among purely Greek cities. Besides, Segesta and Selinus were enemies for much of their history, a pointer to the possibility that it was the Elymians who were responsible for the Greek failure to take over the whole of Sicily at an early date. That is, if any explanation from outside is needed; it is more likely that the Greeks stopped where they did simply because at the time they had no reason to go any further.

Nothing has been said so far about the Phoenicians, the favourite scapegoat (as perennial aggressors) ever since antiquity. The day was to come when Carthage, a Phoenician settlement in Tunisia, and the Greeks of Sicily would engage in prolonged and violent conflict (as later Carthage and Rome). But archaeology has now proved that it is unwarranted to read anything back from the later struggles. Phoenician foundations in Sicily, concentrated in the north-west, were neither numerous nor expansive. Their preference for headlands and off-shore islands gave modern historians the impression that the sole concern was for anchorage and trading-posts. However, recent study has demonstrated that they were proper settlements with an agricultural hinterland. Thus, the first of them, ancient Motya (modern San Pantaleo), a tiny low-lying island just off the western shore in the shallow, sheltered lagoon now known as the Stagnone di Marsala (Figure 4), had its farms on the mainland. The earliest archaeological evidence of the Phoenician presence in Motya is to be dated shortly before 700 B.C., in the same period when similar establishments appeared on the eastern and southern coasts of Sardinia and in Spain. In the seventh century Phoenicians also settled at a place known to the Greeks and Romans as Panormus (Palermo), possibly Ziz in their own language (Plate 7d), and elsewhere in that region, notably a little further east at Soloeis (Thucydides 6.2.6), the location of which is still under debate but is certainly not at modern Solunto, the site of a fourth-century Greek foundation. And if these few, relatively insignificant settlements, are not enough to demonstrate Phoenician disinterest in competing with Greeks for the control of Sicily, further proof comes from the presence of Greek products in Motya and Palermo (and soon of Greek inhabitants, at least in the former). The first faint hint of conflict can be dated to about 580, and then the responsibility must be assigned to Greeks, not Phoenicians.

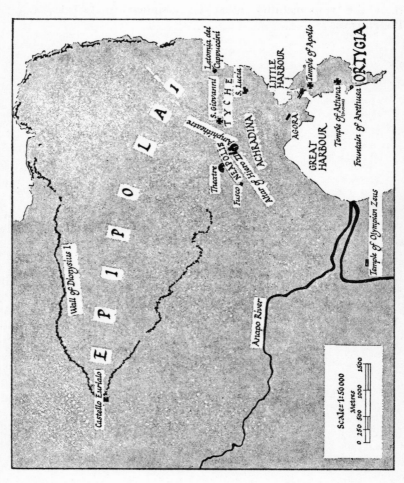

Fig. 1   Ancient Syracuse

Chapter 3

ARCHAIC SOCIETY AND POLITICS[1]

Unreliable and over-imaginative as the foundation stories may be, they are at least evidence of a sort. For the subsequent 250 years the surviving literary tradition about Sicily is hopelessly thin and broken. And archaeology cannot greatly help us reconstruct social institutions or politics. It is demonstrable, as one would have guessed anyway, that the colonists brought with them and retained their dialects and script, their technology, their favourite gods and myths, their cult and burial practices and their calendar, their political and social terminology. In time an occasional Sicel word crept in, but the language remained fundamentally 'pure' Greek as long as Greek was spoken on the island. The impact of native religion was perhaps greater, but that is hard to trace except by implication, for the divine names and the externals of the rituals were, so far as we can tell, thoroughly Hellenized. There were also shifts in emphasis within the Greek traditions. Thus, the popularity of Demeter, goddess of the fertility of the earth, and her daughter Persephone (or Kore), who spent part of the year with Hades-Pluto in the underworld, is no surprise in a region of such fertility: Sicily even challenged the claim of Eleusis (near Athens) to be the place where Demeter first gave man the gift of corn, and Enna was pointed out as the site where Hades seized Persephone and brought her to his house. In the same sort of myth-making process, Heracles got his grand tour of Sicily, which took him all the way to Eryx (to be followed later by Aphrodite) and thereby sanctioned Greek claims to the north-western part of the island. Perhaps it is more than coincidental that the first full-scale literary treatment of that theme known to us is a longer poem of Stesichorus, writing by 600 B.C., whose home city, though not necessarily his birthplace, was Himera, the new Greek settlement which impinged most closely upon Elymian territory.

[1] The term 'archaic' is a conventional and useful label for that period in Greek history which runs from 800 or 750 to 500 B.C. (in round numbers). The following two centuries are called 'classical'.

Stesichorus is a shadowy figure to us, barely discernible behind the handful of scattered lines which survive of his large
poetic output. In antiquity, however, he had an enormous
reputation, among poets as well as laymen, for he was one of

Fig. 2   The Agora of Megara Hyblaea, about 600 B.C.

Key: 1 and 2, Temple. 3, a, b, c, Unidentified sacred area. 4, Unidentified area. 5 and 6, Stoa. 7, Unidentified. 8, Council building.

the great names in the formative period of the Greek choral lyric. He thus symbolizes the important fact that Greek Sicily was, and felt itself to be, altogether and fully Greek, not just a rude, distant outpost. A Greek from Athens or Corinth would have found himself in familiar surroundings in any of the Greek cities of Sicily. Each had its unmistakably Greek central square or Agora, temples and other public buildings, and cemeteries outside the city proper. The most recent excavations at Megara Hyblaea reveal that, though the Agora was not framed by appropriate public buildings until the latter half of the seventh century B.C., the space had been left unoccupied from the eighth-century foundation, as if in preparation for an Agora (Figure 2). As the city grew, streets were set out and then the Agora was 'created' by the erection of two small temples on the southern edge, and a roofed colonnade or stoa on the eastern and the northern side. Each of these buildings blocked off a road. But the western side of the Agora was left open, again in typically Greek fashion; they regularly avoided complete enclosure of the central square (in this instance a trapezoid), for that would make it difficult of access, both for ordinary social purposes and for marshalling the citizenry whenever required.

The oldest of the great Doric temples of Sicily, now a pitiful ruin, was erected in Syracuse near the causeway end of the island of Ortygia (Figure 1); built of sandstone and probably dedicated to Apollo (or to Apollo and Artemis together), it has been dated on stylistic grounds to about 575 B.C., which, if correct, would place it quite early in the history of this type of Greek architecture, not much later than the temple of Hera at Olympia. At Selinus, Himera, Akragas and elsewhere, the initiative first taken at Syracuse (and repeated there in other temples) was followed in the course of a century and a half, resulting in a series of splendid monumental buildings. However, if a visitor from old Greece were perceptive, he would have been perplexed by the rarity of sculpted reliefs on the friezes and pediments (as later, under the tyrants, by the extraordinary size of the temples). He might then have gone on to notice other Sicilian peculiarities, in the carving of the lion rain-spouts at Akragas and Himera (Plate 3b), or in the way sculptors created their figures out of the local stone. Apart from

Selinus in the sixth century, no Sicilian city seems to have developed its own distinctive school of sculpture (Plate 3a). But neither did many cities on the Greek mainland, and the Sicilians were handicapped by the unavailability of native marble. It is difficult to strike a balanced judgment in these matters. Why, for example, should the ruins of little Megara Hyblaea have hidden a surprisingly large quantity of sculpture, far from contemptible in quality (Plate 2a), when so little good stuff has been found in some greater and richer sites? And what significance may one attach to the view of modern experts that there are artistic nuances common to Sicilian work, from the sixth century on, which distinguishes it from that of the rest of the Greek world? It is doubtful that the Sicilian Greeks themselves would have placed much emphasis on these differences. They would have preferred to stress their Greek-ness.

It was made easy for the Sicilian Greeks to keep in step by the continuous traffic which went on between Sicily and the old Greek world. The first colonists attracted further settlers in the following decades and centuries, and the newcomers were by no means all down-and-outs or fugitive criminals. Presumably the tempo and quality of migration at any given moment were determined largely by what was happening at home rather than by Sicilian developments. Our documentary evidence on the subject is so slight as to be virtually non-existent, but there are enough hints pointing to the arrival of skilled craftsmen, of larger groups who went west for the same reasons as the first migrants, of political exiles (including Sappho in about 600 B.C.), and, in the end, of poets, architects and philosophers who came at the summons of patrons. Some were mere visitors; others found the new world disillusioning and returned home; but archaeology has provided sufficient proof of a steady growth in population and in the total inhabited area, which natural increase alone can scarcely explain. At Syracuse, for example, the original settlement occupied both the island of Ortygia and a bit of the mainland in the district of Achradina (probably not physically linked by a causeway before 550 B.C.), and a single cemetery sufficed, located at Fusco on the mainland across the then swamp of Syrako (Figure 1). But by about 640 at the latest, a second necropolis was provided, the so-called Giardino

Spagna near the present church of Santa Lucia, and by 600 still another was established nearby. The way in which the population filled out Akragas, a very spacious city, from, or soon after, its foundation in 580, is further proof both of internal growth and of drawing power.

Apart from migration, there were also continuous commercial traffic and what one might call ceremonial traffic or even pilgrimages, though without most of the usual overtones. Greeks from Sicily shared in the pan-Hellenic sentiment that was gathering around certain shrines, notably at Delphi and Olympia. Obviously it was more difficult and more expensive to go there from Sicily than from places in continental Greece and we have no evidence of the scale of movement, let alone statistics. But it is certain that Sicilian Greeks consulted the oracle at Delphi and that they entered the festival competitions at Olympia (as later at Delphi and the Isthmus of Corinth) when the games began in the seventh century to draw competitors from beyond the immediate neighbourhood. In our incomplete records of Olympic victors for the first two centuries of the games, the first Sicilian named is a certain Lygdamis of Syracuse, winner in 648 of the *pankration*, a brutal contest in which boxing, wrestling and kicking were combined. His grave was pointed out in later times near one of the *Latomie* or quarries, but, since he was also reported to have been as big as Heracles and never to have sweated, he sounds a pretty legendary figure. Tisander of Naxos seems more firmly based on reality: he won the Olympic boxing four times and the boxing at Delphi four times, too, but he brings us down to a fairly late date, between 572 and 558.

Regular travel for ceremonial purposes was perhaps most common between the individual Sicilian settlement and its mother-city. The absence of political controls, or even of political ties in any proper sense, had the positive effect of keeping the way clear for relations in other spheres that were not without meaning even though they had little or nothing to do with politics and power. It was the accepted convention to turn to the mother-city whenever a personality was required for a momentous occasion. Thus, Pammilus was invited from Megara in Greece to act for Sicilian Megara as the official founder of Selinus; one of the three 'founders' of

31

Himera was presumably from Chalcis, one of the two at Akragas from Rhodes. In 492 Corinth provided mediators when Syracuse was threatened by the armies of Hippocrates, tyrant of Gela, and in the desperate troubles of the mid-fourth century Syracuse again appealed to Corinth, and Timoleon was sent to the rescue. Except for this last instance, they were neither political nor military interventions but honorific ones, providing a valued moral authority, paternal but free from force or compulsion. In the same spirit, the new settlements were expected to send embassies regularly to the main religious festivals of the mother-city, with appropriate gifts to the patron god or goddess.

One flaw arose in this sort of relationship from the mixed (though technically Greek) populations which became the rule in Sicilian cities. The original Cretan element in Gela could hardly have felt any particular attachment to Rhodes, for example. Aristotle in the *Politics* (1303a27–28) goes so far as to generalize on the point: "most states which mixed their settlers, whether originally or later on, suffered from sedition". His Sicilian examples happen to be late; more relevant is the case he cites of Sybaris in Magna Graecia on the Italian mainland, founded jointly by Achaeans and men from Troezen, the latter of whom were soon expelled when the Achaean element were further reinforced from home. And generally the 'kith and kin' appeal, frequent though it may have been, and even strong, was never potent enough to override all other considerations. Kamarina was at war with her mother-city Syracuse within half a century of her foundation. The Chalcidian cities in the plain of Catania, in contrast, lived in harmony with each other, as with the Sicels, throughout their independent history.

One of the more puzzling aspects in this matter of inter-relationships is the trading side. Our knowledge of Sicilian commerce for the whole archaic period rests almost entirely on a single commodity, painted pottery. An article of daily use, it is unique both because it is durable and because even fragments can often be identified and dated with considerable accuracy. That is why pottery looms so large in the writings of archaeologists, who are gripped by an understandable tendency to exaggerate its economic importance as well as the firmness of their own speculations. During the first century of the

1 Late Palaeolithic cave drawings, Palermo

2 a. Marble *kouros*, Megara Hyblaea, 1.19 m. tall, mid-6th cent. B.C.

2 b. Silver drachma, Zancle, about 500 B.C. (twice actual size)

obverse

reverse

2 c. Silver didrachm, Gela, early 5th cent. B.C. (twice actual size)

colonization period, virtually all the pottery imported into Sicily was Corinthian, and Corinthian predominance continued even after Rhodian and other East Greek ware became quantitatively significant (from about 650) along with, though to a lesser extent, Etruscan bucchero ware from mainland Italy. Euboean pottery is much more difficult to distinguish (and the subject is still controversial), but the conclusion seems correct that, despite the great Euboean contribution to the first colonization wave, all visible Euboean interest in the west ceased rapidly, by 700 B.C. As for Megara, she never produced exportable pottery, and anyway, by 650 at the latest, Megarian interests shifted to the Dardanelles and the Black Sea region. Finally there was the special case of Athens, a city which played no part in the colonizing activity at any time, but which began to enter the Sicilian markets with especially fine pottery in the sixth century, slowly at first, but after 550 at a rate which drove out all the others within a few years.

What does this bald factual outline mean in terms of policies and politics? Terms like 'commercial rivalry' and even 'commercial imperialism' come easily to mind, but they are not reconcilable with the observed facts. To begin with, Corinthian pottery was about as widely exported in Greece as in Sicily. And when the Athenians 'drove it out', they apparently did so inside Corinth, too, with little noticeable effect on Corinthian strength or prosperity. In Sicily, furthermore, there was not much correlation in the distribution pattern of pottery between colony and mother-city. Corinth had only one colony there, Syracuse, and there is no reason to think that Syracuse had a rôle in spreading Corinthian goods through the island or that Corinth maintained any political relations with Gela or Akragas or Leontini. The seventh- and sixth-century archaeological record is not significantly different in Rhodian Gela from that of Corinthian Syracuse.

Nor can we say much about the carrying trade other than that the Sicilian Greeks themselves were not active participants. Syracuse alone ever had a navy worth mentioning and that not before the fifth century. The absence of a navy implies the absence of a merchant fleet capable of carrying cargoes across the Ionian and Aegean seas. Euboea, Corinth, Rhodes were all early sailing centres and they, as well as other Aegean islanders and later the Phocaeans of Asia Minor (modern Turkey), could all have shared, and probably did, in the exporting to the west. It is also probable that these same people, and especially the Corinthians, cheerfully carried on with Athenian commodities after the Athenian take-over. The Rhodians are the most likely to have brought glass and faience objects and other specialized products from Egypt and Phoenicia, but the Phoenicians themselves cannot be ruled out, just as, in turn, it cannot be said whether or not Greek Sicily was a trans-shipment centre for Greek pottery destined for Carthage, Motya and Malta. Inter-local trade within Sicily seems largely to have been restricted to traffic from Greek communities to the natives in the interior, rather than between the Greek cities.

There is one final puzzle: What did Sicily pay with? Wheat, olives, wine, timber, fruit, nuts and vegetables, and the products of pasturage and the chase were all abundant, and presumably the answer lies there. Only later, when large-scale internecine warfare developed, would enslaved captives have become an additional factor. (Exploitation of the sulphur resources, the only other possibility, is not attested before Roman times and not important before the eighteenth century.) It is unlikely that Sicilian wine and olive oil were in much demand in Greece, with ample supplies of its own, but there came a time when they are known to have been shipped to North Africa, Italy and Gaul in considerable quantities. The later Sicilian Greek historians, Timaeus and Diodorus (13.81.4–5), attributed the wealth of Akragas in the fifth century B.C. to its olive and wine exports to Carthage. We may make due allowance for exaggeration, and a touch of moralizing, in their account of the excessive luxury which prevailed in that city: when Exaenetus scored the second of his two victories in the *stadion* (approximately a 200-metre race) at Olympia in 412 B.C., he was greeted on his return by a triumphal procession of 300 chariots, each drawn by two white horses, "all belonging to citizens of Akragas" (Diodorus 13.82.7). Yet the basic truth of the picture is witnessed by the eight or nine temples that were constructed (one not completed) between 480 and the end of the century, a number exceeded at the time only by Athens in the entire Greek world. In Selinus, where a century of extraordinary

34

architectural activity began much earlier, before 550 B.C., exports to North Africa must also have lain at the root of the prosperity. A large temple, even if constructed of soft stone and not marble, was a considerable burden on the resources, and especially the skilled manpower, of an ancient community, from the quarrying and transport of the stone, sometimes in blocks weighing a ton or more each, to the finishing decorative touches. The ability to carry off such a project not once but repeatedly in a continuing activity, whatever the motivation, is therefore an index of wealth, especially where there were no shrines like Delphi or Olympia to attract rich contributions from outside.

However, for the eastern trade, for the pottery and other goods coming from Corinth and the rest, the main return cargo must have been wheat, supplemented perhaps in a small way by timber, wool, hides, honey, cheese, and an occasional Sicel or Sican slave. The importance of Sicilian wheat to Greece, where wheat shortage was a chronic problem, is well documented from the beginning of the fifth century. That we know nothing about this traffic earlier is presumably just the consequence of the general lack of literary evidence for archaic Sicily, upon a topic on which archaeology can throw no light in the nature of the case. The silence of the sources prevents us from saying anything specific on the subject. Not even the coin-finds help. The idea of coining, that is to say, of officially stamping bits of metal of a uniform weight, started in Asia Minor about 625 B.C., spread rapidly in Greece, but did not reach Sicily until after 550 B.C. The time lag is not surprising; it is really more remarkable that enough silver was available at all. In the sixth century Selinus, Himera, Akragas and Zancle alone had a substantial output of silver coins (Plate 2b), whereas in the next century Syracuse and Gela replaced Selinus and Himera as main mints. Any attempt to link coining closely with trade, and particularly foreign trade, then founders on the fact that scarcely any Sicilian coins have been found outside the island (not even on the Italian mainland), either in systematic excavations or in the accidental discovery of hoards. Corinthian coins are absent from finds in the island in this period (unlike the late fourth century B.C.), precisely at the time when Corinthian pottery dominated the scene. But then, the Phoenicians, Carthaginians and Etruscans did not yet bother to coin at all, and the conclusion is imposed that commerce managed very well by the age-old methods of direct exchange of commodities and of exchange of goods for money in the form of 'unofficial' metal pieces or bars which were weighed and assayed as the occasion demanded. Metal in that form, it goes without saying, never becomes part of the archaeological record. Coinage, a singularly Greek passion, in its early years performed primarily non-commercial functions, of a political and political-psychological character, as becomes clear later in the history of Greek Sicily.

Further, there is no need to posit the existence of a numerically or socially significant mercantile and manufacturing class in Sicily in this period. With the overseas traffic largely in the hands of men from abroad, with a negligible inter-local trade, there was little scope for such a class within the Sicilian communities themselves. Nor would the landowning aristocracy have been averse to dealing directly with foreigners seeking their wheat or other products. Manufacture was undoubtedly handicraft production on a small scale, as everywhere in the Greek world at the time, and it was probably not before the fifth century B.C. that an occasional entrepreneur developed a relatively large establishment with slave labour, like the Syracusan arms-maker Cephalus who migrated to Athens in the middle of that century. None of the Greek-style pottery so common on Sicel sites has been found in the Greek settlements: this shows that they were made either by itinerant Greeks or by the Sicels themselves, and that there were no workshops in the Sicilian Greek cities producing pottery for this not inconsiderable market.

Tenure of land was what mattered most, and again we are faced with a puzzle. It was the rule throughout antiquity that a new settlement, of whatever status, began with a division of land among the colonizing group, and that is what happened in Sicily and Magna Graecia. What we should like to know is the basis on which this was done. Presumably the 'founder' received special treatment, but otherwise was the share-out equal or not? There is a brief old moralistic tale about a Corinthian named Aethiops, a member of Archias' original party, who so lacked discipline that he bartered away his allotment at Syracuse for a honey-cake even before reaching the place (Athenaeus 4.167D). Even if this were by some wild chance a true story, it is not illuminating.

More promising at first sight is a circumstantial account, preserved by Diodorus (5.9.2–5) writing in the first century B.C. but based on older sources, of what happened when Greeks resettled Lipari. About 580 B.C. a joint group from Cnidus in Asia Minor and Rhodes, led by a Cnidian, Pentathlus (a descendant of Heracles, it should be noted), made an unsuccessful attempt to establish themselves in western Sicily. After various adventures, including participation in a war on the side of Selinus against Segesta, they were driven out by the Elymians and Pentathlus was killed. The survivors started for home, put in at Lipari where they were well received by the five hundred people of the old stock who still inhabited the island, decided to settle there, and created a Greek community into which the natives were fully incorporated. What followed, according to Diodorus, fell into three stages, for which he provides no timescale. First, when they were being harassed by Etruscan pirates, they divided the community into two halves, one charged with fighting the pirates, the other with cultivation of the land, which they decided to hold in common. Second, they returned to private possession the land in Lipari itself, where the city-centre was located, but continued to retain the farmland in the other islands in common. Third, they shifted to a system of periodic redistribution of the land by lot at twenty-year intervals.

How much truth there is in this tale is debatable and a firm answer is probably out of reach. It is not a sufficient objection to point out that on the archaeological evidence Lipari was uninhabited at the time the Cnidians arrived, or that other ancient writers, who accept the fact of a Cnidian foundation, which remained in existence, make no mention of the Diodoran details. The main point for present purposes is that Diodorus treats the whole story as most unusual, as a response to a special situation created by piracy. (It is worth adding that there is a serious question whether the Liparans were the victims or the pirates or both). Certainly neither he nor his original source thought for a moment that Lipari was a model of colonial practice, and we are left no nearer an answer to our basic question than before. Most modern historians then argue that, since the world from which the colonists came was one of inequality of property and of a monopoly of political power by the landed aristocracy, that was the pattern most likely to have been reproduced in the new world. Quite possibly. The humbler colonists may have been happy to gain a peasant's holding, conceding the larger claims of their betters. But the argument remains necessarily speculative, and one is free to speculate in another direction, that people who had chosen or had been forced to migrate because of an inequitable condition were not likely to have slavishly repeated that condition when they had a free hand. Some support for this alternative may be seen in the recent discovery that the cemeteries of Megara Hyblaea reveal no significant class distinctions before the middle of the sixth century.[1]

Either way, the Sicilian communities soon enough found themselves in the old Greek pattern. Power grew in the hands of a group of aristocratic families or clans, who had a preponderant share of the wealth, which meant the land, and control of both the priestly functions and the administration of justice. Equally familiar was the endemic malady which the Greeks called *stasis*, a word with a range of meanings running from factional dispute to civil disturbance and outright civil war. Few examples are known from the earliest period in Greek Sicily, all of one type, that of conflict within the oligarchy. Aristotle (*Politics* 1303b17–26) tells how at Syracuse "in ancient times" a personal incident, a squalid quarrel between two young officeholders over a love affair, soon split the ruling class in two and finally led to a constitutional change. What that was he unfortunately does not say nor does he date the conflict precisely. It may, but need not, have occurred about 650, when the Myletid family were expelled from the city and joined in the foundation of Himera. At about the same time Gela also went through some such crisis. What rôle, if any, was played by newcomers or by the poorer classes is not known.

About 600, however, there is the first known instance in Sicily of the class-war type of *stasis* which was widespread in Greece at just that time, and apparently under roughly iden-

[1] M. Cébeillac-Gervasoni, in *Kokalos* 21 (1975) 32–4.

tical conditions and around more or less identical issues. At least, the very little information that has come down about the civil war in Leontini, then (and for some time to come) one of the richest of the Sicilian communities, to judge from the gold ornaments and other treasures found in their graves, suggests that a certain Panaetius was able to seize power by putting himself at the head of the poorer citizens in armed conflict against the traditional aristocratic cavalry. Panaetius made himself tyrant of Leontini, thus introducing the institution round which Sicilian history pivoted for the next three centuries. He was followed in the next generation by the much more famous, or rather infamous, Phalaris of Akragas, who is best dealt with when we come to consider tyranny in detail.

Our understanding of what was going on would be greatly advanced if we could penetrate the legends about the 'lawgiver', Charondas of Catania.[1] Later tradition converted him into a Pythagorean philosopher and attributed to him a bewildering variety of improbable laws and ethical precepts. Comic poets poked fun at his supposed law punishing any second marriage which imposed a stepmother on children of the first marriage. In a mime written by the third-century Herondas of Cos he was 'quoted' by a brothel-keeper bringing a suit against one of his clients. Even his date was forgotten and he was variously placed in the seventh, sixth and fifth centuries. Aristotle knew better on the whole and dismissed much of the legend. He saw Charondas as a moderate (to be bracketed with Solon in Athens) whose law code, marked by unusual clarity and precision of drafting, leaned on the side of the rich against the majority. Aristotle gave the example of weighted fines, invented by Charondas as a device to compel the rich to perform their judicial duties while making it easy for the poor to avoid them. The possibility—and one cannot place the odds any higher than that—is that Charondas, like another famous lawgiver in the west, Zaleucus of Locri in Magna Graecia, was thrown up by the growing social struggles in the seventh or early

[1] The key text on Charondas (and Zaleucus) is Diodorus 12.11–21. It is reprinted, together with all other testimonia and some commentary, in *Inscriptiones Graecae Siciliae et infimae Italiae ad ius pertinentes*, ed. V. Arangio-Ruiz and A. Olivieri (Milan 1925), Appendix I.

sixth century (surely not the fifth) and prevented outright civil war by a compromise, the key to which was a written law code. Whatever else the commons may have demanded and failed to achieve, this action (like similar codifications in Greece and early Rome) was an important gain for them. While the aristocracy monopolized the administration and while the law remained traditional and unwritten, the opportunities for "crooked judgments" were infinite. A written set of laws was a useful brake, and no doubt Charondas also modified some of the individual laws at the same time and perhaps made some constitutional changes. But the governmental structure remained basically oligarchic. If, furthermore, the tradition is to be trusted, his work was then accepted in the other Chalcidian colonies as well, and no more is heard of *stasis* in those communities.

Hoplite soldiers (the heavy-armed infantry), tyrants and lawgivers are all signs that Sicily had entered the difficult transitional stage from the archaic to the classical period of Greek civilization, to the *polis* or city-state period. Ideally a *polis* was a small, exclusive, self-governing community, with an urban centre where the main activities of government, including the state religion, were carried on and where not only the artisans and shopkeepers but also the wealthier classes resided, and with a more or less extensive rural hinterland. How a *polis* was governed was up to a point irrelevant in the concept. It could be oligarchical or democratic, provided only that it was free from outside authority and that the idea of the exclusive community was retained in respect to a variety of rights and duties, political rights in the narrow sense and also, for example, the right to own land. Membership in the community was not achieved by mere residence, not even long-term residence. Not only were slaves excluded but also free men (and their descendants) who came to live there from elsewhere, so that in the more advanced and prosperous, and therefore more attractive, city-states of the classical period, the citizen-body were sometimes outnumbered by the sum of the resident aliens ('metics') and the slaves. On the other hand, there was no distinction in law between the urban and rural sectors. The word 'city' as we have been using it must be understood not as a geographical term but politically, as meaning a community of people, the city-dwellers and the farmers together. In Greek linguistic usage this distinction was brought out very sharply: one travelled to Syracuse but one made war against the Syracusans.

It would be difficult to exaggerate the Greek insistence on local autonomy. By 500 B.C. there were many hundreds of city-states in the Greek world, which extended from the south-eastern corner of the Black Sea to Marseilles. They were all conscious and proud of being Greek and they supported cultural pan-Hellenism, at the Olympic Games, for example. They liked to think that all Greeks should and would co-operate with each other against a common danger. But their passion for local autonomy was equally strong, and often stronger. Even voluntary leagues of city-states were difficult to organize and maintain for long periods. Wars between neighbouring city-states were common. Internal stresses were often the determining factor in external relations. The ideal of a self-governing community was constantly coming up against the reality of gross inequalities, in wealth as in power. Local patriotism had its limits. When *stasis* reached the civil-war stage, the factions tried to destroy each other; to that end, they sought help from outside when they could, among "barbarians" (a term broad enough to include Carthaginians and Etruscans along with Sicels and Elymians) as well as among other Greek states. Patriotism beyond the city-state, Greek patriotism, was not a sentiment one could count on in practice.

Nowhere was the gap between the ideal and reality greater than in Sicily. It would even be fair to say that there the very idea of the city-state proved a failure. Why that should have been the case is perhaps the most interesting question in the classical phase of Sicilian Greek history. The tyrants were the main operative agents of failure, the Carthaginians the main external threat. But it was the Sicilians themselves who converted Carthage into a menace, and that story may just possibly have begun with Pentathlus and his Cnidians in 580. The fifth-century B.C. historian, Antiochus of Syracuse, said that they were driven out of Sicily by Elymians and Phoenicians.[1] If that is right, the reference need mean no more than the inhabitants of Motya, who would not have welcomed a settle-

---

[1] Pausanias 10.11.3; Diodorus 5.9.3 has a different version, omitting the Phoenicians.

ment at Lilybaeum (modern Marsala), controlling the entrance to the bay. Or it might mean that the Carthaginians, rapidly becoming the strongest power among the Phoenicians of the west, added their weight.[1] Friendly communities on the western fringe of Sicily were essential to Carthage, and for that reason the seizure of Motya would have been serious.

Soon there came a threat from a different front. The Phocaeans, who had established a colony at Marseilles which served as a base for trade and piracy all along the French and Spanish coasts, now moved to the western Mediterranean in greater numbers and proceeded to be troublemakers. They set up a base at Alalia in Corsica, harassed the Carthaginians in Sardinia and Carthaginian and Etruscan shipping generally. Possibly the Cnidians at Lipari were making their contribution, too. In the end, the piracy and raiding brought about an alliance and an agreement over spheres of influence between Carthaginians and Etruscans, which lasted for quite some time. Together they crushed the Phocaeans in about 530 B.C. Sardinia was secured for the Carthaginians, Corsica became Etruscan. These operations obviously did not enhance Carthaginian love for Greeks, nor did the futile attempt of the Spartan Dorieus to settle Greeks in the neighbourhood of Eryx, and still no direct conflict arose in Sicily. Selinus and then Akragas continued to grow rich on trade with Carthage. There was no Carthaginian expansion on the island, no forceful interference. Why should there have been?

---

[1] Historians have adopted the convention of employing the adjective 'Punic' (from the Latin) for the western Phoenicians from this point on to distinguish them from the eastern Phoenicians.

PART 2

The Greek Tyrants

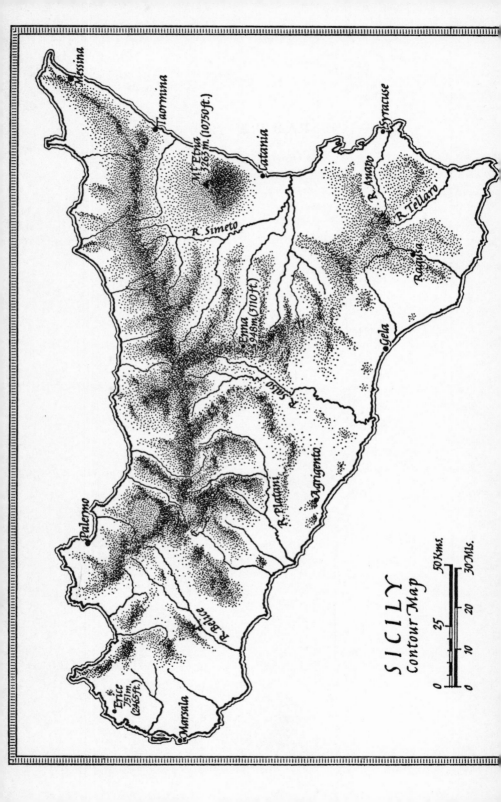

SICILY
Contour Map

Chapter 4

THE FIRST TYRANTS

The growth in population and wealth which characterized sixth-century Sicily was accompanied by increasing unrest and conflict, of the common people against the ruling oligarchies, of one oligarchic faction against another, of one city against another, and, in some areas, of natives against Greeks. Energetic individuals began to capitalize on the troubles, seizing power outside the law, embarking on territorial aggrandizement, making and unmaking vassal-tyrants in other cities, massacring and transplanting populations, enfranchising mercenaries and immigrants in considerable numbers. Tyrants made their appearance early: the shadowy Panaetius in Leontini, Phalaris in Akragas from perhaps 570 to 555, and a few others. But it was the four decades ending in the revolution of 466 B.C. in Syracuse (with similar actions elsewhere) which made up the first age of tyranny in Sicily, an age which foreshadowed so much of later Sicilian history. Wars at home and abroad, ruthlessness in the struggle for power, and a brilliant upsurge of cultural life went hand in hand, at a cost in lives and misery which cannot be measured.

Although some of the tyrants found it useful, especially at the beginning of their careers, to trade on popular aspirations, they themselves belonged to the wealthiest aristocratic class. Phalaris had previously held a high financial post. The brothers Cleander and Hippocrates, who ruled at Gela in succession from 505 to 491, were the sons of Pantares, victor in the four-horse chariot race at the Olympic Games in 512 or 508, the first, so far as we know, of a line of Sicilian princes and magnates to compete (as owners, of course, not as charioteers) in that most expensive, most aristocratic and most glory-bringing of all events in Greek games. Hippocrates was succeeded in the tyranny by the commander of his cavalry, Gelon, member of a family which held the hereditary right to the priesthood of "the gods of the underworld" in Gela, and which traced its descent to one of the original colonists of that city. Gelon, who later transferred his base to Syracuse after capturing it in 485, entered into complicated family arrangements with Theron, tyrant of Akragas from 488 to 472, a man of immense wealth and most distinguished ancestry: the cabal of nobles which overthrew Phalaris was led by either his grandfather or his great-grandfather. Theron took as second wife the daughter of Polyzalus, brother of Gelon, while the latter married Theron's daughter Damareta. After Gelon's death she passed to Polyzalus along with the tyranny in Gela, in accordance with Gelon's will, and another brother, Hiero, who was married to Theron's niece, took power in Syracuse. Gelon, Theron and Hiero were all successful in the Olympic chariot race, but Polyzalus had to be content with a Pythian victory at Delphi.

The predecessors of Hippocrates are mere names except for Phalaris, that remarkable and perplexing figure of myth. A late writer records that he seized power first by misappropriating a large sum entrusted to him for the construction of a temple of Zeus—he used the money to hire a mercenary force of foreigners and slaves whom he installed in an armed camp on the Acropolis; then by taking advantage of a peaceful religious assembly to massacre many males and hold the women and children as hostages. The tale is told circumstantially, but it has too many parallels in the large corpus of anecdotes about Sicilian and other Greek tyrants. As the historian E. A. Freeman observed a century ago, "All these stories of the rise of tyrants are suspicious . . . , differing in detail, but essentially of the same kind . . . . nothing is easier than to put the name of one city and one tyrant for another."[1] Phalaris ruled for some fifteen years, and for that whole period we are informed only that he conducted successful campaigns against neighbouring Sican communities and that he became a model of monstrous behaviour, not excluding a gastronomic taste for infant children. His greatest claim to fame was the hollow brazen bull in which he roasted those who won his displeasure, the first victim, according to the legend, being the smith who fashioned the contrivance ("the only just act which Phalaris ever committed"). The bull was later thrown into the sea, in one version; alternatively, it was removed to Carthage in 406 as spoils of war —there was a famous argument about this among Greek and Roman historians as late as the second century B.C.

[1] *History of Sicily*, vol. 2 (Oxford 1891), p. 82.

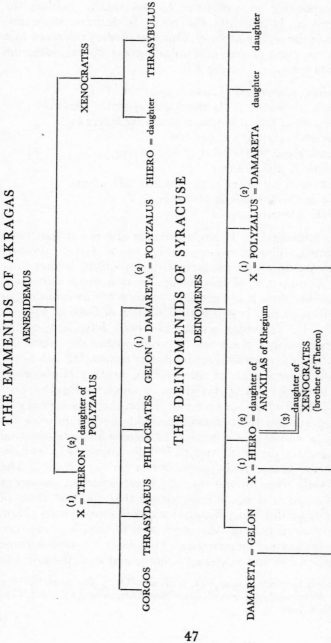

Fig. 3 The Emmenids and Deinomenids

It is impossible to penetrate to the reality behind the Phalaris myth. Historically the myth is perhaps more important than the reality anyway. Our first literary reference to it comes at the close of one of Pindar's great choral odes, the *First Pythian* composed in 470 B.C.

> *The generous achievement of Croesus fades not.*
> *But hateful everywhere is the speech that oppresses Phalaris*
> *the heart without pity, who roasted men in the bronze bull.*
> *Nor lyres under the roof welcome him*
> *as the sweet theme for the voices of boys singing.*
> *Good fortune is first of prizes,*
> *and good repute has second place; the man who attains*
> *these two and grasps them in his hands*
> *is given the uttermost garland.*[1]

That was addressed to Hiero, by whom the poem had been commissioned. The complex ambiguity of Greek tyranny (which cannot simply be equated with despotism) is thus fully exposed. The themes of this particular ode merit closer examination, but first it is necessary to consider in some detail the four decades that began with Cleander in Gela in 505.

Actually, for Cleander we do not even have any of the usual stories, neither of his rise to power within the prevailing oligarchic regime nor of things he did as tyrant. He was assassinated after seven years of rule and his brother Hippocrates then had to engage in a brief civil war in which the loyal support of the popular Gelon was no small factor. Archaeological evidence suggests that the two brothers laid the groundwork for Hippocrates' subsequent conquests in eastern Sicily by erecting fortifications on the northern rim of hills above Gela and by enlarging the army, with special stress on the cavalry. The plains of Gela were among the best horse-breeding regions of the island, and it is not a coincidence that the first coins of Gela, struck at this time, featured a naked cavalryman (Plate 2c). One reason, perhaps the main one, for coining was convenience in paying mercenaries. The silver no doubt came from confiscations and exactions at home and from the sale into

[1] Richmond Lattimore, *Some Odes of Pindar*. Copyright 1942 by New Directions. Reprinted by permission of New Directions Publishing Corporation, New York.

48

3 b. Lion's head, Himera

4. Metopes, Selinus,
early 6th cent. B.C.
Above: Winged sphinx
Right: Europa and
the bull

4 a.
Pebble pave-
ment mosaic,
Motya, probably
about 400 B.C.

4 b. *Tophet* or sacri-
ficial burial-
ground,
Motya

slavery of captives, Sicels at first, Greeks soon thereafter. No racial distinctions were drawn in this respect or in some others: Hippocrates' hired troops included Sicels as well as Greeks. Then, his home base and his army secured, Hippocrates crossed the mountains and invaded Chalcidian territory. Sicilian terrain presented few difficulties to marching armies. Naxos, Zancle and Leontini were quickly taken and placed under vassal-tyrants.

At Zancle the conqueror became involved in complex and confused foreign affairs. In part the situation derived naturally from Zancle's location on the Straits. But the immediate complications followed from the revolt of the Ionian Greeks of Asia Minor against Persian suzerainty. The Persian conquest had earlier made itself indirectly felt in the west: the Phocaean incursions were one consequence; another was the migration of a number of outstanding intellectuals, Pythagoras of Samos much the most famous of them, who, with their disciples, put southern Italy and Sicily in the forefront of Greek philosophical and theological inquiry. Stress must be laid on the indirect effects of Persian rule: it was not so much the Persians that these eastern Greeks fled from, as the political turmoil and civil war which followed within many of their own communities.

The internal troubles of the Asia Minor Greeks flared sharply with the outbreak of revolt in 499. Flight and exile became common and the Zancleans took the occasion, for reasons which are far from clear, to invite Ionian refugees to found a new settlement in Sicel territory on the coast forty miles east of Himera, at a place the Greeks called Kale Akte (Fair Shore), now Caronia Marina. A response came from a group led by upper-class Samians following a disastrous naval defeat in 494. However, by the time they reached Locri in southern Italy, two events had changed the picture. One was the capture of Zancle by Hippocrates, who left the city in charge of a mysterious figure named Scythes. The latter had given up the tyranny in Cos, an island in the eastern Aegean, in order to go to Sicily (with the permission of the Persian king). At about the same time, Anaxilas set himself up as tyrant in Rhegium, which in the sixth century had outstripped Zancle in wealth and cultural achievement. The new situation in Zancle, now in control of so powerful a ruler as Hippocrates, may have frightened

Rhegium; or Anaxilas may have thought, on the contrary, that Zancle had been weakened by conquest. Whatever the explanation, he intercepted the fugitive Samians at Locri and persuaded them not to go on to Kale Akte, but to seize Zancle instead. This they did easily because at the moment Scythes was off with his army on a Sicel raid.

Scythes and the Zancleans summoned Hippocrates, whose first action was to arrest Scythes for failure to protect the city. Next he made a deal with the Samians, leaving Zancle to them in return for half the movable goods and the slaves within the city, and everything outside. Many of the Zancleans he enslaved, but he handed over three hundred of the leading citizens to the Samians to be put to death, a fate which, strangely enough, they were then spared. Scythes also escaped, fled to Himera and from there to the Persian court, where, says Herodotus (6.24), Darius "considered him the justest of the Greeks who had come to him, for, having gone to Sicily with royal permission, he came back from Sicily to the King."

Hippocrates was now ready to try for the greatest prize of all, Syracuse. As for the Samians, they held Zancle for about five years until Anaxilas chased them out and repopulated the city with "men of different origins" (Thucydides 6.4.6), including Messenians from Greece, presumably those who succeeded in escaping during an uprising in 490 of Messenian helots against their Spartan masters. Anaxilas was himself of Messenian ancestry and he now gave Zancle the name it has had ever since, Messina.

Syracuse presented Hippocrates with a challenge more serious than any he had faced before. He had no navy—Gela had no harbour—and without one the capture of Syracuse would normally have been extremely difficult if not impossible. However, there was political unrest in Syracuse and Hippocrates hoped that the lower classes would welcome him as a release from the oligarchy of the Gamoroi. He was disappointed. No support was forthcoming and presumably that is why he accepted the mediation of Corinth in 492. The treaty provided that Hippocrates would release the Syracusan prisoners he had taken in a battle on the Helorus River; in return Syracuse ceded to him Kamarina, which they had once destroyed but which was now flourishing again, as we see from the archaeological evidence. Hippocrates officially became the city's new 'founder' and presumably introduced new settlers. He then went off on another campaign, this time against the Sicels, probably on the slopes of Mount Etna, and he was killed in battle.

Gelon immediately assumed the role of protector of Hippocrates' young sons. But as soon as he was able to reassert tyrannical authority in Gela, he put the boys aside and took power for himself. What he did in the next few years is unclear. Presumably that is when he entered into alliance with Theron of Akragas, which was both political and dynastic through marriage. He may also have helped the latter against Selinus with whom there was chronic conflict for possession of Minoa, a Selinuntine offshoot at the mouth of the Platani River (ancient Halycus), some 40 km west of Akragas. In 488 he won the chariot race at Olympia and dedicated both the chariot and a statue of himself at the shrine. The dedication reads "Gelon son of Deinomenes, of Gela, dedicated (me) to Zeus. Glaukias of Aegina made (me)." Then came his great opportunity. The commons of Syracuse, acting in conjunction with the servile Kyllyrioi, finally did rise against the Gamoroi. The oligarchs retired to the strong point of Kasmenai and in 485 appealed to Gelon for assistance. The revolution had failed to create a stable government in Syracuse—Aristotle (*Politics* 1302b31–2) says the new democracy was falling into anarchy—and no resistance was offered.

Once in control, Gelon decided to transfer his base there altogether (leaving Gela in charge of his brother Hiero) and to make Syracuse a populous and powerful city, well fortified, with an imposing navy and a large army. He achieved his aim with great rapidity and by the most elementary of devices. He moved more than half the population from Gela to Syracuse. He is said to have destroyed Kamarina, which Hippocrates had re-founded only a few years before, and to have transferred its inhabitants to Syracuse. An incredibly stupid attack by the oligarchs of Megara Hyblaea, who were then in the midst of a *stasis* of their own, enabled him to incorporate their territory into his. As for for Megarian people, in Herodotus' words (7.156), "he brought to Syracuse the men of substance, who had instigated the war and therefore expected to be put to death, and he made them citizens; the common people, who had no share in the responsibility for the war and therefore expected to suffer no evil, he also took to Syracuse and there he sold them into slavery for export outside Sicily. . . . He did this . . . because he thought the commons were most unpleasant to live with." At some point he also enfranchised many of his mercenaries, perhaps more than 10,000 as Diodorus says (11.72.3).

In ten years Gelon had made himself the most powerful individual in the Greek world, perhaps in all Europe. The Greeks knew it, and in 481 an embassy arrived to seek his help against the Persian invaders of Greece. Gelon is supposed to have offered to supply the whole Greek army with wheat for the duration of the war, and to send 200 ships, 20,000 heavy-armed infantrymen, 2000 cavalry, 2000 archers and 2000 slingers, on condition that he be made commander-in-chief of the coalition army and navy. The condition was unacceptable and the offer was refused. We do not have to believe the account of the negotiations (Herodotus 7.156–62), and it is unimaginable that Gelon had any intention of responding on any terms to the appeal of Hellenic patriotism against a far-off king who was no threat to him. His interests and his problems lay in Sicily and the west. However, the army figures (though not those for the navy) have a chance of being an accurate catalogue of the total force at his disposal. If so, they indicate a population in and around Syracuse that no Sicilian community was again to equal from the Roman conquest to the modern era. There is some archaeological confirmation, too, for this was the period when the urban settlement spread north and west into the district still known as Neapolis or New Town (Figure 1).

The Gelon-Theron power bloc was now in control of most of Greek Sicily. After Theron took Himera from its tyrant Terillus in 483, only Selinus and Messina stood outside and their prospects of retaining independence looked poor. Terillus was 'guest-friend' of the Carthaginian leader Hamilcar (the first of a number of Carthaginians of that name to be involved in Sicilian history). He was also the father-in-law of Anaxilas of Rhegium, who was still in control of Messina. Terillus and Anaxilas appealed to Carthage for military assistance, presumably with the passive, if not the active, support of Selinus.

And Carthage responded, the first but by no means the last foreign invader of Sicily to be invited in.

The massivity of the Carthaginian response is not easy to understand, except by those who believe in a predestined war to the death between two races. Granted that no one could be certain of the limits of Gelon's ambition, the Carthaginians and the Sicilian Phoenician communities could reasonably fear a direct attack one day on the latter. Yet neither that fear nor any other visible Carthaginian interest in Sicily itself sufficiently explains why three years should have been spent in building up a vast armada, including troops from North Africa, Spain, Sardinia and Corsica, or why the invasion should have been commanded by Hamilcar himself, the sufet or chief magistrate of the city. The answer more probably lies in the larger issues of western Mediterranean politics. The *entente* which had been established between Carthage and the Etruscans was beginning to lose its effectiveness because of a weakening in the Etruscan position. There are hints in our evidence to suggest that after Rome broke free from Etruscan domination in 508, Carthage tried to reshape her alliances and even to intervene directly in Italy. A revival of active piracy was always a threat in such conditions, and there was at least one outbreak based on Sicily when a Phocaean named Dionysius, admiral of the Greek fleet which was defeated by the Persians at Lade, made his way to the island and from there "made piratical raids on Carthaginians and Etruscans, but not on Greeks" (Herodotus 6.17).

Whatever the explanation, Carthage invaded in strength in 480, landing at Palermo and from there proceeding by land and sea to Himera under the guidance of Terillus. Although this was Theron's war in the first instance, it was Gelon who won it, while the invaders had to battle alone, Anaxilas and the Selinuntines mysteriously abstaining. The Greek victory was decisive. Hamilcar was killed, his ships, drawn up on the beach, were burned. Escape was thus blocked and a large number of prisoners were taken and enslaved, many ending up in private hands, the rest in public employment on temples and other works. Carthage paid a large cash indemnity, which enabled Gelon to increase markedly the issue of the new Syracusan coinage he had instituted on a modest scale when he took power five years before. With the spoils he also built temples of Demeter and Persephone in the new quarter of Neapolis, and he made a rich dedication in Delphi. This time the inscription read "Gelon son of Deinomenes, of Syracuse, dedicated the tripod and the Nike to Apollo. Bion son of Diodorus, a Milesian, made (them)."

With the battle of Himera all hostilities ceased abruptly. No move was made against the Phoenician communities in Sicily, nor did Carthage return to the struggle or threaten for another seventy years. Selinus prospered. Anaxilas went off a few months later to win the recently instituted (and short-lived) mule-cart race at Olympia. He was allowed to retain Messina and in turn he seems to have accepted and reconciled himself to the superior power of the Syracusan tyranny. He married his daughter to Hiero, perhaps after Gelon's death in 478; he obeyed Hiero's order to abandon an attempt to conquer Locri; he died peacefully in 476.

Ten years after Himera, in the *First Pythian* already quoted, Pindar referred to Gelon's victory in the context of "gathering back Hellas from the weight of slavery". That this was the 'party line' in Sicily can hardly be doubted, and it marks the beginning of the myth of a barbarian threat to civilization by Carthage which was to play such a role in the following centuries, helping to bring about the very threat it imagined and surviving into present-day historical writing. The diffusion of the myth was encouraged by the coincidence that Persia suffered an equally severe defeat at Greek hands at the same time. Herodotus (7.166) reported that the two victories, at Himera and in the Bay of Salamis, came on the same day; later writers added that the Persians and Carthaginians had concerted their invasions. The immediate beneficiary was of course Gelon, who was heroized. He lived on in the tradition relatively free from the usual stories of tyrannical atrocity, the exception who proved the rule. He was the child of fortune: already as a boy he had been saved from death when he left his classroom to chase a wolf which had snatched his tablet and an earthquake brought down the school, killing everyone within. He was humane and merciful: one of the provisions of the treaty with the Carthaginians after Himera was that they must give up the practice of human sacrifice. (Quite firm archaeological evidence from both Carthage and Motya reveals that the shift from infant to animal sacrifice was a slow process of the late fifth and fourth centuries B.C.—Plate 4b.) His rule was a Golden Age, and when he died the entire population of Syracuse joined the funeral procession.

Hiero seems to have inherited his brother's good credit but he soon began to lose it. He distrusted Polyzalus and actually fought with him briefly. He developed an elaborate secret police. By the time of his death in 467, little more than a decade after he succeeded to the supreme power, the first age of Sicilian tyranny was about to come to a whimpering end. Yet objectively it is hard to discern any fundamental differences between him and his brother, other than in luck and in accidental timing. In 476 Hiero transplanted the people of Naxos and Catania to Leontini, 're-founded' Catania under a new name, Etna, bringing settlers from as far afield as the Peloponnese, and introduced his young son Deinomenes as its ruler. The action provided the centrepiece for Pindar's *First Pythian* and it was also celebrated by Aeschylus, perhaps in the same year (470), with a play now lost, *The Women of Etna*. In 474 Hiero responded to an appeal from Cumae, sent a fleet and defeated the Etruscans in a naval battle in the Bay of Naples which Pindar ranked above the victory at Himera. No one can disprove the claim that Hiero was acting from purely patriotic Greek considerations. If so, it was a unique instance in the history of Sicilian tyranny.

The intensely personal and individual quality of the tyrants' actions cannot be stressed too heavily. There was something self-consciously archaic, even 'heroic' about them, and more than a touch of megalomania. They never balked at atrocities, but words like 'brutality' or 'tyranny' are insufficient in the face of their rapid destruction and foundation of cities, their repeated transplantation of tens of thousands of people. Their dealing with wives and daughters was more than the familiar utilization of marriage for dynastic and political advantage, more than the common royal prerogative to take any woman who caught the ruler's fancy; they entered into multiple formal marriages, flouting the Greek taboo against polygamy, and they escaped unharmed.[1] It is basically meaningless to inquire into

[1] L. Gernet, "Mariage des tyrans", in his *Anthropologie de la Grèce antique* (Paris 1968), pp. 344–59.

55

their constitutional position, either at home or in subject communities. No doubt some sort of governmental machinery existed, including the popular assembly by that time characteristic of many Greek city-states, but ancient writers showed no interest in it and rightly so.

Pindar and other writers sometimes called them 'kings', not as a technical term but rather as the best the language could do to express the reality in friendly tones. The tyrants themselves showed a certain reticence in this respect, as in the wording of Gelon's dedications. Hiero's too: a bronze Etruscan helmet found in Olympia has the metrical inscription, "Hiero son of Deinomenes and the Syracusans (dedicated) to Zeus Etruscan (spoils) from Cumae" (Plate 8a). Coins reveal the same psychology. These first tyrants took much trouble with their coins, employing engravers of the highest artistry and changing the emblems when appropriate. After Theron took Himera, the crab of Akragas immediately appeared on Himeran coins (Plate 7a, b), and Anaxilas commemorated his Olympic victory by introducing the mule-cart on the coins of both Rhegium and Messina. But not once did Gelon or Theron or Hiero put his own name or portrait on a coin, or any title or symbol of office.

This touch of reticence was one facet of a larger concern to be accepted and to have their greatness acknowledged throughout the Greek world, and that at a time when tyranny had effectively disappeared in Greece proper and the once neutral word 'tyrant' had become, in many quarters, strictly pejorative, a synonym for 'despot'. The one entrée the Sicilians had was through their wealth, with their victorious chariots and their very rich gifts and dedications to the major shrines. Pindar's reference to Croesus (as a contrast to Phalaris) was not arbitrary. And they used their wealth to draw to them great sculptors and engravers, poets and playwrights. There was clearly something equivocal, or at least divided, in the Greek response. Tyranny was a bad thing, to be sure, but it was not only a man like Pindar, spokesman for the increasingly anachronistic archaic-aristocratic ethos, who found power on a heroic scale irresistible. Voltaire caught one nuance when, in a contemptuous passage about Sicilian history—"nearly always hating their (foreign) masters and rebelling against them, but not making any real effort worthy of freedom"—he added that under her own Greek tyrants Sicily "at any rate . . . had counted for something in the world".[1]

Moral considerations apart (and not counting the victims), Greek Sicily prospered from Hippocrates to Hiero. The tyrants, their families and close associates undoubtedly took their fair share of the riches. But more than a little trickled down. The end of tyranny saw no cessation in the outward signs of prosperity: in agriculture, in the continuation of the tradition established by the tyrants of minting the finest coins, in the scale and quality of temple-building and of other public works. On the material side, it seemed as if Syracuse and Akragas had the necessary conditions to follow the path of Athens, where tyranny had been overthrown in 508. A beginning was made in 466, but the end-product proved to be weak and short-lived.

[1] *Le siècle de Louis le Grand,* chap. XIII.

Chapter 5

DEMOCRATIC INTERLUDE, 466–405 B.C.

Our knowledge of the wars and revolutions that brought to a close the first age of tyrants is very unsatisfactory. The historian Diodorus, the chief source of information, is notoriously weak on chronology and his tales are often interchangeable between any one situation and any other: the same great battles by land and sea, involving large numbers of citizens and mercenaries, the same conventional picture of excessive and brutal despotism driving a desperate people to revolt *en masse*. Thrasydaeus in Akragas was "violent and murderous" and so was Thrasybulus in Syracuse in the identical words; both embarked upon careers of lawlessness the moment they succeeded to power, the former on the death of his father Theron, the latter after his brother Hiero. Thrasybulus was the third of the four Deinomenid brothers to become tyrant in Syracuse, while Hiero's son Deinomenes retained Etna, and this is yet another example suggesting that Aristotle was right to point to intra-family struggles as an important factor in the downfall of these tyrannies. It is also noteworthy that the break came only after the deaths of the 'heroic' figures. Despite Diodorus, it was the weakness of the next generation as much as their brutality which brought them down. Tyranny by its nature relied heavily on the person of the individual tyrant. Traditional monarchy can survive a weak king and even several in succession; tyranny cannot. What form the new regime might then take was an open question. One possibility, for example, was a new tyranny, but in Sicily at this time it was democracy.

Why that should have been the case is not at all obvious. Such democratic experience as Greek Sicily had had in the previous decades was very limited and unpromising. Yet, as we are given the account, the normally difficult transition required little more than an armed conflict against the tyrants and their mercenaries. We have no names of democratic leaders, no innovators or constitution-makers (like Cleisthenes in Athens). There is no trace of resistance by oligarchic factions except in

58

the late and largely apocryphal biographical tradition about the great philosopher and physician, Empedocles of Akragas, scion of an aristocratic family who is said to have become an active democrat and to have helped break up an oligarchic group known as the Thousand. Where, we should like to know, did the Syracusan Gamoroi disappear to, who had appealed to Gelon in 485 from their retreat in Kasmenai but are never heard of again? More puzzling still is Diodorus' account of how Thrasydaeus undertook an expedition against Hiero, was heavily defeated and then thrown out of Akragas, to be followed (without reference to Empedocles and the Thousand) by a democratic regime which sought and obtained a peace treaty with the Syracusan tyrant. Himera, which had been under Akragantine suzerainty, apparently went the same way. The notion of Hiero as a protector of democracy, even in another and potentially hostile state, is pretty remarkable, yet Diodorus is explicit about it although he represents a heavily anti-Hiero tradition in all other respects. At any rate, Hiero's brother and successor, Thrasybulus, gained nothing from the understanding with the new regime in Akragas, for his overthrow was brought about by a coalition in which the Syracusans were supported by armies from Akragas, Himera, Gela and Selinus as well as a Sicel force. Only mercenaries and the settlers of the new foundation at Etna remained loyal to the Deinomenid tyranny and they had little choice. Thrasybulus was eventually allowed to go in peace and live out his life in Locri, whereas Thrasydaeus fled to Megara in Greece where he was condemned to death and executed. Why the distinction between the two is unknown.

With the expulsion of Thrasybulus from Syracuse, tyranny seems to have been replaced by democracy everywhere but in Etna and Messina, where the change was to come within the next few years. In its Greek sense, democracy meant direct rule by the *demos*, the whole people, and one immediate problem was to determine who 'the people' of any given community were. Years of mass exile and transplantation had left a bitter heritage on this issue, which produced open conflict once the tyrant's hand was removed. Diodorus makes a point of noting, obviously as an exception, the internal peace in Himera from its repopulation by Theron until its destruction by Carthage in

409. Elsewhere the picture was very different. In Syracuse 7,000 of Gelon's 10,000 mercenary settlers were still resident (the numbers are Diodorus' and must be treated with reserve). The new regime soon declared them ineligible to hold public office. They rebelled, were defeated after heavy fighting, and left the city for unspecified destinations. There were similar expulsions in other cities and also the recall of former exiles. Etna was a special case: a combined Sicel-Syracusan attack drove the population out and they reestablished themselves, surprisingly, further inland in Sicel territory at Inessa in the mountains east of Centuripe. Inessa was renamed Etna while Etna became Catania again, repopulated by Hiero's expellees and new settlers, both Syracusan and Sicel. Meanwhile Messina freed itself from Rhegium and tyranny and invited exiled mercenaries (and presumably others) from the various cities to settle. And Kamarina was 'founded' once again by Gela as an independent community.

Kamarina should put us on our guard. It was supposedly depopulated and destroyed twice within a century or so, most recently by Gelon. Yet a man of that city named Psaumis was able to win two Olympic victories in the 450s; he possessed enough wealth to enter the chariot race, the mule-cart race and the horse race in a single Olympic and then to engage Pindar to write two victory odes, the *Fourth* and *Fifth Olympian* (unless the latter was actually composed by a skilful Sicilian imitator). Meanwhile Hiero finally achieved his great ambition in the chariot-race of 468, and probably in the same year one of his lieutenants, Hagesias, who was assassinated after the tyrant's death, won with the mule cart. More remarkable is the career of the long-distance runner, Ergoteles of Himera, who erected a statue of himself at Olympia. The bronze tablet affixed to the base of the statue has been re-discovered by modern excavators; it commemorates no fewer than eight victories equally divided among the four greatest of the Panhellenic games, probably in the decade 474–464.[1] To be sure, a long-distance runner did not require money on anything like the scale of the chariot race, but Ergoteles (or his patrons) could afford to commission a statue

[1] Pausanias 6.4.11; *Supplementum epigraphicum graecum* XI 1223a.

and to engage Pindar to celebrate one of the victories (in his *Twelfth Olympian* which, if written in 470 as usually thought, contains some phrasing to substantiate Diodorus' statement that Himera, and thus Akragas, had become democratic in Hiero's lifetime). These are all hints that, though the turmoil reported by the ancient historians was no doubt serious enough, the fortunate among the wealthier classes still had the leisure, the ambition and the riches to carry on in their traditional style.

All this shifting about of large numbers of people created grave confusion in property relations, as landholdings were confiscated, distributed and re-distributed each time there was another move. There is a firm ancient tradition, still repeated in Roman times by Cicero and Quintilian, that the many lawsuits which ensued led to the development of forensic oratory and the first rhetorical handbooks. Whether the cause-and-effect explanation is correct or not, it is a fact that Corax of Syracuse and his pupil Tisias were the founders of the Greek art of rhetoric at this time and that later in the century Gorgias of Leontini was its most famous exponent in the Greek world[1] Diodorus (12.53.3) says that when Gorgias addressed the Athenian assembly in 427 as head of a delegation from Leontini, "he astonished the Athenians, who were naturally clever and liked words, by the novelty of his speech". Another consequence —at least the Athenians were led to believe it—was a lack of cohesion and solidarity within each city. Have no fear of them, Alcibiades is supposed to have said in advocating the Athenian invasion of Sicily in 415, "for their cities are peopled by a heterogeneous mob. Changes and admission of new citizens take place easily. In consequence, no one is prepared to defend himself as in a genuine fatherland" (Thucydides 6.17.2–3).

The Athenians took Alcibiades' advice, invaded Sicily and were slaughtered by the Syracusans. Yet Alcibiades was not wholly wrong. In Syracuse, the only city about which we have details, the government almost looked like the Athenian. Supreme political authority was vested in the popular assembly, in all the adult male citizens who attended its meetings. There, following free and open debate, laws and decrees were passed, foreign and military policy was decided, and the state's

[1] See George Kennedy, *The Art of Persuasion in Greece* (Princeton 1963), pp. 58–68.

officials were chosen annually, headed by a board of fifteen generals (who were political as well as military figures). There was also, in the universal Greek fashion, a council which did the preparatory work for the assembly. However, the council and the civil officials were not chosen by lot as in Athens but were elected, a procedure which in the Greek view introduced the aristocratic principle and therefore constituted a limitation on full democracy. Nor was there, so far as we can tell, pay for office, and this again reduced the participation of the poorer classes in the daily running of affairs. Hence Aristotle (*Politics* 1304a27–29) classified the Syracusan constitution as a *politeia* rather than a *demokratia*, a distinction which is not translatable in modern language, or in modern thinking either. The conventional and not altogether happy practice among historians is to speak of 'moderate' and 'radical' democracy.

Beneath the political structure, class divisions remained rather sharply drawn. The Gamoroi may have disappeared from the historical record but not oligarchic sentiment. Political and military leadership was drawn from a wealthy élite, and that there was much dissatisfaction is revealed by an unsuccessful attempt about 454 B.C. to set up a new tyranny with the backing of the poor. Fear of tyranny then led the Syracusans to copy the Athenians and introduce ostracism (under the name of "petalism"), a device whereby a leader whose influence was deemed excessive, and therefore dangerous, was sent into a sort of honourable exile for a period of five years (in Athens the period was ten years).[1] However, according to Diodorus, the unexpected effect was to cause the better citizens to withdraw from public affairs altogether, devoting themselves to their wealth and luxurious living, and petalism was soon abandoned.

This charge of debilitating luxury in Sicily was widely bruited in the Greek world—had the oracle not given Syracuse to Archias when he chose wealth? Like Alcibiades' prediction of a lack of patriotic solidarity, it had a measure of truth. The rapid removal of the tyrants had altered the power structure

[1] Diodorus (11.87.1) explains that the procedure was called "petalism" because the Syracusans recorded their votes for banishment on olive leaves (*petala* in Greek), whereas the Athenians employed potsherds (*ostraka*).

and for about a generation Sicily was free, at least overtly, from the aggressive ambitions of the larger cities. That this was the result not of a deep-rooted pacific attitude inherent in the new democracies but rather of a temporary and unavoidable concentration on internal affairs was eventually to become apparent.

Meantime a Hellenized Sicel named Ducetius took advantage of the lull to launch a powerful 'national' movement. Ducetius first appeared upon the scene when he brought an armed force to support the Syracusan attack on Etna. Now, starting from his native Mineo some fifteen kilometres south of the sanctuary of the Palici, he united all the Sicels of the region into some sort of league, with himself at the head, and he attacked and destroyed the two fortified Greek or Greek-dominated centres in the interior, Inessa-Etna and Morgantina. Precisely like the Greek tyrants of the previous generation—and this side of Ducetius deserves stress—he proceeded to found or re-found and fortify certain strategic points in his territory, distributing land allotments and creating an effective fighting force. One new (but short-lived) foundation was Palice, near the sanctuary, which was well located strategically but which also had the obvious, and no doubt greater, merit of putting his movement under the patronage of the ancient native divinities. By 451 or 450 he felt strong enough to take aggressive action, beginning with the Akragantine outpost of Motyon (possibly present Vassallaggi) on the main road from Akragas to the northeast. The Syracusans came to the aid of Akragas but Ducetius was able to take Motyon. The next year Syracuse returned in force under a new general. Ducetius was badly defeated at an unidentified place called Nomae, and at the same time Akragas regained Motyon.

The 'liberation' movement promptly collapsed. Ducetius himself stole into Syracuse secretly with a few followers and sat down as a suppliant before one of the altars. An assembly was called and the unanimous decision was reached to respect the right of asylum. Ducetius was ordered to live in exile in Corinth, at Syracusan expense. But he soon broke his promise, pleading the instructions of an oracle, and with a small band of Greeks he sailed to Sicily. Instead of returning to the interior, he went to Kale Akte, a characteristically Greek coastal site we have met once before, in the story of the Samians at Messina, and there he founded a new city, settled by the men he had brought with him from the Peloponnese together with Sicilians who were attracted to it. Kale Akte has not been excavated but aerial photographs reveal a small urban centre indistinguishable in appearance from any Greek city of the same size and period (Plate 8c). Ducetius died soon after, in 440, leaving behind a successful community which was still prospering when Rome ruled Sicily. By contrast, inland Morgantina remained largely unoccupied for a century. The interior was rapidly subjugated by Syracuse. Some of the Sicel communities seem to have been euphemistically called "allies" while others were garrisoned, but they all had tribute levied on them. The liberation movement was ended but not, for a little while longer, Sicel national consciousness. In 427 and again in 415 the inland Sicels made a last feeble effort to assert themselves, giving Athens such support as they could in her invasion.

During all these troubles Carthage made no move. She had preoccupations elsewhere; besides, with the Sicilian Greeks relations were friendly enough to permit the establishment of an enclave of Carthaginian traders in Syracuse and other cities. In turn the Hellenic element grew constantly stronger in the Phoenician settlements in the west of the island. They all minted Greek or bilingual coins (as did Elymian Segesta and later Eryx), and Greek objects compete in the archaeological record with Punic material (the significance of which is pointed up by the rarity of Greek finds in contemporary Sardinia). Carthage may have exercised a loose hegemony, but they appear to have remained independent communities to all intents and purposes.[1] Thus the earliest treaties between Carthage and Rome permitted Romans to trade freely in Sicily while imposing very severe restrictions on their movements everywhere else within the Carthaginian sphere.

This is not to say that there were no conflicts in western Sicily. Hostility was chronic between Selinus and Segesta and there are hints of open warfare in other places. But these quarrels were no different from the usual inter-city relations

[1] Motya had grown so much that a large new necropolis had to be developed in the Birgi district of Sicily immediately to the north, with which it was linked by a causeway about two kilometres in length (Figure 4).

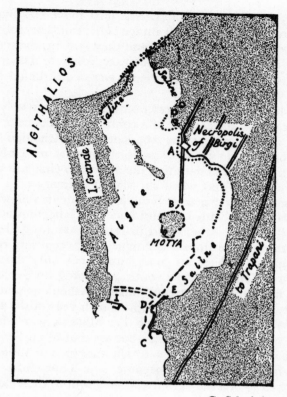

G. Schmiedt

Fig. 4   Motya and its Fortifications
Key: A–B, Causeway. C–D–E, Embankment. I, Breakwater

on the island and had no deeper significance. In the end it was
Syracuse which broke the comparatively peaceful interlude and
from the same motives as under the tyrants. As early as about
445, we are told, Akragas had declared war against Syracuse on
the ground that the latter had dealt with Ducetius unilaterally
and that his return to Kale Akte was a danger. This is a sus-
piciously inadequate reason but there is no way to get behind
it. In any event, though Syracuse won handsomely and peace
was declared, a renewed struggle for power had begun between
the two largest and richest Greek states, both, let it be noted,

originally Dorian foundations. The next move was Syracusan and unprovoked. Taking advantage of her solid control over the Sicels and no doubt of the tribute they sent in, Syracuse prepared a considerable armament; according to Diodorus the cavalry was doubled, 100 triremes were constructed and the infantry was also increased.

What happened in the next decades is unfortunately known to us not within the context of a continuous account of Sicilian history, but rather as an appendage to Athenian history. Athens had begun to show political interest in Sicily as far back as the 450s (not counting the appeal to Gelon at the time of the Persian Wars) when she signed a treaty of friendship with Segesta, of all places. Similar agreements followed with nearby Halicyae, with Leontini and with Rhegium across the Straits. Just what Athens had in mind is far from clear, perhaps nothing more than a willingness to accept any proffered friendship in the west for some future, not fully thought out programme. Then in 427 Leontini, attacked by Syracuse, requested help under the treaty and the Athenians sent a force in twenty ships. Athens was in the fourth year of the Peloponnesian War against Sparta and her allies, a war which was decisive not only for her future but for that of all Greece. Yet she was willing to detach a small, though not insignificant, force to intervene in Sicily because, says Thucydides (3.86.4), "she wished to prevent corn from being sent to the Peloponnese and also to test out whether she was capable of bringing Sicily under subjection". That is only Thucydides' interpretation, of course, and it smacks of hindsight, but it is worth noting that, also according to Thucydides (2.7.2–3), the Spartans had appealed to the various Sicilian states for aid at the beginning of the war in 431. None was forthcoming in the way of fighting power, but there can be little question that Sicilian corn was important to some of Sparta's allies in Greece if not to Sparta herself.

How long the conflict between Syracuse and Leontini had been going on is not known. By 427 much of Sicily had been drawn in, Himera, Gela and perhaps Selinus on the side of Syracuse, and on the other side Kamarina, Catania, little Naxos and, as soon as they could, some of Syracuse's Sicel subjects. Akragas seems to have remained strangely neutral, while in southern Italy there was support for Syracuse from Locri, for Leontini from Rhegium. The fighting went on for more than two years on both sides of the Straits; even Lipari was raided. Underneath there was also serious internal factionalism and class war, notably in Messina, which changed sides in response to her own shifting internal balance, and in Rhegium. Then in 424, apparently on the initiative of Gela and Kamarina, representatives from the Greek Sicilian cities convened in a congress at Gela and made peace. The chief advocate of a settlement was the Syracusan Hermocrates, the only real personality to have survived in the historical record of Sicily in this period. His main argument, we are told, was that Sicily must cease its wars or be swallowed up by the Athenians.

All this is hard to judge. The Athenian generals in Sicily accepted the peace without visible protest and took their forces home, where they were punished for so doing. As for Hermocrates' possibly disingenuous plea for unity, that proved vain. Civil war broke out in Leontini and in 422 the upper classes called in Syracuse. The latter responded and drove the commons out. Where they went is unknown, but some found their way to the mother-city, Chalcis in Euboea, and elsewhere in Greece. Leontini was 'razed' and the victorious oligarchic party migrated to Syracuse. A few were soon dissatisfied, returned to Leontine territory and issued one more appeal to Athens. This time the Athenians were cautious and sent an embassy only, which had little difficulty in deciding that it was best for Athens not to try another armed intervention at that moment.

The scene then shifted to the west of the island. In 416 Selinus and Segesta were fighting again; there were disputes about border territory and others, unexplained, arising from intermarriages. Syracuse was giving support to Selinus and so Segesta appealed to Carthage. There was no response and she turned to Athens, where an embassy pleaded their old alliance, recalled the fate of Leontini, and promised a large financial contribution. The mood in Athens was very different from that of 422; for one thing there had been a lull in the Peloponnesian War for five years and therefore both manpower and resources were available. However, the Athenians were prudent enough to send a delegation to Segesta to look over the situation. There they were elaborately deceived and they returned to Athens with glowing, but false, reports of the wealth in Segesta and in Elymian Eryx. Part of the deception may have been the commencement of work on the magnificent temple at Segesta (which was never finished). In the debate which followed in the Athenian assembly, Alcibiades was the most eloquent spokesman for an invasion; that was the occasion for his sneer about the unreliability of a mongrel population in Sicilian cities. Alcibiades carried the day overwhelmingly and in the summer of 415 Athens dispatched the most splendid and most expensive armada ever to have sailed from a single Greek city, in Thucydides' words (6.31.1)—more than 250 ships, including troop-carriers and supply-transports, and perhaps 25,000 men.

The expedition ended in a total disaster though it need not have. It began to go wrong almost from the start. There was disagreement and ill-will among the Athenian commanders. Alcibiades was soon indicted in Athens on a complex sacrilege charge and left Sicily for exile rather than stand trial. Many months were frittered away seeking further alliances in Sicily or raiding for booty, and perhaps also out of sheer indecision, thereby giving Syracuse badly needed time in which to strengthen her fortifications and her insufficient navy. Both sides were carrying on active diplomacy. In the summer of 414 Sparta sent Gylippus to take charge of the Syracusan forces and with him a small contingent of ex-helots; other troops came from Corinth and Boeotia. Athens sent reinforcements in 414 and another large army in 413 under their ablest general, Demosthenes, who brought the needed resolution and tactical skill to the Athenian army.

All in all, Athens transported some 40,000 men to the island, a majority of them from her own manpower; the rest were men from allied states in Greece, the Aegean islands and Asia Minor, and mercenaries from Crete, Arcadia and Italy (some Etruscans included). In Sicily she was less successful in recruiting than Alcibiades and others had hoped. Segesta and most of the Sicels supported her, but their help was not very important. Other states seemed to have been more frightened of such a large invading force than of their traditional enemy Syracuse. As for Syracuse, she probably mustered another

40,000, including troops from Gela, Kamarina, Himera, Selinus and the Sicels from the region of Kale Akte. Like Athens, she provided the majority of the men herself. And Akragas continued in her neutrality. So did Carthage and the Phoenician sector of Sicily. Carthage made no move when the Athenian fleet sailed past Palermo in full force in 415 to seize the native coastal town of Hyccara, at the behest of the Segestans, and sell off the entire population. Nor did she respond in 414 when the Athenian generals sent an embassy to solicit aid.

The war finally centred on Syracuse, as it should have at the very beginning. Tactically this entailed three separate though interlocked struggles: for control of the great harbour, for control of the heights of Epipolai overlooking the city to the north and northwest (Figure 1), and for a circumvallation which both sides were attempting simultaneously in the standard siege practice. By the time of the final battles in the autumn of 413, Syracuse had gained the advantage. A Greek citizen militia was not well equipped, materially or psychologically, to campaign abroad for two years. Supplies were uncertain, morale began to weaken, there were desertions, epidemic diseases struck. In the end the Athenian generals decided to retreat. The result was a frightful slaughter. Another 7000 were captured and imprisoned in the limestone quarries where many died during the winter. An unknown number were sold into slavery, branded on the forehead with the mark of a horse. The two generals Demosthenes and Nicias were executed. Only a fraction managed to make their way home, and of some of them Plutarch tells a story which is worth repeating even if perhaps not true. They were set free, he writes, because they could recite by heart some of the choruses of Euripides; "for the Sicilians, it seems, had a passion for his poetry greater than that of any other Hellenes outside Greece" (*Life of Nicias* 29.2).

Syracuse celebrated and much booty was dedicated to Apollo in Delphi. But the victory brought no peace either to Syracuse or to Sicily. Internal faction, which had been damped down during the Athenian invasion, now started up with renewed vigour. "The common people," said Aristotle (*Politics* 1304a 27–29), "having been responsible for the victory, now trans-

formed the government from a *politeia* to a full democracy."
Led by one of the generals named Diocles, they forced through
a number of reforms, on the Athenian model ironically enough,
of which selection of officials by lot was the most notable, and
they had the law codified. Their chances were improved by the
absence of Hermocrates, the strongest of the oligarchically
minded political figures, who was commanding a fleet of twenty
triremes (together with two from Selinus) which had been
dispatched to the Aegean to help Sparta against Athens. In
409 sentence of banishment was passed on Hermocrates and he
was ordered to turn his ships over to other commanders. By
then, however, the history of Sicily had taken a new turn.

With the removal of the Athenians from the island, Selinus
returned to the attack on Segesta. This time the latter feared
total destruction and in 410 appealed to Carthage once more,
with the new inducement that she was willing to become a
Carthaginian tributary. Carthage accepted, for reasons we do
not know. That the response was opportunistic rather than the
culmination of a plan is suggested by the small army sent
across: 5000 Libyans who were reinforced by perhaps 1000
Campanian and other mercenaries available in Sicily. The
next spring, however, the Carthaginians returned in full force
under Hannibal and Selinus fell in nine days, so rapidly that
the other Greek cities had no time to send the assistance they
had promised. A massacre followed and Selinus was gutted.
Hannibal then marched his army to Himera, joined by numbers of Sicels. At Himera they found a Syracusan force under
Diocles' command and soon the hastily recalled Syracusan
fleet arrived from the Aegean (no small, though only a temporary, blessing to the desperate Athenians). After some severe
fighting the Syracusans withdrew, and perhaps half the
Himerans were able to escape by ship to Messina. The remainder were captured, tortured and massacred. The Carthaginian army then sailed back to Africa and was disbanded,
which suggests that even now no decision had been taken to
capture the whole of Sicily.

The issue was then forced by Hermocrates. Upon his dis-
missal from his command in the Aegean, he obtained a fund
from one of the Persian satraps, with which, back in Sicily, he
built five warships at Messina and engaged a thousand mer-

cenaries. His party failed to secure his recall to Syracuse and so he went to the west of the island, where he assembled refugees and more mercenaries, bringing the total to about 6000, set himself up as ruler in what was left of Selinus, and proceeded to raid Carthaginian tributaries and dependencies. Syracuse disowned these actions and considerable diplomatic activity followed, including a Carthaginian embassy to Athens. The internal crisis in Syracuse did not slacken meantime: Diocles was banished in 407 and Hermocrates apparently understood this as a signal to return. But when he arrived at the gates of the city with his followers, he was refused admittance, some say because it was now apparent that he wished to become tyrant. He attempted a coup and was killed. Among those of his men who managed to save themselves was a 24-year-old, Dionysius, who was soon to accomplish what Hermocrates failed to achieve and to become the most powerful Greek ruler of the age, the model of the tyrant in subsequent political discussion.

Diplomacy failed and the Carthaginians returned to Sicily in the spring of 406 with their largest army, though Diodorus' 120,000 is not credible. The first target was rich Akragas, unusually prosperous thanks to its neutrality in the wars of the previous decades. The fighting lasted seven months, during which the Syracusans fought well, the Akragantines hardly at all, and recriminations and treason charges were freely thrown about within the ranks of the Greeks. In December Akragas was abandoned and the population transferred to Leontini, unhindered by the Carthaginians who then plundered the city and removed vast quantities of works of art and also, according to one tradition, Phalaris' bronze bull. The effect in Syracuse was a further deterioration in the political situation, which young Dionysius turned to his advantage by having himself appointed to the board of generals (and soon to sole command with plenipotentiary powers). In the spring there began a battle for Gela which went much like the Akragantine a few months earlier. Gela was evacuated and then Kamarina. Syracuse was next on the list but the Carthaginians made peace with Dionysius instead and returned home. Diodorus attributes their action to a severe outbreak of plague (which they then carried back to Africa), and, though one becomes suspicious of the frequency with which plague was conveniently available in

71

ancient Sicilian history, no better explanation of the Carthaginian withdrawal suggests itself.

The treaty with Dionysius marked the first recognition by the Greeks of a Carthaginian *epikrateia* (conventionally, but perhaps imprecisely, translated 'province') in Sicily. According to Diodorus (13.114.1), the Punic, Elymian and Sican settlements were to belong to Carthage; the people of Selinus, Akragas, Himera, Gela and Kamarina were to be allowed to return home on condition of leaving their cities unfortified and of paying tribute to Carthage; Leontini, Messina and the Sicels were to be autonomous; Dionysius was to rule in Syracuse. In the event, the surviving Himerans were settled in nearby Thermae (along with colonists from Carthage and Libya), and Himera itself was never inhabited again, apart from the inevitable squatters[1]; Segesta's new dependent status was symbolized by the abrupt cessation of her coinage; Selinus came back to life as an impoverished settlement with a large Punic component, visible in the archaeological remains; and the eastern cities soon lost their promised freedom. The clause in the treaty which above all others was to remain in force was the rule of Dionysius, in a manner that no one could have envisaged in 406. The democratic interlude was over.

There can be little doubt that it was the Athenian invasion followed by the Carthaginian which brought tyranny back to Syracuse (and thence to the rest of Greek Sicily in a short time). And that suggests an answer to the question already posed regarding the failure of the Sicilian Greeks to make a success of the city-state way of life. Their behaviour was profoundly influenced and disturbed by the fact that they lived in an alien environment. The Carthaginians, Etruscans and others were outside but too near at hand; the Sicels, Sicans and Elymians were on the island itself, and in the case of Syracuse at least, within their own territorial sphere, some as a servile element (the Kyllyrioi), others as tributaries and potential rebels. Then there was the peculiar heritage of the first tyrants, which Alcibiades had stressed. Too many Sicilian Greeks were uprooted, sometimes more than once, and there were too

[1] Greek writers occasionally referred to Thermae as Himera thereafter, and perhaps the inhabitants themselves did so, too, hence Termini Imerese. Archaeology, however, has proved that the old Himera was not rebuilt.

many mercenaries. To function properly as an independent self-governing body, the city-state had to have a strong sense of community and had to maintain a delicate equilibrium between 'the few' and 'the many' (in Greek parlance), between the rich and the poor. These the Sicilian cities failed to achieve. Given time, perhaps they would have recovered from the effects of the first tyrants. But time is precisely what they were not given because of their geographical position and their importance to outside powers.

Chapter 6

DIONYSIUS I

From 405 until the Roman conquest, which began in 264 B.C., the history of Sicily has to be written around the careers and fortunes of five rulers of Syracuse, punctuated by periods of civil war, dynastic strife and anarchy. The sources offer no alternative, and the distortion which results is probably even greater than that produced by the tenacious, though unnecessary, convention of turning the history of the Roman Empire or of England into a succession of individual reigns. Occasionally an archaeological discovery or a rare contemporary document inscribed on stone reminds us that life in Sicily was not all war, rapine and financial extortion by tyrants, but no continuous history can be built out of such scraps, not even a cross-section view of society in Syracuse, let alone Akragas or Messina, in any given decade. Worse still, the first and most striking of the five men, the elder Dionysius, became the focus for both contemporary and later moralizing about tyrants. The tales grew more numerous and more extravagant as the years went on, until all possibility of getting at some sort of balanced picture of the man, his career and his world was destroyed forever. One sample will suffice, from Cicero's *Tusculan Disputations* (5.20):

> Unwilling to trust his head to a barber, he taught his own daughters to shave him. Royal virgins were thus reduced to the servile trade of female barber, cutting their father's hair and beard. He went still further: when they grew up he took away the cutting instruments and decided that they should singe his beard and hair with heated walnut-shells. He had two wives, Aristomache of his own city and Doris of Locri, and before he came to them at night he had everything examined and searched. Around the bed he had a broad trench dug, traversed by a little wooden footbridge; after he closed the door of the chamber, he himself removed the bridge.

The trouble with such material is that it can neither be believed nor corrected nor totally rejected. Modern historians have tried to pick their way through the heap, but their accounts often start from some *a priori* assumption, such as

74

that so great a man could not at the same time have been so great a monster, which is neither demonstrable nor even meaningful. The only reliable course is to abandon the effort to get at Dionysius' personality, and not to stray far from the narrow path of external events. We can do that much thanks chiefly to one man, Philistus, a contemporary and close associate of the tyrant. Philistus was a figure not uncommon among the Greeks, a man of affairs who also wrote history, in his case a history of Sicily nearly half of which was devoted to the reign of Dionysius. The work has not survived, but it was read and much praised for at least five hundred years. The narrative portions of the account we have, in Diodorus and others, ultimately go back to this book, unlike the fiercely negative embellishments and evaluations, which stem from others, and in particular from Timaeus writing a century later.[1]

Nearly all the details that have come down about the early life of Dionysius are probably fictitious. From his education, military rank and associations he seems to have been upper class. He first appeared on the scene in the anarchic situation created by Hermocrates and the Carthaginian invasion. Though only about twenty-five years of age, he seized his chance with such skill and speed that he had Syracuse in his power within a year or so. Aristotle cites him as an outstanding example of the tyrant who attained power by demagogic appeals to the poorer classes, and Diodorus provides documentation to substantiate that view.[2] By unrelenting attacks on the generals and the civil administration, whom he charged with incompetence and even treachery in the resistance against the Carthaginian invaders, he first won appointment as one of the generals, then sole command and finally a private bodyguard. The defeat at Gela and the evacuation of Kamarina produced a brief flare-up against him in his absence, led by the aristocratic cavalry. However, this was not a popular uprising and Dionysius crushed it without difficulty. The democratic system had not struck deep enough roots. Dionysius then remained in power for thirty-eight years until his death in 367, "the strongest and

---

[1] See R. Zoepffel, *Untersuchungen zum Geschichtswerk des Philistos von Syrakus* (diss. Freiburg i. Br. 1965), pt. 1.

[2] Aristotle, *Politics* 1205a26–28; Diodorus 13.91.3–96.4.

longest tyranny of any recorded by history," says Diodorus (13.96.4).

The demagogy which brought him to power did not require Dionysius to base himself on the lower classes thereafter. The situation in Syracuse was such, with the Carthaginians virtually at the gates and the city itself in a civil-war state, that there were many who were ready to accept the strong-man appeal. The very wealthy Philistus backed him from the start. A daughter of Hermocrates became his wife immediately after his first success and he in turn married off his sister to a brother-in-law of Hermocrates. Among his first victims when he became tyrant were Daphnaeus, a wealthy general, and also a leader of the common people named Demarchus. Henceforth Dionysius chose his beneficiaries and his victims on his own grounds, irrespective of class or national origin. He converted the island of Ortygia (Figure 1) into a private fortress, housing his closest associates and his mercenaries there as well as a part of the fleet. Mercenaries remained essential to him throughout his reign, making up the whole of his bodyguard, a significant fraction of his army and also of his navy. Yet it must be recognized that he could command miliary service from tens of thousands of citizens, many of whom he himself raised to that status by enfranchising aliens and by emancipating slaves in large numbers (perhaps this marks the final disappearance of the Kyllyrioi from history).

Dionysius' aim was personal power, at home and abroad, and his measures throughout the thirty-eight years were directed to that end. He collected the normal revenues of a Greek state but he also resorted to every possible device to raise emergency funds when he needed them, just as he freely commandeered labour for arms manufacture and fortification. In turn, he disbursed booty and land when they were available and when there were men he wished to repay for their services to him. In the best Sicilian tradition, he also shifted whole sections of the population from one city to another, even crossing the Straits for that purpose. While campaigning in southern Italy in 389 B.C., for example, he destroyed a small but ancient Greek settlement called Caulonia, near the coast some twenty miles north of Locri. He was in a benevolent mood, however. Though he handed over the territory to his ally Locri, he brought the Caulonians to Syracuse, gave them citizenship and five years' tax exemption. The fate of Caulonia is reflected not only in its coinage, which ceased abruptly, but also at Olympia. Three statues were erected there to a great sprinter who won twelve other races besides the three at Olympia. The first statue commemorated his victory in the boys' race in 392 and he is called "Dikon of Caulonia", but the next time, in 384, he is "Dikon of Syracuse".

Dionysius showed the typical tyrant's unconcern for the mechanics of civil administration, even summoning the popular assembly when it suited him. The former military set-up, however, was changed radically, not only by the injection of a strong mercenary element but also by a new command structure, with all the highest posts in the hands of kinsmen and close personal associates. This stress on his family was a *leitmotif* of Dionysius' reign (also a source of trouble during his lifetime and still more after his death). His first wife, the daughter of Hermocrates, died within a few months, apparently as a result of severe maltreatment by the cavalry during their brief uprising. She was just about the only person close to the tyrant for whose death he was not eventually blamed by one writer or another. Then he began a career of marriage-broking which far surpassed that of the earlier tyrants in its Olympian exuberance (Figure 5). In 399 or 398 he himself took two wives in a single ceremony (and, it is said, he consummated both marriages in the same night): Aristomache of Syracuse and Doris of Locri. The former gave him two sons and two daughters, the latter two sons and one daughter. The elder Locrian son was named Dionysius,[1] the younger Hermocritus after the tyrant's father (not to be confused with Hermocrates). This last is one bit of evidence, and there is more, that Dionysius had chosen, for whatever reason, to place the succession in that branch of his descent, the foreign branch, so to speak, and Sicily was eventually to pay a heavy price for the decision.

The names of the three girls are a marvel of disingenuousness—Aristomache's daughters were called Sophrosyne (Prudence or Moderation) and Arete (Virtue), while Doris's was Dikaiosyne (Justice)—and they were quickly elevated from

---

[1] He was probably the eldest of all the children.

the servile trade of female barber to the aristocratic one of female political pawn. Sophrosyne was married to the younger Dionysius when he was not much more than twelve years of age. Arete was given first to the tyrant's brother Thearidas; then, upon his death, to her mother's young brother Dion; much later, after the elder Dionysius' death, the younger Dionysius took her away from Dion, whom he had exiled, and married her to a mercenary captain named Timocrates. Dikaiosyne was married to another of the tyrant's brothers, Leptines, one of whose daughters by a first marriage was the wife of the historian Philistus. Dionysius' sister Theste, finally, was married to a maternal uncle of the tyrant's first wife.

All this has a certain intrinsic interest, but it is also important as a symbol of how completely personal the rule of Dionysius was, and was meant to be seen to be. In this respect he created something new in the western world, anticipating the practice of Hellenistic monarchs in the centuries after Alexander the Great. If one were to ask the name of the empire which Dionysius acquired and ruled, there could be no answer. He was in effect a monarch, but he was not "king of" any fixed and named region or people, just as, for example, the Macedonian Ptolemies were never called "kings of Egypt" in their own official documents. This kind of ruler was monarch wherever his writ ran, so long as he could enforce it. In *de facto* terms— and it would be meaningless to seek a *de iure* definition—the Dionysian empire at its peak included, counting subjects, clients, colonies and such 'allies' as Locri, the whole of Sicily (except for the extreme western sector from the mouth of the Halycus to Solus east of Palermo) and the toe of Italy to the Gulf of Taranto. He had allies in Epirus in northwestern Greece and among the 'barbarian' Italic peoples of southern Italy, the Campanians, Lucanians and Iapygians, who provided his most reliable mercenaries. He also made incursions into Etruscan territory, but those seem to have been nothing more than raids, such as the looting in 384 of the territory of Cerveteri in central Italy and its rich harbour at Pyrgi (now Santa Severa), which brought him 1500 talents, according to Diodorus (15.14.3–4), enough to hire and equip a large army. North Africa, it is worth adding, was immune from even his raiding parties, let alone his imperial ambitions.

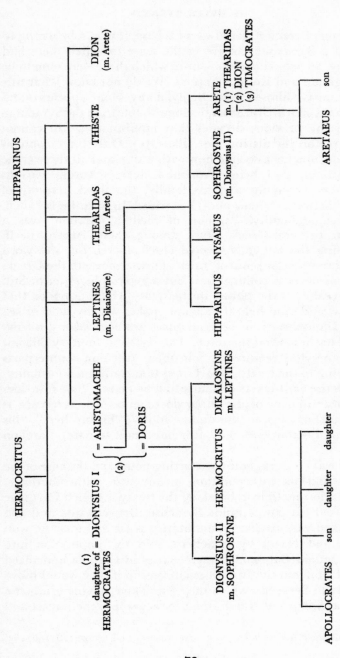

Fig. 5 The Family of Dionysius I

Although Syracuse was always his base, it would be wrong to speak of a Syracusan empire in the sense in which there had been, say, an Athenian empire or in which there were soon to be Carthaginian and Roman empires. We do not know what title Dionysius gave himself inside Sicily, if any. None appears on his coins, many of which are so indistinguishable from the Syracusan coins of the previous decades that numismatists still cannot fully agree on the attributions (Plate 7c). Only three contemporary documents associate him with a title and all three come from Athens, two being Athenian decrees voting various honours to Dionysius and his family, the third a treaty of alliance between Athens and Dionysius.[1] In each he is called, with nice ambiguity, "archon of Sicily". 'Archon' was a common title in Greek cities, among them Athens itself, designating the annually elected chief official, but the word also had the generic sense of 'ruler'. Furthermore, to the Greeks Sicily was never a political unit but a geographical term. Still more revealing is the phrase in the treaty which provided that Athens would send help if "anyone makes war by land or sea against Dionysius or his descendants *or any place where Dionysius rules*". That was what mattered. The civil and military officials of Syracuse were required to join their Athenian counterparts in swearing to the treaty. Apart from that traditional formality, in which the oath-takers certainly had no choice, Syracuse does not appear in any of the three documents. The reference is always to Dionysius, to "his ambassadors", "his brothers", "his sons" (the Locrian ones only, it is important to note), "archon of Sicily".

Sicily was of course both the starting-point and the core of the empire, and its incorporation meant war with Carthage. Dionysius lost no time in breaking the treaty in which Carthage had backed his power inside Syracuse. Between 404 and 402 he attacked various Sicel communities as far as Enna; he won Catania and Naxos by treachery, sold the population into slavery, settled Campanian mercenaries in Catania and razed Naxos; he offered the Leontines citizenship if they would move in a body to Syracuse, which they did. Then, having crushed a mutiny at home and transformed Syracuse into the largest and

---

[1] Dittenberger, *Sylloge inscriptionum graecarum* (3rd ed.), nos. 128, 159, 163.

most heavily fortified of all Greek cities, he began in earnest to prepare for a major war. He not only commandeered labour in his own dominions but he brought skilled Greek craftsmen and engineers from abroad, who helped the cause by making technical improvements in the navy and in siege-engines, including one fundamental invention, the catapult. For ship-building purposes, he made considerable inroads into the forests of Etna and he also imported timber from Italy. He carried on active diplomacy in northeastern Sicily and southern Italy in order to protect his rear when he began his campaign. The marriage with Doris of Locri was part of that diplomatic game. And he succeeded in winning the support of the Syracusan citizenry, many of whom had acquired their property and status from him. Hence, when he was fully prepared, by the end of 398, he summoned the assembly and obtained an enthusiastic decision to go to war. Something of the nature of the appeal is indicated by the way hostilities opened: the Carthaginian merchant colony in Syracuse and Carthaginian ships in the harbour were plundered, possibly even before the formal declaration of war. The other Greek cities followed suit, showing much cruelty to the Carthaginian enclaves which seem to have established themselves in the seven years of peace.

The first military objective was Motya. Other Greek cities contributed men to Dionysius' own large forces. Eryx surrendered on the way. Carthage was not yet prepared and the naval detachment sent to support Motya was inadequate. Nevertheless, the city held out until the late summer of 397 thanks to its island position (the causeway to the mainland having been cut) and its fortifications (Figure 4). The siege tactics and new siege equipment employed on this occasion are said to have served as a model for subsequent commanders, as for Alexander the Great at Tyre. When Motya fell there was a great massacre and much looting. Its Greek inhabitants who remained loyal were crucified. The city itself was destroyed. Though it was later re-occupied (Plate 4), it was never again sizeable or significant. When the Carthaginians regained the territory the next year they preferred to found a new settlement at Lilybaeum, now Marsala, which by extensive engineering work they converted into a powerful, easily defended naval base.

By the time the campaigning season of 396 opened, the Carthaginians had recruited a large army and navy, as usual made up chiefly of mercenaries from North Africa and Spain but supplemented with others hired in Sicily itself. Heavy fighting on land and sea went on for many months all over the island, accompanied by confused political manoeuvres within some of the Sicilian communities. The Elymians remained steadfast on the side of the invaders, and many Sicans and Sicels now went over to them. Thermae-Himera made its peace with Carthage as did its fortified outpost at Cefalù. When the Carthaginians arrived at Messina, part of the population fled but the remainder resisted, only to be heavily defeated and to see their city levelled, walls, houses and all. Syracuse itself was threatened next; the suburbs were raided and there may have been an incipient revolt against Dionysius inside the city (unless the account in Diodorus is just one more piece of the legend), when plague struck the Carthaginians again. Dionysius took advantage of this good fortune to administer a smashing military defeat and the Carthaginian general sued for peace. An agreement was reached—secretly, we are told—whereby Dionysius received an indemnity of 300 talents (all the cash that was on hand) and the small Carthaginian force were permitted to sail home in the night. The mercenaries and the Sicel troops were abandoned to shift for themselves. Dionysius was thus left in effective control of Sicily, except for the old Carthaginian sector and for some centres of resistance elsewhere. The losses in men and materials had been very great, all the more aggravating because they followed so soon after the shattering 409-405 war. No quantitative estimates are possible, and the surviving records have little to report on steps that may have been taken to bring at least the worst hit areas back to life. Messina, we know, was repopulated by Dionysius with Greeks from Italy and exiles from Greece itself, some of whom he soon transplanted further west to found Tyndaris.

For Carthage the defeat was particularly serious because it was followed by a revolt of her subjects in North Africa. However, in 393 and 392 Sicily was again invaded, and Carthage tried a new policy of seeking to win over disaffected elements in both Sicily and southern Italy. Nothing came of the effort, and the peace treaty recognized the authority of Dionysius over the Greeks and Sicels. He was then able to deal with one dangerous trouble spot that had so far held out successfully, Tauromenium (Taormina), a Sicel fortress which he captured and settled with "the most suitable men among his own mercenaries" (Diodorus 14.96.4). There was now peace in Sicily for almost a decade, during which Dionysius was free to concentrate on Italy, winning the southern end with the support of Locri and the Italic tribes against the bitter resistance of a Greek bloc led by Rhegium.

Dionysius was responsible for two more Carthaginian wars on Sicilian soil before his death in 367. The first, which began in 383 or 382, he provoked by diplomatic moves among the Sicans and Elymians which implied that he was aiming to take over the whole of the island. Exactly how long the war lasted is uncertain, since Diodorus telescopes his brief account under a single year. It ended, perhaps in 378, with a great Carthaginian victory at a place called Cronion, apparently near Palermo, where the tyrant lost many men including his brother Leptines who commanded one wing, Dionysius naturally having chosen the safest position and the best troops for himself. He had to pay an indemnity of 1000 talents and to accept a redefinition of the line between the two power spheres, surrendering Selinus, the territory of Akragas west of the Halycus, and Thermae on the north coast. In his last year he tried once again, gained Selinus and Eryx, accepted a temporary winter armistice and died before the next campaigning season. His son then made peace and Sicily was to be free from any serious Carthaginian invasion for twenty years.

Forty-odd years of war, some of it very cruel and costly, left Carthage in control of no more than the original Phoenician-Elymian sector of the island. Sicily paid very heavily for the privilege of having the Carthaginians thrown back after 405. That is as true of the Sicels, Sicans and Elymians as of the Greeks, and by now there seems to have been little distinction among them, though ancient writers continue to refer to them as separate entities. The combination of endless population shifting and normal acculturation had done its work. Even tyranny was as common in Sicel communities as in Greek, Ducetius having set the model at Kale Akte in the previous century. Yet many individuals benefited from the mess, quite apart from Dionysius and his entourage. Among them were many thousands of mercenaries of the most diverse national origins. Although coining had effectively ceased in the other Greek cities, in Syracuse there was a large output, including a considerable gold coinage and magnificent silver coins, notably those with the head of the nymph Arethusa designed by Euaenetus (who also signed some of the dies, a very rare practice among the Greeks—Plate 7c), which were copied not only by Greek cities outside Sicily but also by the Carthaginians in Sicily. The so-called Siculo-Punic coins, struck by both Greek and non-Greek craftsmen in various western mints on the island, leave no doubt about the reason for the extraordinary minting activity, because some of the pieces carry inscriptions in Punic saying "the paymasters" or "the people of the camp" (Plate 7e). And account must also be taken of the mercenaries who were settled permanently, as at Leontini.

Unlike the earlier tyrants, Dionysius also had the interest and the resources to play a role in the affairs of the old Greek world. For a time he continued the cooperative relationship with Sparta that had begun in Syracuse at the time of the Athenian invasion. Sparta seems to have given him some help at the beginning, when his tyranny was not yet secure. Then, in 396, his brother-in-law went to the Peloponnese to recruit men for the war with Carthage and came back with mercenaries as well as thirty triremes under a Spartan admiral. Now Athens had regained enough strength to begin counter-diplomacy, at first without success, but later, as Sparta was becoming visibly weaker, Dionysius seems to have become much cooler. At any rate he failed to support Sparta in a major naval battle off Corcyra (Corfu) with more than ten or eleven ships, which were quickly seized by the Athenians. But after Thebes shattered Sparta in 371, driving the latter into alliance with Athens, Dionysius again contributed useful interventions. In 368 Athens expressed her gratitude by making Dionysius and his sons honorary citizens, and in January of the following year, just before his death, by awarding him the tragedy prize at the Lenaea festival for a play called the *Ransom of Hector*. It is difficult to accept that the triumph came to him for his literary skill alone.

Just what motivated Dionysius in this persistent intervention in Greece escapes us completely. Apart from the valuable military assistance sent by Sparta in 396, no material advantage seems to have accrued to him and only in the world of legends can one seriously believe in long-range imperial ambitions in the east. There is no particular reason, indeed, to look beyond a certain megalomania: the great Dionysius was there to be courted and he would flex his muscles when he felt so inclined, or he might not. He also sought to make his mark among the Greeks outside politics and power. But there was a significant difference from the tyrants of the earlier era: Dionysius had nothing archaic about him. He seems not even to have cared much about victories in the games, although Diodorus (14.109) has a tale about a fiasco in 388 or 384, when he sent to Olympia several elaborately decked out chariot teams and the best rhapsodists (to recite his own poems), in charge of his brother Thearidas. His verses were laughed to scorn, while his horses and chariots met with a series of disastrous accidents during the race. Perhaps that was also the occasion when the orator Lysias, of Syracusan birth (son of Cephalus the armsmaker) but a long-time resident of Athens, delivered a ferocious attack on Dionysius, urging, among other things, that representatives of the impious tyrant ought not be admitted to the sacred festival at all.

Even had Dionysius met with success, there were no longer poets such as Pindar to celebrate a victory in odes. That kind of poetry had disappeared from the Greek scene. Dionysius looked ahead to a new, monarchical world, symbolized by his courtly life, surrounded by his personal bodyguard and retinue, within his private fortress of Ortygia. Yet he was a man of education who wrote poetry and who brought to Syracuse not only poets but also philosophers. In the hard world of politics the image of the frightful despot counted for little: one took one's allies where one found them. Even ideologically, however, not all Greeks were on the side of Lysias. The city-state was in its final decades and disillusioned voices were becoming louder and louder. The influential rhetorical school founded by Isocrates in Athens began to discover virtue in the leadership of an enlightened ruler, a category for which Dionysius seems to have qualified, oddly enough. In 388 or 387 Plato visited Syracuse, and that was the prelude to one of the most fantastic stories in the whole of Sicilian history.[1]

At the beginning of this chapter it was pointed out that our moralizing and mythopoeic sources make it impossible to get any idea what life was like in Sicily during the reign of Dionysius, apart from the slaughter of war. The evidence of the preceding century and again of the following three hundred years indicates that Sicily had a remarkable power of recovery. That is to say, those who survived and who were in the right positions on the right side profited from the wars and then grew richer in peacetime. Syracuse's reputation for high living was still maintained. Cultural life seems not to have been negligible either, though it is curious that Dionysius, unlike the earlier tyrants, did not care to go down in history as a builder of monuments. He erected fortifications rather than temples, theatres or other splendid civic buildings. But what about those Sicilians, and they must have been numerous, who survived without making a good thing out of the troubles? Within a few years of the death of Dionysius there was to be heard the familiar class-war call for redistribution of the land. That conditions rapidly became very much worse is certain, but it does not follow, just because our sources are silent on the subject, that there was not much poverty and unrest among the lower classes already in the time of the elder Dionysius. Large numbers of mercenaries have always been a source of trouble, even after they have been settled on the land as veterans and called "citizens". There is no good reason to assume that Dionysius' were an exception.

For all his power and ruthlessness, Dionysius was unable to weld a national community out of his new citizenry, not even in Sicily. He was undoubtedly the most powerful figure of his day in the Greek world and a match for any non-Greek in the west as well. At times, he commanded considerable financial resources and, by contemporary standards, great manpower. Yet he was never able to go on building from what he had. His career was something of a treadmill rather. Nor could anyone else within his domain build against him. Whatever spark of popular participation in politics there may have been left in

[1] See Chapter 7.

86

Sicily at the end of the fifth century B.C. was extinguished during the years of Dionysius. Henceforth Sicilians were to be subjects rather than citizens. All further political action took the form of destructive dynastic struggles, conspiracies and civil wars. From time to time the people were still summoned to meet, and there were even elections and decrees. But they were mere pawns in the power game, pulled about by adventurers when it suited their purposes. These adventurers and their armed mercenaries made the real decisions, not voters in the assembly.

Chapter 7

PLATO, DION AND DIONYSIUS II

The death of Dionysius immediately exposed the flaw in a power structure that rested so heavily on the abilities of one man and the backing of mercenaries, a weakness which was exacerbated by the complex family situation he had himself created. Dionysius was unusually lucky with the members of his family whom he placed in positions of trust and command. Dion, the brother of his Syracusan wife and the second husband of his daughter Arete, served him loyally and was handsomely repaid. He seems to have been a diplomatic expert, sent to Carthage on at least one mission. Leptines, a brother of the tyrant, was a military chief and apparently a competent one. Yet suspicion hovered and Leptines was for one period removed from command of the navy and sent off to a minor garrison post in Thermae. A contemporary Greek military writer, Aeneas Tacitus (10.21–22), gave this example of the correct tactic in cutting down a popular figure. Outright banishment, he pointed out, might lead to revolution. Even Philistus, the most faithful of them all, suffered temporary eclipse, perhaps on account of Leptines, whose son-in-law he had become.

Dionysius had publicly designated his son of the same name as his successor, and the latter stepped in without difficulty, assembling the people of Syracuse and obtaining a vote of loyalty from them. The younger Dionysius, then less than thirty, lacked his father's energy and drive, opting for a soft, luxurious life—his drunkenness was famous—with perhaps a taste for poetry and philosophy. He seems to have preferred to live in his mother's native Locri, leaving the cares of the empire and command of the mercenaries in the fortress of Ortygia to others. Dion, some ten years older and now head of the Syracusan wing of the elder Dionysius' family, was a man of wholly different quality—educated, haughty, ambitious, cold and cold-blooded. Within less than a year he and the young tyrant fell out. The blow came when Dionysius obtained (so he said) a copy of a letter from the Carthaginians

88

designating Dion as their agent in Syracuse. Dionysius dared not take the extreme steps such a document, with its suggestion of treason, called for. Instead, Dion was allowed to depart for Greece and to receive the income from his extensive Syracusan properties. He remained in Greece nearly ten years and hardly anything is known of him in that period, except that he spent some of the time in Athens in the circle of Plato's Academy. Nor is anything substantial known about events in Sicily during the decade.

In 361 or 360 Dionysius felt able to declare Dion a proper exile and to confiscate his wealth. Arete was handed over to her third husband, the commander of Ortygia. Dion then prepared for a coup, in cooperation with his brother Megacles and another distinguished exile named Heracleides. He failed to win support from the many Syracusan exiles in Greece, not more than twenty-five or thirty of whom were willing to join him. But he did acquire a remarkable assortment of comrades-in-arms, including at least two members of the Academy, Timonides, who kept a log of the venture which he sent to Plato's nephew Speusippus (later Plato's successor as head of the Academy), and Callippus, who was to assassinate Dion. No doubt they did not all share the same motives, but there is no denying the affinity which a number of men trained in the Greek philosophical schools were beginning to show for tyranny, maintaining that only the wise ruler, the philosopher-king, could lead the Greek states onto the path of virtue and morality.

Dion sailed for Sicily in 357 with a thousand hired troops and went straight to Minoa at the mouth of the Halycus River, a Carthaginian dependency governed by one of his friends. Dionysius and the ever faithful Philistus, his commander-in-chief though in his seventies, were in Italy and they were either fooled by Dion's manoeuvre, expecting him to make for the straits of Messina, or they were simply unprepared for the move at all. With the help of the governor of Minoa (and at least the benevolent neutrality of Carthage, which he surely knew he could count on) Dion marched on Syracuse, picking up support along the way from several communities who saw a chance to break from Syracusan suzerainty. The Syracusans welcomed him and the mercenary garrison was strangely inactive, so that he was able to enter the city unopposed and to set up his camp inside, in Achradina. Philistus brought a navy from Italy, overran Dion's lax defences, and massacred many mercenaries, but was finally driven out. Next he attacked Leontini, a city of mercenaries settled by the elder Dionysius, which had recently revolted from Syracuse, but he failed again. Meantime Heracleides had arrived from Greece with twenty triremes and military reinforcements and in a naval battle Philistus suffered his final defeat. The sources disagree as to whether the old man committed suicide or was tortured to death. His dismembered body was dragged through the streets of Syracuse and then cast out unburied.

There followed a decade of fighting, savage and confused, in which the original dynastic conflict was almost submerged. At times control of Syracuse was divided between Ortygia and the rest of the city. The empire was crumbling rapidly. A number of adventurers saw the opportunity to strike out in their own interest, if not in Syracuse then at least in other cities. The large mercenary contingents played their own game. Ability to pay and employ them was, in the final analysis, the decisive factor. Class conflict came out into the open and demands for confiscation and redistribution of land were raised in a number of cities. There was a continual shifting of sides, depending on which individual or which class had the upper hand in any particular community. Only in Syracuse itself did the intra-family struggle for power remain the central theme.

Amidst all the confusion, the one institution which was not effectively challenged was one-man rule. Whatever truth there may have been in Dion's claim that he had come as a liberator who intended to replace tyranny by some form of constitutional government, it was widely believed that he was in fact aiming for the tyranny himself. There can be no doubt that by temperament and conviction he was bitterly opposed to popular rule. The lower classes distrusted and opposed him and they found leaders to speak for them, or at least to pretend to do so, in Syracuse and elsewhere. Heracleides, in particular, broke with Dion and came forward as their spokesman. Early in 354 Dion managed to win control of Syracuse (and to regain

Arete). One of his first acts was to have Heracleides killed. Later in the same year Dion was himself assassinated by Callippus, whose own motives seem to have been purely personal. He arrested Arete and her mother Aristomache, who were later released and then drowned on their way to Greece. Callippus kept control of the city for thirteen months, until he was driven out by Dion's nephew Hipparinus, the elder son of Dionysius I by his Syracusan wife. Callippus retired to the tyranny in Catania, while one Hiketas, also a member of Dion's entourage, took power in Leontini. Several years earlier a man named Andromachus (father of the historian Timaeus) collected survivors from Naxos and took Tauromenium from the mercenaries settled there by the elder Dionysius. Thus the petty tyrant returned to Sicily. In Syracuse Hipparinus lasted some two years when he died mysteriously, to be succeeded by his brother Nysaeus. In 346, finally, Dionysius II regained Syracuse briefly.

By then the eastern half of the island was a shambles, its population sharply reduced and its prosperity gone, · with warring factions ready to call in Carthage once again. The ·ath of Dionysius I, unlike the end of the Deinomenid ᵗᵃnny a century earlier, tore Sicily apart. The sordid details would not be worth even a few pages of narrative were it not for the remarkable saga of Plato's interventions which goes with it. This is a tale of which there is not a trace in the narrative we have in Diodorus nor, interestingly enough, in Aristotle's references to Dion's manoeuvres, which took place in his lifetime![1] The account comes in the first instance from several letters in a collection of thirteen letters supposedly written by Plato, some of which are certainly spurious, and then in detail from Plutarch's life of Dion, which drew heavily on the letters. It goes like this, stripped of such dubious picturesque tales as that of Dionysius I getting rid of Plato in 387 by sending him to the slave market at Corinth, where several philosophers were present by a happy chance so that they could buy his freedom. In 388 or 387 Plato journeyed to southern Italy on a private visit, primarily to establish contact with the Pythagorean philosophers, whose outstanding figure, Archytas of Tarentum,

[1] Diodorus 16.6–20; Aristotle, *Politics* 1312a4–6, 33–9; 12b16–17.

exercised a considerable influence on his later philosophical development. In Syracuse he met young Dion, then about twenty, quickly perceived his deep inner qualities and won him over to philosophy and the life of virtue. Dion bided his time for more than twenty years and then seized the opportunity when the elder Dionysius died. He persuaded the tyrant's son to invite Plato to Syracuse with the express purpose of educating Dionysius II on the proper course for the philosopher-king. The visit was a failure, Dion was sent off to Greece and Plato returned to Athens in despair. Five years later Dionysius invited Plato once more and the aging philosopher tried again. And again it became evident that the younger Dionysius was only playing with him, finally releasing him after several unhappy months. In 354, when Dion was assassinated, some of his friends wrote to Plato for advice on their next steps. In reply he sent them the long letter which appears as the seventh in the collection. The following year they made another inquiry, after Callippus was ousted, and the eighth letter came back. All in vain, of course, and the saga ends at that point.

There are obvious difficulties. Dion's alleged conversion to the Platonic way of life in 387 produced no visible external effects while he served the tyrant for twenty more years and grew rich and powerful in the process. The seventh letter, despite its verbosity, has remarkably little practical advice, though that was its ostensible purpose. It is largely a disquisition on metaphysics interlarded with generalities about the rule of law, the need for selecting good friends carefully and the good government Dion would have established had he been permitted to. The eighth letter has only a little more practicality, including the suggestion that the intra–family dispute be settled by a compromise, a triple kingship of Dionysius II, Hipparinus and Dion's son. Not a word is said about how the mercenaries, adventurers and petty tyrants could be made to accept this simple round-table solution. More useless and empty advice in a desperate civil-war situation would be hard to imagine. Nevertheless, despite the air of unreality that pervades the tale, despite some serious inaccuracies in matters of fact which appear in the two letters, despite the silence of Aristotle and Diodorus, most modern historians accept the saga. But a dogged minority continues to insist on the discrepancies and improbabilities, concluding that the saga is largely, perhaps wholly, fictitious (apart from the early, private visit by Plato in 387). Possibly it was put out by the Academy to explain away the participation of such 'Academicians' as Dion and Callippus in the unsavoury affairs of Sicily. *Their* involvement, at any rate, is certain, and they did not flinch at betrayal and murder.

Insofar as the actual history of Sicily is concerned, it does not very much matter which side one takes in the controversy among modern historians. Judgements of Plato's practical sense and of the political teaching in the Academy will be affected. So will judgments of Dion and his plans. But Dion was not in power, not even in Syracuse, long enough to accomplish anything, whatever his intentions. Events in Sicily took their own turn, whether with or without Plato's intervention. The saviour came not from Athens but from Corinth, and he was a man of military action, not a philosopher.

Chapter 8

TIMOLEON AND AGATHOCLES

The return of Dionysius II to Syracuse in 346 brought him neither security of tenure in that city nor a renewal of power elsewhere in Sicily. Even our very imperfect sources record the names of seven other tyrants during the next five years: Hiketas in Leontini; Leptines, who had murdered Dion's assassin Callippus, in Apollonia and Engyon (probably modern Troina); a 'barbarian' mercenary captain named Mamercus, perhaps a Campanian, in Catania; Nicodemus in Centuripe; Hippo in Messina; Apolloniades in Agyrium; and Andromachus in Tauromenium. The latter two are referred to as 'rulers' rather than tyrants for no better reason than that Agyrium was the native city of Diodorus and Andromachus was the father of Timaeus. Even if it were true that they had been invited to take power, the distinction is meaningless. Genuine political behaviour was no longer possible in Sicily, though the continuing strife between the wealthy 'aristocrats' and those clamouring for land redistribution created the fleeting illusion from time to time that an adventurer had acquired a basis of support and a programme, an illusion that could be strengthened by an occasional meeting of the assembly or an election. But only the mercenaries really mattered, whether Sicilians or outsiders. The difference between an adventurer or *condottiere* and a tyrant was whether or not he managed to seize and hold effective control of a city or district. And the size of a mercenary force was now often numbered in the hundreds, never more than one or two thousand, a sign not only of the break-up of the old concentration of power in Syracusan control but also of a considerable drop in both population and financial resources throughout the island.

Inevitably there was an appeal to Carthage, who responded, despite difficulties at home, perhaps in the belief that it was to her advantage to help keep the island disunited. The old monotonous tale seemed about to repeat itself when a startlingly new twist developed. Hiketas and his supporters, in exile in Leontini, begged Corinth for help. And this time the mother-city, which had never before interfered in the domestic affairs of Syracuse, broke a precedent of centuries and sent a small army under Timoleon. That many Greeks were available as individuals for the adventure is understandable. The fabric of Greek city-state society was wearing thin, there was widespread poverty and misery, and there were intimations of the forthcoming conquest by Philip of Macedon, marking the end of classical Greece. The eastern Mediterranean regions were filled with men, many of them exiles, who sought their fortune by arms and who had neither principles nor scruples nor political loyalties. However, it is far from obvious why Corinth as a political body sanctioned the move and recruited the men, a decade after Dion had been allowed to embark without any positive assistance. Corinth was a shadow of its past, battered by more than half a century of warfare and by several bitter civil-war episodes from which the ruling oligarchy, one of the most tenacious in Greece, emerged victorious. What did Corinth hope to gain from military intervention in Sicily at a time when the home front was beleaguered? No satisfactory answer has ever been produced. The force sent with Timoleon was small, furthermore, perhaps 700 mercenaries in the first instance, followed by another 2000 infantrymen with 200 cavalry a little later, mustered with the help of such Corinthian satellite-colonies as Ambracia and Leucas, and not equipped with funds. Corinth could not manage more.

The choice of Timoleon is equally opaque, except from the vantage-point of hindsight. "Some god," wrote Plutarch (*Life of Timoleon* 3.2), "put it into the proposer's mind, it would seem." His subsequent success in Sicily was beyond all reasonable anticipation, and he climaxed it by retiring from office. That act alone, unheard of in this age, could have been enough to win him the hero-cult which arose in Syracuse after his death. But he had more. His proverbial luck gave him as his first and most loyal ally in Sicily the father of the future historian Timaeus, and it is Timaeus who is behind the morality-tale which passes for an account of Timoleon's career in our surviving sources, in particular in Plutarch's 'biography'.

Of his pre-Sicilian activity little is recorded. He came from one of the leading families in the Corinthian oligarchy, but his only memorable action was the assassination of an older brother who was alleged to be attempting a coup with a view to tyranny. Whether Timoleon was himself the assassin, as Diodorus has it, or he stood by, weeping while two accomplices used their swords, in Plutarch's version, cannot be resolved. Clearly there were circles in Corinth which had doubts about the purity of Timoleon's motives. He spent the next twenty years in retirement, and when he was mysteriously chosen to lead the Sicilian adventure, despite his relatively advanced years, he was told by one Corinthian leader, in the kind of saying Plutarch could never resist, "If you struggle well, we shall credit you with having been a tyrannicide; if badly, a fratricide" (*Life of Timoleon 7.2*).

When Timoleon landed first at Rhegium and then on the beach of Tauromenium in 344, there was an understandable lack of enthusiasm in Sicily, save for Timaeus' father Andromachus. His force was small, his funds low, his goals ambiguous at best. Yet within six years he had defeated and destroyed all opposition and he was master of the island. Dionysius II was the first to give up the struggle, and he was allowed to retire to Corinth. His family were less fortunate: while the tyrant was making his final weak stand in Syracuse there was a Locrian uprising in which his wife, sons and daughters were maltreated and murdered. Leptines also abdicated and joined Dionysius in Corinth. Hiketas and his relations were executed; Mamercus was apparently crucified; Hippo was tortured to death in the theatre at Messina before a large audience including children who were brought from their schools; Nicodemus and Apolloniades were expelled (but their personal fate is unknown). Only the ever faithful Andromachus was permitted to remain in power.

The Carthaginians fared as badly. Their first army, under Mago, for some reason refused to give battle at Syracuse when Timoleon was heavily outnumbered. They withdrew and sailed back to Africa, where Mago committed suicide. In the summer of 339 (or possibly 341) another force arrived at Lilybaeum, made up not only of African subjects and mercenaries but also, most unusually, of several thousand picked troops of their own (called the Sacred Band by the Greeks). This army was smashed by Timoleon at the Crimisus River, perhaps to be identified with the Belice near Segesta. Though

5 Cathedral, Syracuse

6 Citadel of Eryx

his forces were smaller, Timoleon won through surprise moves, superior tactics, and, we are told, the smiles of Fortune in the shape of a torrential rain. Carthage abandoned the struggle, gave up enormous quantities of booty (a tithe of which was dedicated by Timoleon to Poseidon in Corinth), and made peace on more or less the old lines of the days of Dionysius I, withdrawing to the *epikrateia* west of the Halycus River line.

For all this activity Timoleon had no legitimate Sicilian authority. Were it not for the myth which has been created about him, he would be called a tyrant. And rightly so: he had seized power with a mercenary force and he depended largely on mercenaries throughout; he was autocratic and ruthless and brutal and faithless (otherwise known as 'diplomatic') precisely like his allies and opponents, who frequently interchanged roles in their relations with him. Among his chief aides were adventurers of the *condottiere* type, such as Deinarchus and Demaretus who not long afterward returned to Corinth and acted as agents there for Philip of Macedon. A fair number of his mercenaries are said to have partaken, some years earlier, in the 'Sacred War' during which Delphi was pillaged. They were now killed by the Carthaginians, Plutarch relates (30.4–5), and he calls that action the one which more than any other broadcast to the world the good fortune of Timoleon. The tale is as transparent as the habit with which Plutarch regularly restricts Timoleon to passive participation in tortures and executions, as in the assassination of his brother many years before.

Presumably that is all the contemporary Greek world saw in Timoleon: his name is not mentioned in any surviving work of his time. Yet the picture cannot be left at that. Although Timoleon's position and procedures were not fundamentally different from those of other tyrants, he alone emerged with a programme aiming to secure the future of Sicily. When he retired in 337 or 336 because of his age and his blindness, he had taken two major steps of reconstruction. His removal of nearly all the petty tyrants was followed by a dramatic destruction of the palace-fortress in Ortygia and of similar structures elsewhere. Then a "legislative commission" was summoned to Syracuse from Corinth to "revise the laws of Diocles". Apparently neither Dionysius I nor anyone else had bothered to alter the democratic constitution formulated near the end of the fifth century, allowing it to continue a paper existence.

Paradoxically, both Plutarch and Diodorus go on to say that, having revised the late fifth-century democratic constitution, Timoleon reintroduced democracy at Syracuse. Most modern scholars now agree, but there is a strong case for the view of an older generation of historians, that the Timoleontic reform was oligarchic. Plutarch's reliability as a witness on this subject is revealed by his assertion that Corinth was a democracy at that time. He himself, in his *Life of Dion* (53.2), explained that the latter had gone to Corinth for advice because "he had observed that the Corinthians governed more oligarchically, transacting little public business in the assembly". Diodorus is inconsistent and imprecise. The key question is not whether or not a popular assembly remained in existence in Syracuse, as it did, but where the power of decision lay. Assemblies often continued to meet even under tyrannies, in Sicily as elsewhere. On balance, Diodorus' account may be thought to assign the real power to the undemocratic Council of 600, which is what one might have guessed from Timoleon's Corinthian background. At the head of the state there was now placed an official chosen annually from the priesthood of Olympian Zeus. There is precedent in other Greek states for such a post, but the practice was not common. Perhaps the post was purely ceremonial, but the suggestion cannot be dismissed that Timoleon was seeking to reinforce his new machinery of government with a religious sanction. This was his one governmental innovation which survived, for more than three hundred years. The rest, whether democratic or not, quickly broke down. The Council of 600 took complete control and *stasis* returned to Syracuse.

What happened elsewhere in Sicily is unattested. The removal of the petty tyrants left a vacuum, and it seems improbable that the new governmental form was essentially different from the Syracusan. Inter-city relations are also obscure, but Timoleon's idea seems to have been a Syracusan hegemony over a loose federation of autonomous cities. At least that is the implication from coins carrying the legend, "of the allies".

More important, Timoleon renewed the base in the sense that

98

he brought to Sicily large numbers of immigrants from Italy and from many places in the old Greek world, gave them land, and thereby returned extensive deserted territories to cultivation. In two mid-third-century B.C. documents found in the temple of Asclepius in the island of Cos, off the Asia Minor coast, Cos is called "co-founder" of Kamarina and apparently also of Gela.[1] The reference cannot be to any occasion but the present one, and the texts thus bear witness to the wide territory from which the newcomers were drawn. (There was also some internal migration, not all of it voluntary, to strengthen Syracuse immediately.) Plutarch seems to think that the final total of immigrants was 60,000. There is no way to control the figure or to determine the spread of the re-population, but recent archaeology has demonstrated that for once the literary sources are guilty of understatement.

Not much can be said about Syracuse because of the difficulties of excavating there systematically. Everywhere else, however, the testimony of the spade is conclusive that Timoleon inaugurated an era of urban growth and prosperity. Not only were Akragas and Gela raised from mere squatters' hamlets to large, functioning city-states, but the whole hinterland behind the south coast saw a similar development, as did Kamarina, though on a proportionately smaller scale. Even Megara Hyblaea, which had been deserted ever since its destruction by Gelon about 483, was re-constituted. There was a revival in Segesta (for what it is worth, Diodorus (20.71.1) says its population was about 10,000 when attacked by Agathocles in 307), in Morgantina and in Lipari. At Scornavacche on the left bank of the Dirillo between Vizzini and Chiaramonte in the province of Ragusa, where there had once been a tiny Greek enclave in Sicel territory, destroyed in 405, a new settlement of Greeks reappeared and continued for half a century, chiefly engaged in pottery manufacture for local consumption. Two old Phoenician outposts were also apparently resettled at this time as Greek communities, Solus on the north coast and Minoa on the south coast, the latter renamed Heraclea and peopled, at least in part, with migrants from Cefalù.

Diodorus (16.83.1) notes that the new prosperity led to a

[1] R. Herzog and G. Klaffenbach, *Asylieurkunden aus Kos* (*Abh. d. Deutsche Akad. d. Wiss.*, Berlin, 1952 no. 1), nos. 12–13.

revival of monumental building, a practice which had almost completely ceased ever since the Carthaginian invasion at the end of the fifth century. In many places, temples were renovated, theatres and other public buildings were enlarged or newly constructed, city-walls were built or extended. The funds, according to Diodorus, came from greatly increased agricultural production, and he must be right about that, too. Sicily was a basically agrarian society; hence growth or decline in the urban sector, which archaeology can reveal, is primarily a function of success or failure in the countryside. Presumably the main markets for agricultural exports were in Greece. Coins of the Corinthian type flooded Sicily for the next few decades, becoming the normal currency of the island, which had virtually ceased to mint its own silver coins during the previous period of breakdown. Some of these new coins were minted in Sicily itself, the great majority in Corinth and her dependencies on the Greek mainland and islands. The phenomenon is not easy to explain. Although Corinth may have participated in the renewed trade with Sicily, she did not dominate it. Nor is there any reason to imagine that, as an act of altruistic friendship, Corinth accepted responsibility for replenishing low Sicilian stocks of coined money. A more plausible suggestion is that Timoleon issued, or obtained, Corinthian *pegasi* (as they are called) in order to pay his mercenaries, and that, after the revival of Sicilian grain exports, Greeks interested in that trade preferred *pegasi* to their own local coins for payments on the island.[1]

Finally, there are inferences to be drawn about the distribution of land to the immigrants. We assume that there was no equality of assignment, that among the retired mercenaries and the immigrants there were favoured individuals who were given large tracts. No other assumption is consistent with the rapid breakdown of both stable government and social peace which soon followed (and with the conception of Timoleon as an oligarchic legislator, if that is correct). Plutarch closes his biography with the standard fairy-tale ending: "Using the constitution and the laws which he established, they lived happily

---

[1] I follow the analysis of R. J. A. Talbert, *Timoleon and the Revival of Greek Sicily* (Cambridge 1974), chap. 9, with a modification proposed by C. M. Kraay in *Numismatic Chronicle*, 7th ser., 13 (1973) iv–x.

for a long time." On the contrary, there was some popular opposition in Syracuse even while Timoleon was still holding power; class war broke out not long after his retirement; Corinth sent one more 'saviour' (Acestoridas) to preserve the oligarchy and Carthage also provided support. By 317 Agathocles had begun his long reign in Syracuse.

None of this is in the least surprising. The autonomous, self-governing Greek city was beyond redemption even in old Greece and there was surely no hope for it in Sicily, where it had never grown strong roots. What is puzzling is that this round of familiar Sicilian troubles, between Timoleon and Agathocles, did not seriously disturb the new prosperity or further growth. Thus all the examples Diodorus gives of the revival of monumental building date from the reigns of Agathocles and Hiero II; a flourishing pottery industry in decorated 'red-figured' ware grew up in several eastern and southeastern centres and continued at least to the end of the fourth century; the remarkable fortification at the northern edge of the territory of Syracuse, now known as Castello Eurialo (Figure 1) was probably transformed into an independent unit under Agathocles.[1] The ambitious theatre at Morgantina is another, recently discovered example, but the most dramatic evidence of all comes from Gela. Under Timoleon the revived city centred about the original Acropolis, at the eastern end of the low plateau. It then grew so rapidly that it had to spread all the way to the other end, over-running the ancient cemetery which, in the old days, was outside the city proper. A new city-wall was built at that end, culminating in the splendid fortification wall on Capo Soprano which was recovered from the sand in 1953-4 in virtually perfect condition (Plate 9a). Its completion also dates from the reign of Agathocles.

Ancient writers tended to bracket Agathocles with the elder Dionysius, though Agathocles comes out worse, thanks to Timaeus whom he banished from Sicily to Athens (there to spend the next fifty years writing his vast erudite history). Even Diodorus, who joined the general chorus—"none of the

[1] F. E. Winter, "The Chronology of the Euryalos Fortress", *American Journal of Archaeology* 67 (1963, 363-87). Extensive alterations and additions were made later, especially during the Punic Wars.

tyrants before him displayed such cruelty to his subjects"
(19.1.8)—but who also had at his disposal friendly accounts
written by Agathocles' elder brother Antander and by Callias
of Syracuse, a sort of court historian, was moved to a rare
comment (21.17.1): "in the greater part of his history of
Agathocles, [Timaeus] lies about the ruler because of his
personal enmity." What is obscured by these polemical moral
judgments of the ruler's personality is the profound change
which had occurred in the world outside Sicily, a change to
which Agathocles responded and which stamped his career
with novel traits in the long history of Sicilian Greek tyranny.
In simplest terms, the new situation was the emergence following Alexander the Great of Hellenistic monarchy in the eastern
Mediterranean and in Egypt. Neither Greece nor Italy and
Sicily could ignore the strength and ambitions of the kings of
Macedon and Epirus and of the Ptolemaic dynasty in Egypt,
with its interests in Libya also impinging on Carthage, at least
potentially.

Agathocles' father, a potter, came to Syracuse from Thermae
in Timoleon's time. Agathocles himself was then about
eighteen, and much is made in the hostile sources of his
poverty and his practising his father's trade. He himself is
said to have boasted of his craftsmanship, for reasons which
will have to be looked at. But working potters did not become
army officers in that oligarchic world, let alone generals (as
did his brother Antander), and the conclusion seems forced on
us that the family was one of prosperous entrepreneurs, who
left their workshop in the hands of a slave overseer while they
devoted themselves to more gentlemanly pursuits. Upon the
death of Timoleon, young Agathocles threw himself into the
internecine warfare which ensued and spent more than twenty
years as a *condottiere* in both Sicily and southern Italy, getting
off to a good start by marrying a wealthy widow. During
those two decades there were interventions by Carthage
and by Corinth in Sicilian affairs once again (Acestoridas
was for a time general in Syracuse). In 317 Agathocles,
possessed of a private army and a reputation as a defender of
the masses against the oligarchs, made his successful move to
power in Syracuse (perhaps not his first), aided by several
thousand veterans from Morgantina and other inland cities.

The putsch was achieved by a two-day popular uprising in which, according to Diodorus (19.8.1), more than four thousand were slain, persons "whose sole offence was that they were of better birth than the others", and another six thousand were exiled. Agathocles then called a halt to the slaughter and looting, summoned the Assembly, entered it in civilian clothing and laid down the generalship to which the commons had earlier elected him. Given the lower-class composition of the Assembly after the putsch, the offer was naturally rejected. Instead Agathocles was voted sole command, with plenipotentiary powers, and he promised immediate cancellation of debts and redistribution of land.

That these social measures were actually carried out is unattested but probable. The loss of the twenty-first book of Diodorus' *History*, save for some excerpts, leaves large blanks in the record, including the whole of Agathocles' domestic activity as ruler. What does come through, however, is that he did not drop his popular appeal once in power. His boasting about his skill as a potter may not be very significant, but it is a pointer nonetheless. Diodorus claims that he needed no bodyguard and expressly draws the contrast with Dionysius: in the Assembly, he writes, the populace itself took the role. Most important of all is the fact that Agathocles' reported atrocities were always selective, directed against the wealthy and the oligarchically inclined. The only exception was the massacre in Segesta where, in 307, Agathocles' attempt to extract money from the wealthier citizens met with resistance, for which the whole population was made to suffer. Apart from that one occasion, his activity outside Syracuse was regularly class based, reversing the policy of Timoleon. From about 305 to his death in 289 he seems to have been so well entrenched that he was able to drop terror as an instrument altogether. His fortifications were defences against external attack, not citadels against revolts, again in contrast to Dionysius. In the following century the historian Polybius could write (9.23.2): "Do the historians not record that Agathocles of Syracuse, after having the reputation for extreme cruelty in his first coup and in the establishment of his rule, is considered to have become the gentlest and mildest of all once he thought that his power was secure over the Sicilians?" And Sicily prospered again, as has already been noted from the archaeological evidence.

The price was a cruel one in the first ten or twelve years. Not only were the oligarchic factions in some of the cities, notably Akragas, Gela and Messina, able and willing to resist but they had the backing of Carthage, still in pursuit of her policy of keeping an equilibrium among the forces in Sicily. In 311 Akragas was saved from Agathocles by the arrival of a Carthaginian fleet. The tyrant replied by invading Carthaginian Sicily; open war followed, in which Carthage won the support of most of Greek Sicily and soon had Agathocles bottled up in Syracuse. He then made his most daring move. On August 14, 310 he sailed out of the harbour with some 14,000 men, mostly mercenaries, in sixty ships and he landed southwest of Cap Bon six days later, the first European to invade North Africa in force. The defence of Syracuse he left to his brother Antander after having taken the precaution to kill off and despoil many men of wealth. From below Cap Bon, where he burnt all his boats, he made a swift and lucrative march towards Carthage. The rich, well-irrigated territory was largely undefended, Carthage having had no reason in the past to fear invasion from that direction. Within a few months Agathocles was in Tunis, which remained his main base for the duration of the expedition.

The curious situation was thus reached in which both Syracuse and Carthage had hostile armies at their gates. The enemy general at Syracuse, Hamilcar, had to send some of his forces back for the defence of Carthage and he was badly defeated by Antander. He was captured and tortured to death and his head was sent to Agathocles in Africa. Everything was going sensationally well but Agathocles was short of manpower. So he negotiated an alliance with Ophellas, one of Alexander the Great's old officers who now governed Cyrenaica, technically under the suzerainty of Ptolemy of Egypt but *de facto* independently. The agreement was that Ophellas was to have North Africa for himself while Agathocles was given a free hand in Sicily. This was presumably the occasion when Ophellas optimistically issued coins carrying both the silphium and the date-palm, symbols of Cyrene and Carthage, respectively. His contribution to the war included a cavalry force, chariots and ten thousand infantry, some recruited in

Greece, men who were looking not only for booty but also for land on which to settle. Many potential settlers came along from Cyrene, too, so that the march westwards took on something of the character of a great trek.

Ophellas had hardly arrived in Agathocles' camp early in 308 when the Sicilian king had him assassinated for reasons we do not know (the sources predictably attribute this to pure faithlessness on Agathocles' part, which seems out of character and pointless) and took over his army. Utica and Hippo Acra (Bizerta) on the coast west of Carthage were taken, providing Agathocles with a captured fleet, a naval station, and shipyards which he promptly put to work. An attempted coup inside Carthage, to which Agathocles was allegedly a party, failed. Carthage remained safe from capture despite all setbacks, if for no other reason because of her naval superiority. Meanwhile the Greek cities in Sicily were on the loose again, led by Akragas. Agathocles personally rushed to the rescue early in 307 with 2000 men, defeated Akragas and other rebelling subjects, and then crossed back to Africa where the situation was deteriorating rapidly with the army in a mutinous mood, no doubt because the funds had run out. In 306 he sued for peace; Carthage, no more interested than before in expanding her Sicilian possessions, accepted. The treaty re-established the status quo in Sicily, though Carthage kept Heraclea Minoa and Thermae in her *epikrateia* as well as Solus and of course Selinus and Segesta. In the same year, according to one account (Livy 9.43.26), Carthage and Rome signed yet another treaty in the series which went back to the old days of Etruscan domination. One provision, not a new one, allowed Romans to trade in the Carthaginian *epikrateia* in Sicily (but not in Sardinia). This was largely a formality, since Roman trading interests were still slight, but it is worth mentioning as a reflection of the rapid expansion of Roman power in central Italy, and shortly in southern Italy as well.

The rest of Sicily quickly fell to Agathocles and this is probably the time when he took the step which all his predecessors had avoided. He assumed the royal title and "Agathocles" appeared on coin-legends without the name of Syracuse (Plate 9b). Some modern historians have sought complicated explanations of the constitutional position, but it is to be doubted that anything was significantly changed inside Sicily by the new titulary, or that there was any sanction other than power. Agathocles, too, ruled wherever his writ ran, precisely like Dionysius who never called himself King. What is significant, however, is that Agathocles was following the new Hellenistic practice, and abroad, at least, the title was no doubt helpful in his dealings with other monarchs. That he cut something of a figure abroad is evident. He extended his domain into Italy; he captured Leucas and Corcyra, giving the latter as dowry when his daughter Lanassa was married to King Pyrrhus of Epirus, cousin and only surviving kinsman of Alexander the Great; he himself had as his third wife a daughter (or perhaps stepdaughter) of Ptolemy. Much wealth flowed in from various sources, enough to maintain large armies and navies. But on his death the whole enterprise died with him. Never again in antiquity was a Sicilian ruler able to play an independent role in Mediterranean power politics.

PART 3

Roman and Byzantine Sicily

Chapter 9

BETWEEN CARTHAGE AND ROME

Agathocles was assassinated in 289 B.C., at the age of seventy-two, the victim, it seems, of family feuding over the forth-coming succession to the throne. The next decade saw the familiar pattern of strife and anarchy that had followed the removal of each Syracusan strong man. Only two developments require attention. A conflict broke out inside Syracuse between the citizens and a large corps of Italian mercenaries who called themselves Mamertines after Mamers, the Oscan form of Mars, god of war. The latter were bought out and offered a haven in Messina, which they promptly took possession of, killing or exiling many men, dividing among themselves the women and children and the property. The procurement of wives by seizure is mentioned regularly when the Mamertine tale is told by an ancient writer,[1] though this must have happened repeatedly ever since tyrants began to import mercenaries and to settle them in one town or another. Presumably the stress here is to emphasize the uncivilized character of the Mamertines: once established in Messina, they embarked on a career of marauding and banditry, in between more formal fighting, which made them a force to be reckoned with and ultimately the agents who brought Rome to Sicily.

Mamertine raiding even reached the south coast, at Kamarina and then at Gela. There they were followed in 282 by Phintias, tyrant of Akragas, who razed Gela and moved the population to present-day Licata, where he founded a new city named after himself. The hinterland had been inhabited for centuries but Licata had not become an urban centre or a *polis*. Phintias set it up in proper Greek style, with a city-wall, an Agora and temples and then he dropped out of the historical record. As for Gela, it disappeared as a city until Frederick II refounded it as Terranova in 1230, though the surrounding land never went out of cultivation and in some periods was extensively farmed. Akragas was strong enough to contest

---

[1] e.g. Polybius 1.7.3–4; Diodorus 21.18.1.

Syracuse for hegemony again, and that is the second post-Agathoclean factor of some importance, for it promptly brought Carthage back to Sicily. When Syracuse defeated Akragas about 280 and proceeded to make incursions into the west of the island, Carthage sent a major expeditionary force and soon they were at the gates of Syracuse again, Akragas having failed to join the other Greek Sicilians in the struggle.

Now it was the turn of Pyrrhus, king of the Molossians of Epirus in northwestern Greece, to make his mark in the history of Sicilian warfare. Pyrrhus was one of the most remarkable of the post-Alexander generation of Greek adventurers. Based on the unpromising land of Epirus, he was a dedicated military man—Hannibal is said to have ranked him first of all commanders in shrewdness and professional skill—who also knew how to play the diplomatic game and how to create the right mythical image. He boasted descent from Achilles and Heracles, and before the attack on Eryx he made a special vow to the latter, whose ancient exploits there sanctioned a Greek claim to the site. Among his wives were a step-daughter of Ptolemy I of Egypt, the daughter of Agathocles (whom he divorced), and the daughters of at least two local Balkan rulers. Timaeus completed his life's work with an account of the wars of Pyrrhus, and Plutarch thought him worthy of a biography.

Pyrrhus began his career in the troubled affairs of northern Greece and Macedon, but without achieving the power which was his one aim in life. In 280 he saw a new opportunity and turned to Italy, responding to an appeal from Tarentum for help against the threatening Romans, now in control of most of the peninsula. In Italy he scored two sensational victories over the Roman armies. But his own troops were so depleted—hence the phrase 'Pyrrhic victory'—that he welcomed a clamorous invitation to go for easier game and intervene in Sicily.

"Sicily is near", he is said to have told his Greek confidant, Cineas, "and stretches forth her hands, a prosperous and well populated island, easy to capture. For *stasis* and anarchy are everywhere in the cities, and the bite of the demagogues, since the death of Agathocles" (Plutarch, *Life of Pyrrhus* 14.4).

Pyrrhus crossed over to Sicily in the autumn of 278 with 10,000 men, landing at Tauromenium where the then tyrant, Tyndarion, helped him and remained his loyal ally, in a curious echo of the Timoleon story. The enthusiasm appears to have spread rapidly, so that he was able to treble his forces and increase his fleet to 200 ships. Soon he was King Pyrrhus in Sicily, too, as his coinage in gold and silver testifies. Whether he was King *of* Sicily, as some historians hold, may be doubted. Pyrrhus was a typical Hellenistic ruler: he was king of the Molossians by tribal right, but elsewhere his rule was personal, not national, as his Sicilian subjects quickly learned. Within less than two years he defeated the Mamertines and threw the superior Carthaginian forces out of the island except at Lilybaeum, which proved impregnable so long as Carthage controlled the sea. Pyrrhus besieged Lilybaeum for two months and then gave up, partly because many Sicilians were turning against his autocratic rule, even hoping the Mamertines and Carthaginians might free them from their liberator. He returned to Italy in the autumn of 276, just two years after his arrival at Tauromenium. A defeat by the Romans at Benevento the following year ended his western adventures. Rome was now at liberty, helped by an understanding with Carthage, to complete the conquest of Magna Graecia with the capture of Tarentum in 272.

Meanwhile one of Pyrrhus's Syracusan henchmen, Hiero, seized power in his native city, reorganized the mercenary army, and in time also came to an understanding with the Carthaginians. He was then in a position to prepare properly for an attack on the Mamertines, even enrolling a new citizen force alongside his mercenaries, and in 269 he scored a major victory, although the Carthaginians, continuing their game of keeping Sicily divided, stopped him from taking Messina itself. Hiero now assumed the title of king and he held it for 54 years without serious challenge, dying in 215 at the age of 92. Early in his career he solidified his political position at home by marrying Philistis, daughter of a leading aristocrat named Leptines, who was almost certainly the great-grandson of the historian Philistus and great-great-grandson of Leptines, brother of Dionysius I. This marriage is reminiscent of Dionysius' first marriage, with the daughter of Hermocrates, and Hiero may well have been conscious of the precedent. Certainly he traded on the coincidence that he had the same name as one of the fifth-century Deinomenid rulers and he called his eldest son Gelon. There is some evidence that he actually claimed Deinomenid descent. The claim is dubious, but the survival power of some Sicilian families through generations of war, anarchy and assassination, as exemplified by Hiero's father-in-law, must not pass unnoticed. Nor should the longevity of the tyrants themselves.

Kingship was now a familiar and established institution among the Sicilians, as among the Greeks everywhere. Hiero went further than any predecessor, not only by regularly employing the royal title in public documents but also by putting his portrait on coins, complete with diadem (Plate 9c). Surprisingly, his coins still more often portray his wife Philistis with the title of queen (Plate 9d), under the unmistakable influence of the Arsinoe coins of Ptolemaic Egypt, and eventually Gelon appeared as co-regent, again a Ptolemaic practice. And Hiero re-established residence in a large fortified palace-citadel on Ortygia (which later became the headquarters of the Roman governors). Yet Hiero was not simply a further extension of the Syracusan trend; he was a different kind of ruler in important respects. For one thing, he soon abandoned all military adventures and any idea of extending his realm, which at its maximum embraced the eastern sector of Sicily from Tauromenium (later lost to him) down to Noto, but devoted himself to its management and his own enrichment. His interests in the eastern Greek world were fundamentally different from the power politics of his predecessors; hence his two daughters were married to Syracusan aristocrats, not to foreign rulers. To be sure, he maintained the traditional respect for Olympia. Although his name is not recorded as a victor there, that seems to be a mere gap in our admittedly incomplete records, for he issued coins portraying the goddess Nike (Victory) as a charioteer (Plate 9d), and he set up at least six statues of himself in Olympia, the largest number of any single individual. But fundamentally his concern was with markets for the agricultural and pastoral produce he controlled, which explains the particular interest in Egypt and Rhodes.

All this reflects the entry of Rome into Sicilian affairs. A Dionysius or an Agathocles was able to play a rôle in Mediterranean power politics even in the face of Carthage, but no Sicilian ruler could do so against both Carthage and Rome.

7 a. Tetradrachm, Akragas, before
middle of 5th cent. B.C.

7 b. Didrachm, Himera,
c. 480–470 B.C.

7 c. Decadrachm, Syracuse, Dionysius I

7 d. Tetradrachm, Panormus,
c. 400 B.C.

7 e. Tetradrachm,
"Siculo-Punic",
c. 350 B.C.

SILVER COINS (*actual size*)

obvers

revers

8 a. Etruscan bronze helmet, dedicated at Olympia by Hiero in 474 B.C.

8 b. Copper coin, "King Antiochus" of the slaves (2½ times actual size)

8 c. Kale Akte from the air.

Hiero initially allied himself with Carthage in 264, but he did not wait to be crushed or even to suffer a military defeat before deciding that he had chosen incorrectly. By mid-263 he swung and signed a treaty with Rome, being let off with a relatively small indemnity in return for a Roman guarantee of his authority within his own realm. There is some reason to believe that pressure from the Syracusan aristocracy helped him see the light, and there are no signs of objection at that time from the subject-cities either. The alliance (or symbiosis) was one of the most long-lived of the period. Hiero remained faithful to Rome until his death forty-eight years later, helping her on a large scale with corn and other supplies. Syracuse and its dependent states thus escaped the horrors of the First Punic War and of the early years of the Second, and Hiero personally escaped the usual threats and conspiracies.

Henceforth the history of ancient Sicily is part of Roman history, with the most profound effects not only on Sicilian politics but also on its economy and civilization. Henceforth, too, we are subject to grave difficulties in trying to penetrate the veil spun by the triumphant Roman historical tradition. There were accounts which viewed affairs from the opposing side, such as those of Philinus of Akragas or of Hannibal's Greek secretary, the Spartan Sosylus, but they have been drowned out. Philinus was at least made use of and discussed by Polybius and then cast aside; Sosylus' work he dismissed (3.20.5) as being like the "common gossip of a barber's shop". Three kinds of bias, in particular, require the closest watch: belief in the inevitability of a war to the death between Carthage and Rome (as successor to the Greeks in this myth); the focusing of attention on the places and the issues which mattered to Romans; and the glorification (and, insofar as possible, the whitewashing) of Rome, of her motives, her behaviour, her values. Thus, the faithful Hiero could do no wrong, whereas his successor Hieronymus, who broke with Rome and took Syracuse into the Carthaginian camp, managed to accumulate in his thirteen months of rule as many vices and atrocities as Dionysius I, although he was no more than a child, fifteen or sixteen years of age. And the wars between Rome and Carthage are known to history only by the wonderfully one-sided name, Punic Wars.

To be sure, Roman leadership was far from monolithic and the frequent conflicts over policy, sometimes very sharp, save the historical record from being irredeemably distorted. Polybius, at least, retained a measure of critical judgment. The most problematic action of all was the one which touched off the First Punic War in 264; the war-guilt question was still being debated in some Roman circles a century later, when Polybius was in Rome and writing his history. For reasons which are not very clear, the Mamertines in Messina suddenly decided to eject the Carthaginian garrison protecting them from Hiero and to appeal to Rome instead. No doubt they stressed their kinship, being of Italic stock, but this could not have weighed very heavily at that moment. Only a few years earlier the Romans had had to expel from Rhegium another Campanian force, which they had themselves installed there, because the soldiers had turned to marauding in the best Mamertine fashion. Yet Rome now gave a positive response to the Mamertines and it is hard to discover why. The inevitable argument, after the fact, that a Carthaginian presence on the straits of Messina was a threat to Italy, is anachronistic; Carthage had never in the past shown the slightest ambition to move into Italy, nor did the rather tame behaviour of her army and navy in the region suggest that a new and bellicose policy was on its way. Besides, Rome and Carthage had on several occasions negotiated treaties with each other, most recently when Pyrrhus invaded Italy. The Roman Senate, in the end, refused to come to any decision about the Mamertines and it was popular pressure which forced the issue. A relatively small army was instructed to cross over to Sicily, with Syracuse (a Carthaginian ally for the moment) as its target; it managed to slip by the Carthaginians and Syracusans and land successfully, and the First Punic War was under way, though no one thought of it in such terms yet.

Not even the most hotheaded of the war party in Rome intended anything but a season's campaign or two. No preparations were made for a major war against the other great power in the western Mediterranean. Both the preparations and the ambitious war aims came later, as the war grew. Polybius dates the turning-point in 261, after the Romans had captured Akragas. That seems too simple and schematic, but he is right to the extent that only then did Rome take the indispensable step of creating a fleet, without which no one could hope to contend with Carthage on equal terms. Carthage had quickly responded in force to the Roman invasion of Sicily, for, as always, control of western Sicily was essential for her navigation. With Lilybaeum and Panormus to look after the fleet, she proceeded to establish a military base at Akragas, the greatest city in her Sicilian 'province', and a secondary one at Heraclea Minoa. It was these which Rome first attacked. Afterwards, when a Roman navy came into being, the war spread not only to the northwest and west of Sicily but also to North Africa. It was a war fought without a respite for nearly a quarter of a century, until 241, in which neither side gave way to the other in ruthlessness or determination. Rome and her Italian allies (whose participation was compulsory) lost at least 100,000 men, 500 or more warships and equipment beyond counting. No wonder the ancients believed the First Punic War to be the most destructive thus far in their history. Or that they had to find war aims, even if retrospectively, commensurate with the effort and the costs. Against the outlay must be balanced very considerable sums that poured into the Roman treasury (and the pockets of individual soldiers) from captives and other booty, and after the victory from the Carthaginian indemnity.

In all this carnage the Sicilians themselves provided victims rather than manpower. Rome took Akragas in 261 after a six-month siege and sold off 25,000 of the inhabitants. That was the native city of the anti-Roman historian Philinus, it is worth remembering. Carthage returned seven years later, after a storm had destroyed the Roman fleet returning from Africa, tore the walls down and burned the city. In 258 Kamarina was taken by Rome with siege equipment provided by Hiero; most of the population were sold into slavery. Then it was the turn of Panormus, where 13,000 were sold while another 14,000 were permitted to ransom themselves at a fixed price per head. In 250 Carthage razed Selinus and transferred the inhabitants to Lilybaeum, marking the end of Selinus as an inhabited centre until a small Christian settlement was established there in the later Roman Empire. Lilybaeum now became the concentration point of the war. Rome converted Panormus into a main base of her own and in 250 she put Lilybaeum under siege, which the city was able to withstand, thanks to the Carthaginian navy, for ten years—one more demonstration of what this single Sicilian promontory meant to Carthage. A naval defeat in 241 finally forced Carthage to surrender. She agreed to a large indemnity, to a total withdrawal from Sicily, and to a commitment not to make war on Hiero in the future.

Hiero's prudence had paid off handsomely. The Sicilian losses just mentioned are by no means complete, but even if we had all the details, including the endless commandeering and destruction of crops and cattle along with the killings, enslavements and physical ruin of many cities, the picture as a whole would not be significantly altered: the First Punic War was a disaster for western and southern Sicily, not for Hiero. His territory was effectively untouched from the moment he joined the Roman side, and though he contributed supplies and materials to the Romans, he was not called upon for men and he and his people no doubt made their profits out of the vast booty thrown on the market year after year. In the end, too, his rule was sanctioned by both Rome and Carthage, and he quickly showed that he was happy to see Carthage remain a force as a counterweight to Rome. No sooner had the war ended than North Africa erupted in a barbarous four-year revolt of the mercenaries and Numidians (the setting for Flaubert's *Salammbô*), which threatened the very existence of the Carthaginian state. Hiero responded generously to appeals for supplies, "being convinced," explains Polybius (1.83.3), "that it was to his advantage, for the sake both of his rule in Sicily and of his friendship with Rome, that Carthage should be saved." Polybius went on to call this a wise judgment and to add, rather puzzlingly, that Rome also honoured its pact with Carthage in the same crisis. In 238, while Carthage was still struggling with the rebellion, Rome seized Sardinia, an action, says Polybius (3.28.1) which was "against all justice", one for which "it is impossible to discover any reasonable pretext or cause".

The next two decades in Sicily are almost a complete blank in the available records: the sources on which we are compelled to rely had their attention concentrated elsewhere. All of Sicily, apart from Hiero's dominion, was now a Roman possession. A new administrative and imperial situation was thus created for Rome. In the previous centuries her acquisitions had been solely in Italy, and by a series of *ad hoc* measures, in the form chiefly of 'alliances' and 'half-citizenship', she had evolved a viable power structure. But Sicily and Sardinia were possessions, not allies in even the most euphemistic sense, and a new machinery was required to organize and administer and exploit. Details are almost completely lacking about the first steps taken—the full-fledged provincial system was still some decades in the future—but it is certain that both islands (Hiero's territory always excepted) were required to pay an annual tribute, chiefly in corn, that Roman officials were installed, and that Lilybaeum, at least, was turned into a Roman naval base. In Carthage, meantime, the Barca family—Hamilcar, his son-in-law Hasdrubal, and then his son Hannibal—had taken the stage, planning vengeance against Rome. Eyes were turned to Spain, where a new Carthaginian empire was being built. This was the base from which Hannibal crossed the Alps in 218 to initiate the Second Punic War.

From the beginning Sicily was important in the second war as a barrier between Hannibal in Italy and the home base in North Africa. The Romans were able to raid Africa from Lilybaeum and southern Italy from Messina, while disrupting direct communication by sea between Hannibal and Carthage. Hiero helped supply the Roman forces in Sicily and on at least two occasions sent substantial gifts to Rome itself. In 216 a convoy arrived at Ostia from Syracuse with 1000 mercenary archers and slingers, 300,000 *modii* (about 26,000 hectolitres) of wheat and 200,000 of barley, and a gold statue of Victory which was placed in the temple of Jupiter Optimus Maximus on the Capitol. The next year 200,000 *modii* of wheat and 100,000 of barley were sent. Each contribution followed a terrible Roman defeat in Italy, the first at Lake Trasimene, the second at Cannae. But not everyone in Syracuse was so loyal, not even in the ruling family. Hiero's son and co-regent, Gelon, was rumoured to be negotiating with Carthage. He died suddenly and "opportunely", the old man died soon after, and the half-century symbiosis came to an end. For a year Syracuse was beset by palace plots and civil disorder while Rome and Carthage carried on complicated diplomatic moves with the various parties. Strong anti-Roman feeling now showed itself, not only among the subject-states of Syracuse (the authority of Syracuse over them had been reinforced by Roman power) but also among the commons in Syracuse and among the communities in Roman Sicily. Hiero's successor, his young grandson Hieronymus, supported by Hiero's sons-in-law, eventually came to a formal understanding with Carthage, including a commitment by the latter, no doubt tongue-in-cheek, to turn the whole of Sicily over to Syracuse after the Romans were defeated.

Hieronymus was promptly assassinated at Leontini, but Syracuse was not to be moved. Direction of affairs was now effectively in the hands of two emissaries of Hannibal's, Hippocrates and Epicydes, whose good Greek names were legitimately come by: their grandfathers, exiled by Agathocles, settled in Carthage and gave their sons Carthaginian wives. Full preparations were made, with popular backing and a good mercenary army. When the Romans invaded in force under Marcellus, they found that they could neither take the city by storm nor blockade it against the Carthaginian navy. For two years Syracuse was kept under siege, but neither superior manpower nor the most sophisticated assault techniques and equipment availed, by land or sea. Archimedes was the fertile genius of the defence and he provided the Romans with a face-saving explanation of their long frustration. The Romans, wrote Polybius (8.3.3), "failed to reckon with the ability of Archimedes, nor did they foresee that in some circumstances the genius of one man is more effective than any number of hands."

More than Syracuse was at stake. The whole war now turned on Sicily and everyone knew it. Had Syracuse and the Carthaginians succeeded in throwing the Romans out, Hannibal could have been reinforced with men and supplies, Philip V of Macedon might have decided to make a genuine contribution, and Rome would have faced defeat. Marcellus responded with vigour and brutality. Megara was totally destroyed again, a revolt in Enna was followed by mass butchery, while Carthage, in turn, re-established herself at Heraclea Minoa and Akragas. Altogether, Carthage despatched some 40,000 troops, including 6,000 cavalry, and 200 ships to Sicily between 214 and 211. In 212 Syracuse at last fell to Rome, thanks primarily to treachery by a cabal of nobles. The city was given over to the soldiers for looting and Archimedes was killed, though we are assured that this was contrary to Marcellus' orders. Marcellus then proceeded to ship back to Rome not only the customary booty but also vast quantities of statuary and paintings, some torn from the walls of the temples and other public buildings. For that he earned the censure of Polybius and the hatred of the Sicilians generally, so much so that the Romans were persuaded to replace him for the final operations by another general, M. Valerius Laevinus. From that date, says Livy (25.40.2), began the Roman admiration for Greek works of art.

Only the Carthaginians in Akragas had still to be dealt with, and in 211 the city was betrayed by the Numidian mercenaries. The population was sold off with the booty, and the remaining Sicilian cities either were taken or surrendered promptly. In 210 Laevinus reported to the Senate in Rome that not one Carthaginian remained in the island, that every Sicilian refugee had returned, that agriculture was in full swing again for the benefit of both the Sicilians and the Romans. That he exaggerated a bit is not too important. The return of the land to full tillage required attention: Laevinus himself seems to have devoted much of the year 209 to touring the island for this purpose. But the fact is that by then Sicily was able to supply the Roman army at Tarentum with its corn needs and that Lilybaeum was again available as a base for operations in Africa. The Second Punic War actually dragged on until Hannibal's defeat at Zama in North Africa in 201. It destroyed Carthage as a power, left Rome in control of the western Mediterranean, poised for world conquest. That is the war's place in the history-books. In the process, however, the same war not only put an end to the last vestiges of independence in Sicily, but it re-directed much of Sicily's external economic relations to Italy as well.

Most of Sicily had already been subordinate to Rome for a generation. Only Hiero's kingdom had remained independent, and his reign is hard to evaluate. After the assassination of Hieronymus, the assembly met and voted that the royal house should be extirpated. The decision was carried out summarily, one of Hiero's daughters and her two children even being dragged from their household sanctuary to be put to death. Such incidents support the view recently put forward that throughout his reign Hiero depended on a pro-Roman oligarchy, while the commons were basically hostile. Certainly the final defence of the city took on the character of a great patriotic struggle, in which the role of Archimedes is worth special comment. He had been admitted to Hiero's inner circle. He is reported to have found the principle of specific gravity when presented by Hiero with the practical problem of detecting whether a goldsmith had cheated in making a cup out of a gold and silver alloy. One of his mathematical treatises, the *Sand Reckoner*, was dedicated to Gelon. Yet, on any interpretation of his role in the siege, he devoted himself wholeheartedly to the war against Rome, despite his late patron's lifelong loyalty to Rome. The Roman record in Sicily, after all, had not been an endearing one, beginning with the treatment of Akragas in 261.

Hiero's association with Archimedes was more than just an accidental personal attraction. He was a businessman and technocrat, in a sense, and for that it is hard to find a precedent in the history of Greek tyrants. If his public buildings were typical of Sicilian tyrants in their megalomania—his great altar near the theatre at Syracuse (Figure 1) measured 199 by 23.5 metres—his direct interest in the engineering was his own. He once had constructed the greatest seagoing vessel of antiquity, the "Syracusia", which he sent off to Alexandria laden with perhaps 2000 tonnes of merchandise, tonnage probably not equalled until the nineteenth century.[1] The ship was useless for any purpose other than conspicuous display; Alexandria was the only harbour which could take it and so Hiero gave it to Ptolemy as a gift on the completion of its maiden voyage, and we hear no more of it. He is also credited with a manual on agronomy. In that field, at least, he knew how to be superpractical; not only did he possess large estates of his own but he

[1] Modern estimates of this super-freighter's capacity run as high as 4,200 tonnes, but I follow the conservative calculation of L. Casson, *Ships and Seamanship in the Ancient World* (Princeton 1971), pp. 184–6. He gives the best text and an annotated translation of the sole ancient source, Athenaeus 5.206d–209, on pp. 191–9.

claimed a tithe of all the crops produced in his kingdom. Although modern scholars have repeatedly suggested that this was an old tax in Sicily, going back to the Deinomenids, the evidence, such as it is, points to its being a Hieronic innovation and to his having worked out the collection procedures with skill and precision. To hold the stores he constructed a vast fortified granary on Ortygia, and he then used the crops both for straight business transactions as an exporter and for political purposes, as in his gifts to Rome. There is no suggestion of a monopoly, whether in corn or in the horses and pigs that were shipped as far as Egypt, but Hiero clearly was the greatest single beneficiary, and he also collected a harbour-tax on all other shipments. Fundamentally he has to be ranked with the contemporaneous Hellenistic monarchs in the Greek East, though a minor one, not with the Greek rulers of an earlier age. And, it is worth repeating, the necessary security was provided for him by Rome.

Hiero began his career in a war-torn, wasted Sicily. He was immediately approached for patronage by a young Syracusan poet named Theocritus (16.85–99): "Would that dire necessity send the enemy, few in number, from this island across the swelling sea of Sardinia, announcing the death of loved ones to children and wives. . . . Would that the cities which the hands of the enemy have utterly laid waste be dwelt in again by their former citizens. May the abundant fields be tilled, while countless tens of thousands of flocks, growing fat in the pastures, bleat over the plain. . . . Let the minstrels bear the highest praise of Hiero across the Scythian sea. . . ." The memory of Pindar and Simonides and an earlier Hiero was clearly in Theocritus' mind, but this Hiero was not interested in patronizing the arts, then or later. So Theocritus left Sicily forever, going first to Cos and then to Alexandria; the last great Sicilian literary figure to write in Greek (Diodorus can hardly be called a literary figure) produced his bucolic poems, a Sicilian genre in origin, as a voluntary exile. Half a century later, at Hiero's death, Sicily was again war-torn and devastated, but this time enemies over the sea were in firm and permanent control.

Chapter 10

THE FIRST ROMAN PROVINCE

Sicily was "the first to teach our ancestors what a fine thing it is to rule over foreign nations". So Cicero (*II Verrine* 2.2) in 70 B.C. at the trial of Gaius Verres for gross extortion and malfeasance as governor of Sicily. After Cicero's opening speech for the prosecution Verres decided that defence was futile and he went into voluntary exile. For political reasons of his own Cicero proceeded to publish a 400-page book in the guise of five lengthy court orations, which were neither delivered nor even written for delivery. That book is our main source of information on the internal affairs of the province under the Roman Republic, and its limitations as evidence are pretty obvious. Cicero selected what suited his purposes. Every advocate did, but with Verres no longer there to reply and no court sitting to hold any reins, Cicero was free to suppress or distort information, perhaps on occasion to invent, beyond the normal practice in advocacy. Both he and his readers fully accepted the implications of "what a fine thing it is to rule over foreign nations". His model of rectitude, against whom Verres was measured and found wanting, was no other than Marcellus, the conqueror of Syracuse, widely condemned by earlier writers and characterized by Appian (*Sikelika* 5), a late but by no means stupid historian, as a man "nobody would trust except under oath", whom even the Roman Senate had agreed to withdraw from Sicily because he was intolerable to the Sicilians.

In particular, Cicero went all out to create the impression of a peaceful, prosperous, essentially unchanging Sicily—until Verres became governor and turned the island into a desert in three years. Yet nearly a century and a half had passed since the capture of Syracuse in the Second Punic War. Neither conditions nor institutions remained static through all those years; Cicero himself mentions new regulations when it suits him. Perhaps nothing in his performance is more disingenuous than the repeated self-satisfied assertion that the tax system of the Romans was just a continuation of Hiero's system, implying that the fortunate Sicilians were therefore paying what they had always paid and had gained the blessings of peace to boot. Even if the stated facts were all correct, which they are not, the contention fudges a number of important distinctions. For one thing, only a small part of Sicily was subject to Hiero and paid tithes (and other taxes) to him. Diodorus' skimpy references to Carthaginian taxation, all to the fifth century, sound more like a fixed monetary tribute levied on the cities (which could, to be sure, have been onerous enough). Independent Sicilian communities levied taxes, too, but there is surely a difference, both psychologically and substantively, between such payments, the yield of which was on the whole expended locally (as also in the case of Hiero), and the goods and money which the Romans carried away without a similar return.

Whatever the antecedents, the base of the Roman tribute system was one tenth of the wheat and barley crop, paid in kind and shipped straight to Rome, a tax on wine, olives, fruit and vegetables which was probably also a tithe, and a pasture-tax in cash. The grain tithe has been estimated, on the basis of Cicero's rather ambiguous statements, at about 3,000,000 *modii* (825,000 bushels) a year. In addition Rome reserved the right to take a second tithe by compulsory purchase, at a price the Senate fixed unilaterally, whenever Rome required it.[1] This was done in 190 to supply a Roman army fighting in Greece, again the following year and in 171 for the army in Macedonia. These instances have been preserved accidentally. There is no way to guess how often the practice was repeated, until a law of 73 B.C. seems to have made it a regular, annual occurrence. And there were still further compulsory purchases, again at unilaterally fixed prices, for the maintenance of the Roman governor and his staff. Even if fair market prices were decreed, there was scope for chicanery in such prerogatives. Nor was the remainder of the crop at the free disposal of the Sicilians: exports were permitted only to Italy, unless a special licence were given by the Roman Senate, as it did in 169 at the request of a Rhodian embassy. No wonder Roman writers loved to quote Cato's dictum that Sicily was the "Republic's granary, the nurse at whose breast the Roman people is fed".

[1] The principal sources for what follows are, respectively, Livy 33.2; 37.50; 42.31; Cicero, *II Verrine* 3.163; Livy 43.2.11-12; Polybius 28.2; Cicero, *II Verrine* 2.5.

Rome also collected a 5 per cent ad valorem duty on all goods shipped in or out of any Sicilian harbour. This was a money-raising device in the purest sense, without any idea of protectionism, and exemptions were given only for the tithes and for personal goods carried by voyagers. Finally, there was an obligation on the several communities to provide ships, with their crews, for a small navy whose function was to protect the harbours against pirates. That completes the list of contributions levied by Rome but the Sicilians had local taxes of their own to meet as well. Although denied armies and the right to conduct foreign affairs, which had drawn so heavily on public funds in the old days, the Sicilian communities still had to carry the full cost of their public buildings, water supply, cults, festivals and other amenities. Some was borne directly by individual wealthy citizens, a traditional practice among Greeks; the rest came from taxes, for which by Verres' time two censors in each community drew up a quinquennial census. Both the office and the procedure were Roman, not Greek.

'Community' in this context has to be understood as a Roman administrative notion, for which the Latin word was *civitas*. When Augustus' lieutenant Agrippa was collecting material for his "map of the world" towards the end of the first century B.C., Sicily seems to have been apportioned among 68 *civitates*, including the islands of Lipari and Malta (Pliny, *Natural History* 3.88–91). Although this number was probably not absolutely stable, the figure would not have fluctuated much in the preceding two centuries. Among the 68 were such good old urban centres as Syracuse, Messina, Agrigentum (to use its Roman name now) or Lilybaeum, but also Imachara, Apollonia, Cetaria, Ietai and other such localities, not genuine cities (whatever the extent or wealth of their agricultural holdings) by any norm other than administrative convenience. In Cicero's day eight were "free and immune", Messina, Tauromenium and Noto by "treaty", Centuripe, Halaesa, Segesta, Halicyae and Panormus by unilateral grant of the Roman Senate or people. That is to say, they were autonomous, at least notionally, and their own citizens were exempt from the tithe (but not always from the naval obligation and never from compulsory purchases). They make up a curious group. If there was a common denominator among them, it is lost among the missing details of the two Punic Wars and their aftermath and of the two slave wars in the latter part of the second century B.C.[1] The Romans had long since become expert in employing a complex mechanism of rewards and punishments in their march to world empire, and they made the appropriate modifications as they created for the first time a method of provincial rule. Messina's high status, at least, is easily understood, for Cicero regularly calls it "the city of the Mamertines", as the renowned wine of the district was always known as "Mamertine wine". The case of Segesta is different, requiring a sentimental explanation with strong enough political overtones to overcome any suggestion of frivolity. Segesta was originally an Elymian settlement, and the Elymians and Rome both now claimed a Trojan origin, the latter through Aeneas.

From Rome's point of view the main function of the *civitates* was to supply the preliminary information on which levies were based. The actual collection of the tithes was farmed out by a procedure which seems to have been taken over from Hiero's. The tithe for each *civitas* was auctioned locally every year, the potential bidders having at their disposal a list prepared by the community of the landholdings and of those who worked it (for the tax fell on them and not on the owners in cases of tenancy). The tithe was then collected by the tax-farmers on the threshing-floor after the harvest, and disputes were settled by an established court procedure. The effect of a local auction in relatively small units year by year was to keep the tax-farming in the hands of Sicilian men of affairs and away from the great Roman companies who were to collect the taxes in Asia. Occasionally a *civitas* entered the auction and farmed the taxes itself, and here and there a Roman name appears, usually someone who had migrated to Sicily. The whole machinery clearly helped the growth inside Sicily of a core of provincials with a stake in Roman rule. It is to be doubted, however, that this was the main Roman calculation. Lacking any previous experience with provincial rule, Rome simply took over an existing procedure. Besides, the companies of Roman publicans had not yet become so powerful in the third

[1] See Chapter 11.

century and the early second, when the Sicilian system was established. As they grew in importance they won concessions. The not insignificant Sicilian pasture-tax and the harbour-tax were farmed at Rome, and in 75 B.C. wine, olive oil and other products were separated from corn for tax purposes and the collection was handed over to them as well.

Local administration, like local taxation, was left to the Sicilians in principle, even among the communities that were not formally "free and immune". Rome had neither the manpower nor the desire nor any good reason to take on that burden, in Sicily or elsewhere in the empire. What little information we have suggests a great diversity in the details, the end-product in each community of centuries of more or less autonomous development. There were differences, above all, between old *poleis* like Syracuse or Agrigentum and such communities as Panormus or Drepana which had not been properly Greek anyway. Private law was not interfered with or Romanized; Diodorus makes a special point of this on one occasion (13.35.3). There is even a suggestion that communities were permitted to retain the traditional Greek rule that land ownership was barred to non-citizens, including fellow-Greeks from the next town. In the eight favoured cities, in particular, this would have remained an important privilege. Everywhere there are signs that councils and assemblies continued to meet and to transact business, though in a very low key. At the same time, there was an unmistakable preference for oligarchy, even in communities in which popular assemblies maintained a shadowy existence and ceremonial functions. Latin writers regularly translated the several Greek words for 'council' by *senatus*, and the Roman Senate was indeed the model now, pathetic though the imitation had to be. Cicero's constant reference to the nobility of the leading men in Sicily may not prove much: they were his witnesses and one wonders how they would have come out were he counsel for the defence. But Livy was equally free with the label, and behind him stood Polybius. Rome always found oligarchies more amenable than democracies in subject states.

In practice, autonomy meant freedom from Roman interference so long as Rome chose not to interfere (or was not asked to). Interventions were variously motivated and took various forms, legal and extra-legal. The rarest was a general regulation for the province as a whole, such as the *lex Rupilia* of 131, following the suppression of the first slave revolt. How much ground it covered is unknown: all that survives is Cicero's brief summary (*II Verrine* 2.32–34) of provisions specifying the court procedures, and by implication the law to be enforced, in private suits, differing according to the civic status of each of the parties. This was an old problem in Greek history because of city-state autonomy; now there were further complications in the provinces with the influx of Roman immigrants carrying on agriculture and business in communities in which they were both 'foreigners' and members of the imperial nation at the same time. That was the situation for which the *lex Rupilia* laid down the rules.[1] More common were interventions into specific local situations. In 197, for example, the Senate instructed the governor to bolster the population of imperishable Agrigentum by transplanting settlers from elsewhere in Sicily. Four years later another governor, one of the Scipios, promulgated the rules of cooptation into the Agrigentine senate and specified that the representatives of the new settlers must not constitute a majority in that body. Nothing is said about the initiative for these measures, but in 95 B.C. Halaesa, one of the 'free' communities, asked the Roman Senate to resolve a dispute over cooptation into its own senate and was given new regulations, including a minimum age of thirty and a bar to practitioners of "infamous professions".

These are examples of official interventions from Rome itself. However, in the ordinary affairs of the Sicilians, Rome was personified in the local tax-collectors, the two Roman quaestors (financial officers stationed in Lilybaeum and Syracuse) and the Roman governor, with their staffs, retainers, servants and hangers-on. The normal term of office was one year, extended on occasion for special reasons: Verres had three terms because his designated successor was preoccupied with the Spartacist slave revolt in Italy. Various factors entered into their selection, but neither a capacity to govern well and equitably nor a knowledge of Sicily was among them. Nor was a one-year tour of duty conducive to good administra-

---

[1] For the following measures, see Cicero, *I Verrine* 2.122–4.

tion. Some governors proved to be reasonably honest and competent, others not. They were all responsible to the Senate in Rome and that august body was happy to make the annual selection and then to forget all about Sicily unless its attention was forced. And even then it was rare for anything to happen. In 210 a Sicilian delegation made a desperate appeal against the return of Marcellus (Livy 26.29–32). They produced a long, well-substantiated list of charges and met with much sympathy. Marcellus was not a beloved figure in Rome: he had been denied the customary triumph for his capture of Syracuse and received only the lesser honour of an ovation. He himself now proposed that Laevinus go to Sicily in his place, but that is all the amends the Sicilians received. Marcellus was too powerful politically. The Senate confirmed all his acts, including the one which forbade any Syracusan to reside in Ortygia because it was too easily defended on the land side and too easily contacted by sea. (That order was still in force in Cicero's day: *II Verrine* 5.84.) The incident foreshadowed the tyrannical power which governors could exercise in the future, and sometimes did.

It is pointless to argue, with some historians, that very few governors of Sicily were prosecuted for malfeasance (none is known earlier than 114 B.C.)[1] and that even these were probably victims of Roman political in-fighting. Only rarely was a Roman, of sufficient standing and power to achieve a governorship, brought to trial and found guilty for other than Roman political reasons. Verres is proof enough. On any reading of Cicero, Verres and his gang were a remarkable collection of rogues. They cheated, lied, embezzled, robbed, conspired, suborned and terrorized in all possible directions in their dedication to the cause of personal enrichment. They even flogged and tortured Roman citizens publicly. Yet nothing happened. In 72, the second year of his governorship, a rich and influential Sicilian, Sthenius of Thermae, made a personal appeal in Rome. He won the support of the two consuls and one of the tribunes, was listened to sympathetically in the Senate (in which Verres' father sat), and left empty-handed. Verres was re-appointed once again, and then his luck turned

[1] Cicero, *Letters to Friends* 9.21.3

when Cicero intervened. Still it was a near thing. Verres had the support of the powerful Scipios and Metelli, his counsel was Q. Hortensius, a very distinguished advocate and consul-elect for 69. Had the delaying tactics of the Verres party succeeded in postponing the trial to 69, he might have escaped after all. However, the manoeuvres failed and Verres retired to an affluent life in exile from Rome, enjoying his outstanding art collection for another 27 years.

It is not suggested that Verres met with approval in leading Roman circles. But when values clashed, the fundamental interests of Roman rule and the close personal ties within the ruling class normally overrode all other considerations. The authority and *dignitas* of a provincial governor counted among the fundamental interests. It is also not suggested that anyone in Rome expected an official not to enrich himself during his term abroad. Cicero himself had been quaestor in Lilybaeum in 75 and his claim to have won universal approval for his honesty and fair-dealing need not be questioned. How much he brought back that year is unknown, but in 51 and 50 he was governor of Cilicia, again honest and equitable, and his profits, legally gained, amounted to 2,200,000 sesterces (*Letters to Friends* 5.20.9). That may have been no remarkable sum to a Pompey or a Crassus; in Sicily it would have looked large enough. In the *Verrines*, Cicero himself calls the 3,000,000 sesterces inherited by a certain Heraclius of Syracuse a "great fortune". The only question, and a difficult one, was where to draw the line between lawful enrichment and extortion.

Private Roman exploitation was another factor in "what a fine thing it is to rule over foreign nations". At the head of Marcellus' ovation in 211 there marched two traitors, Sosis of Syracuse and a Spaniard named Moericus, who had played an important part in delivering the city to the Romans. They were each rewarded with Roman citizenship and a gift of 500 *jugera* (about 125 hectares) in Sicily. Moericus and his Spanish soldiers were settled in an inland community called Murgentia (perhaps the same as Morgantina), which had revolted to the Carthaginians. As for Sosis, he was allowed to select his allotment, in Livy's words (26.21.10–11), "from Syracusan land which had belonged either to the king [Hiero] or to enemies of the Roman people, and he was to choose any house he wished in Syracuse belonging to someone who had been put to death under the laws of war." Livy's categories are significant and precise. The Romans repeated in Sicily a practice they had developed in their Italian expansion, that of confiscating in the name of the state the landed property of declared enemies, sometimes of whole communities (Leontini), more often of specific individuals or families (as in Syracuse). This *ager publicus* was then either given to deserving individuals, like Sosis, or to veterans, as in 199 B.C. in Sicily, or it was leased in large allotments at rather nominal rents.

How much land the Roman state acquired in Sicily in this way is unknown, and the subsequent history of the Sicilian *ager publicus* is most obscure. Cicero has confused it so effectively that no historian has been able to produce a convincing account. That a large part of the Leontine territory was still *ager publicus* in Cicero's day is probably the only thing to be said without too much risk of contradiction, which is saying very little. By one means or another, a number of Romans and south Italian 'allies' and 'half-citizens' quickly moved in, as owners or tenants, occupying large and profitable holdings in fertile plains and in the extensive pastures of the interior. The Sicilian phase of the Second Punic War had not only disrupted agriculture, but it had also permanently removed many landowners. Among those who seized the opportunity were members of the second estate in Rome, the "knights", although apparently no senators at this time. Other Romans migrated to the bigger maritime cities for business reasons. The numbers added together were not great, probably a thousand or two in the final count, but their wealth and influence were disproportionate. In main cities they were organized informally, in what was called a *conventus*, which had no corporate standing in the law but which provided the judges for many civil disputes and would in general have had little trouble in lobbying Roman officials. It is not surprising that the *Italici* of Halaesa erected a monument to the governor, possibly Scipio Asiaticus, in 193.[1] Perhaps the worst of Verres' crimes was his inability to leave the Romans in Sicily alone.

Superficially the situation when the Romans completed their

---

[1] *Corpus Inscriptionum Latinarum* 1[2] 612.

conquest in 211 seems reminiscent of the days of Timoleon. Armies and battles had ruined cities and devastated the countryside both times. Massive reconstruction was required, and both times it was achieved. But there were two important differences. The reduction of Sicily to a colonial position is the first and its implications are straightforward. The second is more problematical: now there seems not to have been the manpower shortage which Timoleon overcame through his successful appeal for immigrants. A sufficient slave labour supply was apparently at hand, although lack of statistics frustrates us on just this sort of essential question. Nothing is known in detail of the destiny of the men, women and children who were sold off by the tens of thousands during the third-century wars. It is only because of the special circumstances that an ancient writer bothers to mention that the Carthaginians captured at Himera in 480 were put to work on the temples in Akragas. Otherwise we must guess: a few were ransomed, more were carried abroad by slave dealers, the rest ended up as slaves inside Sicily. This would create no moral difficulties, no problems of conscience, either for Romans or for the more fortunate among the Sicilians. Anyway, an inexhaustible new reservoir of slaves was tapped once Rome began military operations in Greece and the Near East. As early as 210 the population of Anticyra near Delphi was carried off by a Roman army, and from then on the practice was continuous while the numbers soared. At the end of the Third Macedonian War in 168, seventy towns and villages of the Molossians in Epirus were destroyed and 150,000 inhabitants enslaved. When the armies left off, private slavers (called 'pirates') moved in, sweeping a great net through Asia Minor and Syria.

Cheap slave labour poured into Italy and Sicily in the second century B.C., encouraging the wealthy to increase their holdings in farms and pasture. Sicily was now well on its way to becoming the classic land of large estates, the *latifundia* of the Romans. However, by referring to *latifundia* in this period, one cannot avoid speaking in a rather imprecise way, not so much of very large single units in a geographical sense but more often of the concentration of numbers of separate farms in the possession of one man. In Sicily the growing concentration often took the form of tenancy rather than ownership. Cicero (*II Verrine* 3.108) explicitly calls this a custom among rich Sicilians, the Centuripans being the largest body of "cultivators", taking up farms on lease everywhere on the island (their citizens numbered 10,000). Why Centuripans? He does not say and we cannot even guess intelligently. Their immunity from the tithe in Centuripe gave them an obvious financial bonus, but the immunity did not extend to land they farmed in other *civitates*. Some of the leasing was necessitated by the survival of an amount of Roman *ager publicus*, as in Leontini where at the time only one Leontine was on the tithe-roster, but that cannot be the sole explanation for this otherwise mysterious phenomenon.

An enumeration of Verres' victims (or alleged victims) reveals that the Roman-Italian takeover did not give this favoured group anything like a monopoly of the *latifundia*. Many Sicilian landowners prospered under Roman rule, and on as great a scale. Even the masses of the population seem to have found a livelihood, chiefly on the land, minimal no doubt but with some security. One test is the absence of serious emigration, despite the frequent savage warfare, not counting the captives sold abroad, of course. We hear of exiles fleeing to Carthage and elsewhere and of Sicilians living in Rome for one reason or another. Otherwise it is remarkable how few Sicilians tried to make their fortunes abroad in an age of mobility. Sicilians had taken no share in the great Greek trek into Syria, Egypt and other Near Eastern areas in the half-century after Alexander the Great. One may see in Timaeus the *reductio ad absurdum* of insularity, sitting among his books in Athens for fifty years, indifferent to the profound transformations going on around him, his erudition and his emotions directed wholly to the west. Then Roman expansion stimulated another eastward move, this time of many thousands of traders, moneylenders and businessmen from Italy, and again hardly a Sicilian took the opportunity although fellow-Greeks from Magna Graecia joined in early and profitably.

The vaunted peace which Rome brought to Sicily, in sum, had the beneficial material effects claimed for it. Rome and the Romans took a heavy tribute but under the Republic they did not pauperize the island. There is no contradiction between the idea of an economy dominated by slave-worked *latifundia* and Cicero's statement (*II Verrine* 3.27) that the multitude of Sicilian farmers were smallholders for whom a single yoke of oxen sufficed. In a population of, say, half a million on the land, 3000 holdings of 500 *jugera* and more would account for the bulk of the agriculture and pasture, especially on the best acreage, and still leave place for Cicero's little men. These are notional figures but they serve to illustrate what has often been the landholding balance in this kind of economy. Modern estimates of the total population of Sicily in Cicero's time range between 600,000 and 1,000,000. There is no way of dividing the total among the urban and rural sectors. The 10,000 citizens of Centuripe included the farmers in its territory as well as the city-dwellers. Panormus, Catania and Syracuse were probably larger, but on any count no city was comparable to the Syracuse of Dionysius I, and some—Gela, Selinus, Himera—were dead. On the other hand, population was thicker on the ground in the interior and in such hitherto insignificant districts as the southeast. Literary references and archaeological surveys complement each other to reveal that the still heavily wooded island was thoroughly cultivated, with market gardens, orchards and small allotments filling in the spaces among the *latifundia* and the sheepfolds. Inland communication was good enough and it is a fair assumption that the Romans improved the main roads. On the urban side, there was some geographical redistribution. The northwestern area, especially Panormus, became much more heavily settled and it is tempting to attribute this development to the economic progress in Spain and then France under Roman rule, which opened a new field for Sicilian trade.

The precise economic position of the mass of the free population is unknown. There are no signs of discontent among them such as were visible under Timoleon or Hiero II, a silence which could reflect no more than hopelessness arising from fear of Roman power (and the indifference to such matters in the sources of information available to us). But the slaves in Sicily rose, in the latter part of the second century B.C., in two revolts which, with that of Spartacus in Italy, were far the greatest slave uprisings in antiquity and perhaps in the whole of history. Fear alone thus seems an insufficient explanation, though it could never have been wholly absent or very far beneath the surface. The acceptance of imperial rule has always been a complex social and psychological phenomenon, and so it must have been in Sicily too. Verres had support inside Sicily and not only among his gang. Not even Cicero could conceal that; indeed, he saves some of his most mordant rhetoric for "the city of the Mamertines" which, like Syracuse, had refused to join in the prosecution. The most remarkable aspect of the whole episode is, in the end, Verres' ability to get away with what he did. There was no Roman army in Sicily, no genuine police force (other than the Venerii, as the Romans called them, slaves belonging to the temple of Aphrodite in Eryx), nor enough Romans and Italians altogether to have withstood concerted opposition. Yet the resistance to Verres was isolated, spasmodic and totally ineffective. One must conclude that Rome had successfully carried out its time-tested policy of winning over key sections of the subject population, and that the ultimate power and ruthlessness of the ruling state, though kept in the wings, took care of the rest.

Rome and Italy, it must not be forgotten, were a foreign nation to Sicilians. Language was the obvious test. All Sicilians now spoke Greek as their mother tongue, whatever their origins in the distant past. Even the majority of the slaves were Greek-speaking. Possibly there were still pockets of Sicel or Sican speech in the hinterland, and the men named Hannibal and Himilco who put up a Greek tombstone or two in the west may have talked Punic among themselves, as some Mamertines no doubt retained their Italic dialect. But these would have been insignificant survivals. It was Latin which was intrusive and alien down to the end of the Republic, a fact which the Romans accepted by not trying to impose it even for administrative purposes. Verres employed interpreters. Diodorus, a man of education and learning, made a special point, in the introduction to his *History* (1.4.4), of informing his readers that he knew Latin "because of contact with the Romans in the island". Writing at the end of the Republic, he still thought of himself as a Greek. Cicero explained in the *Verrines* the peculiarity of the Greek calendar, still in use throughout Sicily. Among the main functions of the calendar was the liturgical one of fixing the many sacrificial and festival days, which were also Greek. Sacred heralds toured the island summoning the cities to send representatives to Delphi and other pan-Hellenic shrines. An occasional Sicilian still turned up among the Olympic victors. Temples and large stone theatres remained Greek in style, with such changes and adaptations as were characteristic of the Hellenistic world. The theatre at Segesta, according to some authorities, marks a transitional stage, perhaps about 100 B.C., as do the Roman-style houses which begin to appear in Agrigentum at about the same time. Even the latter do not yet show signs of Roman building techniques replacing the traditional Greek methods of construction. The amphitheatre, finally, did not make its appearance, at Syracuse and elsewhere, until the imperial period.

One Sicilian 'export' remains to be noticed, a most unusual case of religious syncretism and diffusion. On the steep acropolis of Eryx (Plate 6), where there had once been a native cult-centre according to the literary tradition (though no archaeological traces have been found), the Carthaginian Astarte (or Tanit) received homage. The Greeks identified her, as elsewhere, with Aphrodite and elaborated a myth that Eryx was the son of Aphrodite and a native king named Butas, thus explaining why Aphrodite specially favoured the sacred precinct, in which Heracles also had an interest. Every year the goddess and her doves flew across to North Africa for a few days, and a daughter-shrine was established in Tunisia at Sicca Veneria (modern El Kef) inland near the western boundary of Carthaginian territory. The temple at Eryx possessed an unusual number of slaves, and at some stage, which cannot be fixed, sacred prostitution became a feature. This is a mysterious business, for the practice was rare among the Greeks and the only attested example among the Carthaginians was precisely at Sicca.

Eryx and Segesta both went over to the Romans in the First Punic War. In 217 B.C., when the second war had become critical after the disaster at Lake Trasimene, the Sibyl instructed the Romans to seek the help of Aphrodite at Eryx, no doubt because Aeneas, who was coming more into the picture as founder of Rome, was another of her sons. The general Fabius Maximus vowed to dedicate a temple to her at

Rome, which he did two years later. That temple was not relegated to the precinct where other foreign gods were housed but was built on the Capitol itself. For her feast-day Venus Erucina was assigned April 23, the day, closely associated with Jupiter, when the new wine was celebrated. In 181 B.C., during a war with the Ligurians, a second temple was erected to her outside the Colline Gate. There, according to one liturgical calendar, the "day of the whores" was celebrated. Further evidence of the cult has been found in Pozzuoli, Herculaneum and Potenza. In Sicily itself the Roman Senate, which seems to have taken over the administration of the temple at Eryx, granted the seventeen "most loyal cities" the privilege of wearing gold ornaments and gold-trimmed garments in the sacred processions and of providing an armed guard for the goddess. How and when the Venerii came to acquire their police function is not known. Temple prostitution apparently continued at Eryx, though it was not repeated in Rome where the rites were fully Romanized—Diodorus (4.83.6) says that when Roman officials visit Eryx "they put aside the gravity of office and enter into play and intercourse with women amidst great gaiety".

In this complex fashion the conquest of Sicily proved a powerful stimulant in the evolution of the most famous of all Roman myths, the Aeneid.

Chapter 11

THE GREAT SLAVE REVOLTS

Following his brief account of Aphrodite at Eryx, Diodorus
(4.84.3) proceeds to the myth of Daphnis, son of Hermes and a
nymph, who dwelt in the "Heraean" mountains,[1] where he
pastured large herds and bestowed upon the Sicilians the gift
of bucolic poetry, "which has remained in favour in Sicily until
the present day". It is a region, he explains, so rich in vines and
fruit-bearing trees, with sweet-water springs, that tens of
thousands of Carthaginian soldiers had been able to sustain
themselves there during one of the wars, which he neglects to
identify. Under the Romans the area, still very productive,
was a concentration-point for great numbers of slaves primarily
employed on the *latifundia*, and it was at Enna, the geographically dominant site, that the first of two major revolts began
soon after the middle of the second century B.C. It caught the
slaveowners and the authorities unprepared, and no wonder.
Rebellious slaves have always fled or committed sabotage and
on occasion small bands have rioted, but a large-scale revolt of
any duration is an extreme rarity. The formal requirements of
planning, organization and discipline are too great, and the
difficulties are intensified by the psychological demoralization
that is so characteristic of the condition of servitude. Where an
exception occurs, one must seek the peculiar circumstances
which permitted the general rule to be broken. Ancient
writers found them, after the event, in the combination of very
large numbers of slaves and excessive brutality by the masters.
Hence Diodorus, reflecting his main source on the subject, the
Stoic philosopher (and teacher of Cicero) Poseidonius, who
was an adult contemporary of the second revolt, commented
that, though the unthinking majority were surprised, "for
those who could correctly judge affairs, the course of events was
not illogical" (34/35.2.25). Hence, too, the unexpected com-
passion of the narrative.

Beyond doubt the concentration of slaves in Sicily at the

[1] "Heraean" is the ancient name for the mountainous formation running
southeast from the Madonie across Sicily.

time was extraordinary, their treatment in many cases monstrous: they were branded, chained, beaten, ill-fed and overworked. These were necessary factors for a revolt; they were not of themselves sufficient. The Sicilian revolts helped spark off smaller, short-lived uprisings in Italy and Greece; and in Athens, at least, the slaves were then far fewer in number than they had been in the classical era when there had never been a revolt.

The story really begins in the Hellenistic East. Greece itself, after interminable and sometimes large-scale warfare, had fallen to Rome. In 146 the Romans razed Corinth, having first looted it on a scale that Verres must have envied. Further east, in Asia Minor, Syria and Egypt, the political system and the equilibrium of power created by Alexander's successors were in a state of ugly dissolution—dynastic struggles, civil wars, uprisings and political anarchy. The immediate beneficiaries were the ubiquitous slavers, who bought up war captives and political victims as well as seizing free men, women and children by the thousands. The majority of these chattels were sold to eager buyers in Italy and Sicily (after 150 B.C. especially through Italian merchants based on the free port which the Romans had established on the island of Delos). The new situation thereby brought about in Sicily was the sudden concentration of large numbers of new slaves, many of them men of education, some of high birth, and nearly all Greek-speaking. This last is important: ancient writers had warned against homogeneity among the slaves in the past, correctly appreciating the advantages, to the free men, inherent in a diversified slave population who could not easily communicate among themselves because of linguistic and other cultural barriers. In Sicily they now could, and they also had leaders who could organize and channel the more spirited among them, who could plan and, when necessary, impose a measure of discipline. That new combination of factors, added to mere numbers and brutal treatment, was decisive.

It is futile, of course, to seek accurate totals or even proportions. The newcomers were thrown in with an already sizeable slave population of mixed origins. There were other distinctions among them, too, of occupation and status. At the one extreme were the herdsmen and shepherds, probably the most brutalized of them all, arms-bearing and solitary, without education or specialized skills, brigands when the opportunity arose. More numerous still were the agricultural workers, among whom there were also gradations, from the chained labourers to the privileged, though nonetheless servile, bailiffs (the Latin *vilici*). And there were the urban slaves, craftsmen and domestics, the latter a rapidly increasing and on the whole more favoured group, catering to the growing demands of luxurious living and conspicuous consumption. Just how these categories differed in their behaviour during the revolts is unanswered in the available material apart from tantalizing hints, but it appears that the pastoral and agricultural slaves provided the mass of the insurgents, though possibly fewer of the leaders. Messina and Syracuse, for example, refused to rise and could not be captured. In the second revolt there appears to have been a conscious effort by the leaders to keep their men out of the cities; because of the corrupting effects of urban idleness and luxury, we are told, but perhaps there were other powerful reasons, for, later on, the slaves in Morgantina actually helped defend the city against the besieging rebels.

The straight narrative we have of the revolts is a truncated one, consisting mainly of Byzantine excerpts made in the tenth century of books 34–36 of Diodorus, which have otherwise perished. It is therefore impossible to present the story in proper chronological sequence; there are visible gaps; and there is no check on the numbers said to have been involved, which would have been guesses in the first instance anyway. It is not even certain when the first revolt began, but the year 139 B.C. seems a little better founded than 135, more commonly given in modern histories. The spark was ignited on the estates of the very rich Damophilus of Enna, "who surpassed the Persians in the sumptuousness and costliness of his feasts" (34/35.2.35). His desperate slaves came to a decision to kill their master. But first they sought the advice of Eunus, one of the new slaves, the chattel of another citizen of Enna. Eunus came from Apamea in Syria, a large city on the Orontes River and the chief arsenal of the Seleucid kingdom which had been established in the more eastern regions of Alexander's empire. (By a happy coincidence, Apamea was also the native city of the philosopher-historian Poseidonius.) We are not told what duties Eunus performed; instead there is much detail about his considerable reputation as a magician, miracle-worker and prophet. The gods spoke to him through dreams and he was a devotee of the Syrian goddess Atargatis. All this gave him something of the court-jester role and an appropriately special status in his owner's ménage, but it also gave him charisma among the slaves, which he knew how to exploit to the full. What he was now asked, specifically, was whether the gods approved the plan to kill Damophilus. His reply was personally to lead 400 slaves into the city, where they were joined by many urban recruits in a quick riot of pillage, murder and rape. Damophilus and his even more vicious wife Megallis were away at their country villa nearby. They were soon brought in and a discussion was held in the theatre. The pleas of Damophilus were beginning to sway many—the Uncle Tom psychology is to be found universally among slave populations—until two of the leading rebels took matters in hand and chopped him down. Then Eunus was proclaimed king, with absolute powers.

Eunus immediately summoned an assembly and began to reign in earnest. His first task, after bestowing the title of queen on the Syrian slave woman, also from Apamea, with whom he was cohabiting (another indication of his favoured status among slaves), was to decide the fate of the slave-owners in Enna. On his orders, Megallis was handed over to her female slaves, who tortured her and then threw her from the battlements, while her daughter, who had always tried to shield the victims of her parents' brutality, was escorted safely to relations in Catania. For the rest, Eunus drew a simple distinction: all those who could be usefully employed in manufacturing arms were put to work in chains, the others were summarily executed. Meantime a companion revolt had begun in the Agrigentine district, led by a herdsman named Cleon, originally from the Taurus region of Cilicia in Asia Minor. Eunus, who within three days had organized an army of 6000, which then grew to 10,000, summoned Cleon to join him as commander-in-chief. The latter promptly accepted, in a show of responsible behaviour which astonished and dismayed the enemy, and he contributed more than 5000 men to the cause. Starting with this nucleus, Eunus ultimately won control of Morgantina and

Tauromenium in addition to Enna, and presumably of much of the territory between these strong points and some elsewhere. His forces are alleged to have reached 200,000 at one stage, which is suspect—other texts say 60,000 and 70,000—but there is no doubt that he won a number of battles against Sicilian militias mustered by successive governors, and that the revolt was not crushed until 132, after Rome finally found an efficient commander in the consul P. Rupilius, who had 20,000 or more trained Italian soldiers under him.

Most remarkable of all was the way Eunus set about creating a carbon-copy of the Seleucid monarchy. He called himself Antiochus, the name most common in the Seleucid dynasty (in 139 Antiochus VII regained the throne from a usurper), wore the diadem and other insignia, and minted copper coins in Enna bearing the head of Demeter, an ear of corn, and, in abbreviation, "King Antiochus" (Plate 8b). Cleon held the title of *strategos;* there was a royal council and a bodyguard, and when it was all over and Eunus was found hiding in a cave, he had with him his court butcher, baker, bath attendant and buffoon. None of this can be dismissed as a mad farce. The slaves were not seeking a social revolution; they were not abolitionists nor was there a 'communist international' behind the spread of the rebellion to other parts of the Mediterranean world, as was at one time seriously believed by some historians. One must not probe too deeply into their aims because it is unlikely that any of them, including Eunus, had thought through a programme. They were out to liberate themselves and to take revenge, and then they expected to live as free men in the only kind of world they knew. One of the initiators of the second revolt, a Cilician overseer named Athenion, is reported to have said that, having divined from the stars that he would one day be king of Sicily, he had to spare his territory and its crops and cattle. Eunus' men were under similar orders not to burn down farmhouses, destroy agricultural tools and crops or kill farm workers. How, then, was their Sicily to be organized? The obvious answer was the kind of state in which men like Eunus had grown up, a Hellenistic monarchy. And they did well enough with it, building a viable army which was victorious until the Romans sent in regular troops in force, and even then they fought bravely and many chose the honourable end of suicide rather than capture.

Eunus, as King Antiochus, was thus the indispensable figurehead who made possible the scale and tenacity of the first revolt, both as king and as wizard. The assurance of divine support which he promised, the care taken not to damage the sacred precinct of Demeter in Enna (and her retention on his coins), perhaps also the unusual and therefore portentous activity of Mount Etna in 140 and again in 135—these are all pointers to the buttressing role of religion, of 'the gods' rather than of any particular divinity or cult. That distinction has to be made, for, on the basis of the reference to Atargatis, some historians have suggested that the revolt was a religious and nationalist movement in the full sense, drawing analogies with Messianism and even with the peasant revolts in central Europe during the Reformation. That seems doubtful. The sources do not speak in such terms and it is significant that Eunus stopped one step short in his Seleucid monarchy-building: he made no move towards ruler-worship. It is also significant that, although the second revolt repeated the pattern of divinely sanctioned kingship, then the leadership was not even Syrian and the trappings of office were as much Roman as Hellenistic. The leaders of the second revolt also turned to the ancient native gods, the Palici—and it is surprising that these traditional protectors of Sicilian slaves were not called upon in the first uprising, assuming that we are not faced with a mere gap in the surviving information. In sum, the slaves sought the help of any and every divinity available, rather than of one in particular. And it seems improper to speak of a 'religious *movement*' for activities which had, in this sphere, neither a specific goal nor a specific cult in view.

Our judgment would be better based if we had any idea how the production of food and arms was organized during the years of fighting. Mere reference to the protection of farm equipment, to Eunus' putting the slave-owners of Enna to work on arms, and, in the second revolt, to Athenion's selecting only the best fitted rebels for military service while the others were sent back to agricultural production—which is all the information given us—does not add up to enough. A considerable drop in production was inevitable. There were depredations, in which the landless free poor took a hand (that seems to have been their chief contribution to the stormy events). Distribution probably suffered even more. Although nothing is said about grain shipments to Rome, except for a possible hint of failure in 138, it is hard to imagine that the tithe was being regularly collected in the regions in which the rebels were most active, and M' Aquillius, the proconsul who suppressed the second revolt, had to lend corn to the cities in Sicily itself. The slaves were in no sense Sicilian patriots: the enemy was the rich slaveowner, whether Sicilian or Roman—the first revolt was touched off by the slaves of Damophilus, a Sicilian, the second by several bands in separate actions, including one belonging to a Sicilian of Halicyae and another to a Roman knight nearby.

Yet somehow the rebels secured enough food and equipment both times to fight on for some years, no small achievement even if one accepts the shorter chronology of the first revolt. The slowness of the Roman response is noteworthy. True, Rome was heavily engaged in fighting elsewhere, especially to put down the long drawn out Spanish struggle for independence known as the Numantine War, and at home there was a deep crisis developing which erupted in the tribunate of Tiberius Gracchus in 133 B.C. Yet the slave revolts in mainland Italy were stamped out quickly and with the utmost severity, so that the Poseidonian explanation, that the Romans failed to appreciate the proportions of the Sicilian outbreak, may be accepted as another factor. When the full truth finally dawned and a large enough legionary army was sent in, the slaves had no chance. All the harbour-towns had remained open, so that there was no difficulty on that score. And, though not even a Roman army could easily storm such natural citadels as Tauromenium and Enna, the slaves had no way to relieve a siege. In the event, both cities were betrayed. Slaves were no more immune from that than free men: that is how Marcellus had captured Syracuse. The rest was a relatively easy mopping-up operation.

Those taken at Tauromenium were tortured and then flung from the battlements. More thousands were killed at Enna (or killed themselves), though Eunus, who managed to escape for a time, was mysteriously allowed to die in prison. Then there was an end to vengeful punishment on the whole, for the compelling reason that the society required slaves in order to recover and to resume the accustomed way of life. As the

Christian apologist Orosius noted five hundred years later, "If we consider the unfortunate losses in the fighting and the still more unfortunate gains in victory, the winners lost in proportion to the numbers of those who perished among the vanquished" (5.9.8). The following year (131) Rupilius issued his *lex* for the province, which presumably dealt with more matters than just the court arrangements already mentioned in connection with Verres. That it dealt with fundamentals may safely be denied: the slave *latifundia* went on, unchanged and soon restored to their normal level of production and profit, with new owners or tenants replacing those who had lost their lives in the rebellion. No Roman had any intention of legislating against the free use of one's wealth or the maximum exploitation of one's slaves.

The slaves struck again, probably in 104 B.C., when Rome, not rid of her internal troubles, was further preoccupied with a major threat to northern Italy from the Germanic Cimbri and Teutones. Rome requested military assistance against the latter from Nicomedes III, a client-king of Bithynia in Asia Minor, and was rebuffed with the complaint that no young men were available thanks to the activities of the slave-hunters protected by Roman officials and tax-farmers. The Senate then ordered the release of any 'allies' who had been reduced to slavery. The promulgation of this decree in Sicily led to immediate chaos: so vast a crowd of slaves appeared before the governor in Syracuse demanding their freedom that, after granting it to some 800 of them in a few days, he called a halt to the proceedings and commanded the rest to return to their masters. Instead of obeying they marched off to the shrine of the Palici and raised the banner of revolt. For the second time it was new slaves who were the initiators of a major uprising.

An immediate response came from the other side of the island, starting with small bands acting independently but soon in an organized movement. Again two leaders came to the fore: the Cilician Athenion in the area between Segesta and Lilybaeum, whose first troops were the 200 slaves in his charge, and in the region of Halicyae and Heraclea a man named Salvius of undefined nationality (perhaps Italian), an expert at taking auspices and perhaps not a slave himself. Salvius had more military skill than any other slave commander in either revolt and he was the dominant figure at first, becoming king under the Greek name of Tryphon, and later, after sacrificing to the Palici, giving himself a Roman aura, wearing the purple toga and appointing lictors who bore fasces. He even built himself a royal fortress-city at Triocala—which has not been located: opinions divide between the region of Caltabellotta and a site further west—with moated walls, a palace, a large Agora and a council-house. For a time he and Athenion fell out and the latter was imprisoned, but then they were reconciled and fought together in harmony. When Salvius was killed in battle, Athenion succeeded him to the throne, fulfilling the prophecy he had read in the stars.

Although the rebel army was smaller than in the first revolt —40,000 is the maximum figure recorded—they were probably better equipped and better trained, and the fighting ranged more widely over the island. Hardly a district was immune. But the Romans were better prepared, too, and they did not repeat the casualness with which they had greeted the previous outbreak. The slaves were unable to capture a single major city; attempts at Lilybaeum, Morgantina and Messina all failed, and there is no indication that Enna was even tried. It was at the siege of Morgantina that both the rebels and the defenders appealed to the urban slaves for support. The latter won out, offering freedom as a reward, a promise which the Roman governor subsequently failed to honour. At the same siege the Romans are reported to have taken many women captive; if the statement is to be trusted, it is the sole reference to the participation of female slaves apart from the killing of Damophilus' wife at Enna in the first revolt.

However, if the Romans were prepared, they also suffered from incompetent commanders and apparently from a measure of failure of nerve. At Morgantina, Salvius routed a Roman sally into his camp and offered to spare any soldier who dropped arms and surrendered. Some 4000 accepted and it is a pity that we do not know their fate; only 600 were killed in the battle. Finally M' Aquillius took charge and the end came quickly. He was rewarded with an ovation in 99 B.C., not a triumph which would have been too great an honour for a victory over slaves. The closing episode crowned the whole tragic story. A thousand slaves who were still holding out surrendered on a promise that their lives would be saved. They were double-crossed and sent to Rome for combat with wild beasts. It is said, relates Diodorus with some caution, that the captives chose an honourable and heroic alternative, killing each other or committing suicide before the altars in the circus where they were intended to entertain Roman spectators.

This time there was little question of what to do with the surviving rebels, since most of them died in the fighting— 20,000 allegedly in one engagement. Replacements for the lost slaves were soon found, and the only preventive step we know the Romans to have taken was the prohibition of arms-bearing by slaves, a measure as unenforceable then as at any other time. Again the damage cannot be estimated, but the reasonable suggestion has been made that it was less than that caused in Sicily by either of the two Punic Wars. (There is no indication that Rome felt constrained, after either revolt, to offer relief in the form of a remission of the tithe, as it did in Catania, for ten years, following a damaging eruption of Mount Etna in 122 B.C.) The island's repeatedly demon-strated powers of recovery showed themselves once more. When Verres arrived in 73 B.C., twenty-six years after the end of the second revolt, he found a rich land ripe for plunder. Among the regions dwelt on at length by Cicero in his detailed indictment were some which had been centres of the revolts: Enna and the Heraean mountains, Morgantina, and places in the west and southwest.

Verres was soon faced with dangerous new tensions among both the slaves and their masters. In the year of his first praetorship the gladiator Spartacus organized a revolt at Capua in southern Italy which ultimately brought together some 90,000 slaves. Both at Rome and in Sicily there was understandable fear of a backlash effect, especially when in 72 B.C. Spartacus, having failed to lead his men northward out of Italy, concentrated them in Lucania and threatened to invade Sicily. Plutarch (*Life of Crassus* 10.3) quotes him as saying that only "a little fuel is needed to rekindle" the Sicilian fire. His plans were not realized because the pirates on whom he counted did not produce the shipping needed to bring the rebels across the Straits. But the danger was real and there were always fugitives to contend with. Verres took steps at the ports and in this matter he performed his duties effectively. Otherwise the Senate would presumably not have renewed him in office, whatever his backing or their tolerance of his peculations.[1]

Spartacus was crushed in 71 and the age of slave revolts was at an end. However, Sicilian and Italian slaves were soon to have one last opportunity to assert themselves, in the very different and unusual role of recruits in the navies during the civil war which brought the Roman Republic to its close.

[1] See E. Maróti, "*De suppliciis,* Zur Frage der sizilianischen Zusammenhänge des Spartacus-Aufstandes", *Acta Antiqua* 9 (1961) 41–70.

Chapter 12

SICILY UNDER THE ROMAN EMPERORS

Once Verres was dealt with, Sicily returned to its normal place in the Roman scheme of things. Although neither the individuals nor the communities he had pillaged were compensated for their lost money and treasures, the island recovered rapidly, its farms and pastures productive as before, feeding Rome and creating wealth for large landowners and men of affairs, not even seriously disturbed by the civil war between Caesar and Pompey which soon erupted in Rome. The Roman factions of course recognized the strategic possibilities of Sicily, unchanged from Hannibal's day: a naval bridge to North Africa and a potential base of attack on Italy. Hence, earlier in the century, the party of Sulla had made certain to hold the island in their struggle with the Marians, and now Caesar, in 49 B.C., took control of it after he crossed the Rubicon. Neither time did fighting ensue in Sicily itself: the Roman opposition was too heavily engaged in Rome and Italy, the Sicilians were impotent even if they leaned towards one side or the other. When Asinius Pollio arrived as Caesar's emissary, the governor there, Cato, protested and that was the end of the affair. Cato had no troops; Sicily quietly 'joined' Caesar's camp and it was from Lilybaeum that his men sailed to attack the Pompeians in North Africa.

Everything changed, however, with Caesar's assassination in 44 B.C. In the confused situation that followed, Pompey's son Sextus organized an army and a fleet in Spain. Upon learning that his name was on the proscription list drawn up by the new triumvirs—Antony, Octavian and Lepidus—he went on the offensive. Selecting Sicily as his base, he captured Mylae and Tyndaris without much trouble, then Messina; after that, Syracuse and the other cities apparently acknowledged his authority without further struggle. Within a few months Sextus Pompey had become a major force in the civil war between the triumvirs and Brutus and Cassius. He was joined by a large and heterogeneous following, including remnants of his father's faction, men who looked to him to preserve

148

some vestige of 'republicanism', victims of the proscriptions and confiscations of the triumvirate, adventurers, pirates and tens of thousands of fugitive slaves, chiefly from Italy. The flow of slaves was so great that "the Vestal Virgins prayed over their sacrifices that the desertions might be checked" Dio Cassius 48.19.4). It was largely slaves who manned the ships which gave Sextus Pompey control of the seas, and thus a flow of war materials and riches (his piratical activity cannot be discounted), and the power, which he did not hesitate to employ, to disrupt the movement of corn to Rome. All shipments from Sicily came to an end and Italy was blockaded against seaborne supplies from elsewhere. Even the armies of the triumvirs fighting outside Italy were threatened with food shortages.

The primary responsibility for dealing with Sextus Pompey fell to Octavian, the future emperor Augustus. He could do little, first because Brutus and Cassius had to be beaten in the east, then because he was for a time engaged in fighting the partisans of his fellow-triumvir, Antony, in Italy itself. A decision was eventually forced by the Roman populace. Faced with famine, they rioted and demanded that a settlement be reached with the master of Sicily. At a conference held in 39 B.C. near Misenum, the naval base in the Bay of Naples, the reluctant triumvirs agreed, among other things, to recognize Sextus Pompey's authority in Sicily, Sardinia and Corsica, and to grant freedom to the slaves in his service. For his part, he promised to lift the blockade, to resume shipment of the tithe (possibly in arrears as well), and not to recruit or accept fugitive slaves in the future. That there was much good faith on either side may be doubted, but the agreement deserves to be recorded as evidence that Sicily was still vital to Rome. Disputes quickly arose and then war, fought in Sicilian waters and on the island itself. The fighting was destructive on a scale comparable with the Punic Wars, despite its short duration, involving possibly 200,000 men and more than 1000 warships. The coastal cities of Tyndaris and Messina and the area between them were especially hard hit, but the damage was by no means restricted to that sector. Nor did it come to an immediate end with the defeat and flight of Sextus Pompey in 36. Octavian was merciless. He levied a 1600-talent cash indemnity on the island. Those cities which had surrendered to him were pardoned, the resisters severely punished. It is a pity that our sources, with their customary concentration on the few leading personalities and on individual battles, give hardly any details. Most of the 30,000 captured slaves were restored to their owners; the remaining 6000, whose owners were not found, were impaled. The entire population of Tauromenium was deported. And that about exhausts our information. How and why the Sicilians divided on the issue, or why they took sides at all, remains a mystery. That the future of Sicily would have been significantly different had the war gone the other way seems most unlikely.

The defeat of Sextus Pompey (who was soon captured and executed in Asia Minor) was celebrated in Rome as a major event. And Octavian was now free to deal with Antony. In 31 B.C. victory in the battle of Actium left him in sole command of the Roman empire. Four years later he had his position formally regularized by the Roman Senate and people and he assumed the name of Augustus. Characteristically, he tried to fudge the record by minimizing and distorting the nature and strength of Sextus Pompey's challenge. That is why he claimed only an ovation, not a triumph. In the account of his career which he prepared for posthumous publication, the so-called *Res Gestae*, Augustus wrote (25.1): "I freed the sea from pirates. In that war, I captured some 30,000 slaves who had fled from their masters and taken up arms against the republic, and I handed them over to their masters for punishment." A more dishonest statement will not be found even in that disingenuous document. Sextus Pompey is not mentioned at all; the opposition is reduced to slaves and pirates, though Octavian had himself employed 20,000 freed slaves in his navy and though among those who had joined Sextus Pompey were members of the senatorial and equestrian orders, including, for a brief period, Ti. Claudius Nero, accompanied by his wife Livia (whom Octavian took as his own wife not long after) and their child, the future emperor Tiberius.

Sicily in 36 B.C. was in bad shape once again, not unlike the condition after Timoleon had defeated the Carthaginians and their allies. Many men had been lost, both in the countryside and in the cities, and there was much land lying temporarily idle because the owners were dead or missing, or because Augustus had confiscated it in reprisal. A portion, presumably large, was retained in the imperial domain. Another large tract, probably in the fertile plain of Catania, was given to Agrippa, the genius who presided over many of Augustus' successes and who, in particular, master-minded and led the victory over Sextus Pompey. On Agrippa's death most of his holdings passed to the emperor by will, including, we assume, the Sicilian estates (the manager of which, a certain Iccius, was the dedicatee of one of Horace's poems, *Epistles* I 12, in 20 or 19 B.C.). Smaller holdings were given to discharged Italian veterans of Augustus' legions, the size scaled according to army rank. These men then performed a double function: they replaced some of the destroyed man-power in Sicily and they constituted a loyal leavening in the population, concentrated in the districts of the chief northern and eastern ports. Elsewhere in the empire Augustus often bought land for his veterans and it is possible that he did so in Sicily, too, if his confiscations proved insufficient for the total need of the resettlement scheme.

On this base Augustus erected a new administrative super-structure, part of his reorganization of the empire. Caesar had begun the process when he granted "Latin rights" to the Sicilians *en masse*—a status which, among other things, meant full Roman citizenship for any man who held one of the annual municipal offices. Had Caesar lived, the effect in a few decades would have been the Romanization, in this political sense, of thousands of the richer Sicilian families. Cicero, Sicily's traditional friend and protector, disapproved, only to learn of more extreme measures taken by Mark Antony four or five weeks after Caesar's assassination: Antony announced that Caesar had prepared a bill making all Sicilians Roman citizens and that he was putting it into operation. A lie paid for by a huge bribe, wrote Cicero (*Letters to Atticus* 14.12), and he may well have been correct. Anyway, the intervention of Sextus Pompey and the war which followed brought an end to these manoeuvres. It is pointless to speculate on the formal status of the 68 (or so) Sicilian communities in the years 44–36 B.C.—Roman generals and armies were making all the important decisions. Once Augustus gained sole control, a new situation was created, first by the bitter fighting and soon by the new Sicilians, the veterans, Roman citizens to begin with, as the franchise had by this time been extended to all Italians (including the population of old Magna Graecia).

There are uncertainties in our knowledge of the Augustan settlement in Sicily, as of the dates when it was introduced. Although he surely made a start in 36, at least in Tauromenium, the basic land allotment could not have been accomplished overnight. Further steps were taken when he visited the island in 22 or 21 B.C., the first stop on a tour of the empire. Besides, he did not have to appear there personally in order to make administrative changes. In the end, six cities—Tauromenium, Catania, Syracuse, Tyndaris, Thermae and Palermo—had the status of a Roman *colonia*, a technical term in Roman public law with virtually none of the negative overtones of our word 'colony'. At this time the status of a Roman *colonia* was normally proof of a substantial inflow of Roman veterans, and it is virtually certain that this was the case with the six honoured Sicilian cities, which would suggest, in turn, that they had all either been decimated in the war with Sextus Pompey or been punished by Augustus afterward. Just how the surviving Greek inhabitants of these cities were ranked is a debatable question: the aristocracy presumably shared in the privileged status, but possibly not the others. The question is important, for, by definition, all citizens of a *colonia* were full Roman citizens, employing Roman law in their private affairs, having special protection in the criminal law (such as immunity from torture), eligible for administrative careers right to the top of the Roman hierarchy.

Messina and Lipari and possibly a few others (Lilybaeum, Agrigentum, Halaesa) became Roman *municipia*, which differed in status from the *coloniae* only by being somewhat less honorific; their citizen-body was not infused with Roman veterans; they were simply being rewarded for their services. Individual Roman citizens, it should be added, were to be found everywhere, not only in the 'Roman' cities. Only Centuripe, Noto and Segesta were returned to the Latin status. The rest continued as they had been ever since the Roman conquest, allowed to run their own domestic affairs as "peregrine" communities, subjects of Rome.

Comparison of this catalogue of privileged cities with the Republican list reveals considerable overlapping, but also some interesting changes. Although tradition and sentiment still counted for something, they mattered less than current behaviour and imperial requirements. Segesta is worth looking at more closely. Previously "free and immune", Segesta was now not elevated to first-class honours, and that may reflect a decline in Roman interest in the Elymian-Trojan link. The temple of Aphrodite at Eryx, which Segesta had somehow taken under its wing and for which the Roman Senate had once assumed responsibility, was allowed to fall into decay. The Segestans appealed to Tiberius to rebuild it and the emperor agreed "gladly", but apparently not very effectively, for Claudius had to come to the rescue again. Centuripe was a different case. Its earlier privileges rested on economic considerations, on the role of the Centuripans in large-scale farming. By chance we know that Centuripe actively supported Octavian against Sextus Pompey; yet the reward was not Roman or "municipal" status, only Latin, and no obvious explanation comes to mind.

None of the privileged statuses any longer carried automatic exemption from Roman taxation (not to be confused with local taxes for purely local purposes). Even Roman *coloniae* were taxable outside Italy unless an exemption was expressly granted. No such concession is recorded for any of the Sicilian cities; if the argument from silence has any standing, in this instance it suggests that exemptions were not given. The tax system, furthermore, was basically altered: the tithe was abolished and replaced by the *stipendium*, a levy assessed in money on landholdings (and possibly also a poll-tax). Augustus' reasoning included merely formal administrative considerations, but it may also have been a response to a new situation in corn production. The steady growth in the rural economy of North Africa, and the acquisition of Egypt, provided new sources of corn for the populace in Rome, a special concern of its rulers to the end of antiquity. Sicilian grain seems in consequence to have become somewhat less indispensable to Rome for a period. Nevertheless, Sicily is shown (symbolically) with Spain, Africa and Egypt in a large floor-mosaic of the middle of the first century A.D. at Ostia, the port of the city of Rome, celebrating the four main corn-growing provinces. The considerable produce from the emperor's own estates (as later from the papal estates) continued to be shipped to Rome. By a lucky chance there has been preserved in Ephesus a group of plaques honouring a local notable, Gaius Vibius Salutaris, for his many acts of civic philanthropy; earlier in his career (at the end of the first century A.D.), it is recorded, he headed a quasi-official corporation in charge of purchasing grain in Sicily "for the people of Rome".[1] And casual literary references of a more general nature to this continuing importance of Sicilian grain keep recurring, for example in a Greek oration addressed "to Rome" by Aelius Aristides in the late second century, or in a Latin poem, *Against Symmachus* (I 940–4), by Prudentius at the end of the fourth. Other scattered texts indicate the export of wine, wool and horses.

Our knowledge of the history of ancient Sicily is reduced to casual references for most of the next six hundred years. Roman writers such as the historian Tacitus or the imperial biographer Suetonius hardly mention the island at all; by contrast, the source material down to the Augustan settlement appears rich in retrospect. In the two centuries after Augustus, administrative changes in Sicily were minor ones, leaving little trace in the surviving documents. Later reforms in the imperial system as a whole naturally included Sicily, too, such as the extension of Roman citizenship to virtually the whole free population of the Empire in 212, or the reorganization of the provincial structure and the tax system by Diocletian and Constantine at the end of the third century and early in the fourth. The province of Sicily now became a subdivision of the diocese of Italy under the vicar of the city of Rome. Despite these later administrative shifts, Sicily had effectively lost its identity, other than geographical, at least to the outside world. To the emperors and the senatorial aristocracy, Sicily had from the early imperial period become an outlying district of Italy.

That attitude was strengthened by a negative factor: Sicily herself gave no more trouble to Rome. There is only one isolated reference to an outbreak of "banditry" in the 260s,[2] hinting at a peasant uprising with the participation of slaves. Significantly, not only are such movements known from con-

---

[1] Dessau, *Inscriptiones Latinae Selectae* 7193, 7195.

[2] *Historia Augusta: Gallieni duo* 4.9.

temporary Gaul, but there they continued to plague the Roman rulers into the fifth century, spreading into Spain as well, whereas they were not repeated in Sicily. No legions were stationed in Sicily until the Vandal troubles and no naval force. Augustus permitted Roman senators to visit the island without first obtaining his permission, a privilege continued by subsequent emperors and extended to Narbonnese Gaul by Claudius, but to no other province down to the third century. Presumably the privilege was used by absentee landowners to have an occasional look at their estates. Otherwise Mount Etna and Syracuse were tourist attractions of some importance, the latter one of the *villes d'art* of the western Mediterranean despite all the depredations. But few emperors cared to visit the island, apart from Caligula, who seemed to enjoy Syracuse, Hadrian, who spent most of his time travelling in the provinces, and Septimius Severus, who was governor of Sicily before he became emperor in 193.

In the fifth century Sicily returned for a time to the mainstream of imperial history, in consequence of the barbarian invasions and the division of the Empire into a fragmented western half and an eastern half with its capital in Byzantium (Constantinople). Once again, after more than six hundred years, Africa was the invasion base. In 429 a relatively small but mobile and well-organized Germanic tribe, the Vandals, conquered North Africa. Their king, Gaiseric (or Genseric), had vast ambitions, which he pursued with energy and skill for the next fifty years, employing his naval power and such diplomatic possibilities as were available in a complicated game involving the rulers of Italy, the Byzantine emperors and the Goths, another Germanic people, who were pressing into Italy and eventually gained the throne there.[1] Sicily was the point of concentration because of its location and its wealth. Gaiseric raided the island for the first time in 440. Five years later he occupied Corsica and Sardinia and sacked Rome itself for a fortnight, but he was beaten off Sicily. He failed once more in 456, but pillaging continued until finally, in 468, he succeeded in taking military control of the island. Nothing is known about the Vandal period and it lasted only about eight years, when

[1] The available sources about the Vandals are coloured by hostility to their Arianism, to be noted in the next chapter.

another German, Odoacer, who had gained the throne in Italy, bought Sicily back from Gaiseric for an annual payment of tribute. That move initiated an important period of peace in Sicily, briefly interrupted when the eastern general Belisarius captured it for the Byzantine emperor in 535 with a fighting force of fewer than 10,000 men, who met little resistance; again in 550 when Sicily was the scene of fighting between the Goths of Italy and an army from Byzantium. The year 535 may be said to mark the end of Roman rule in Sicily, which was thereafter a Byzantine province until the Arab conquest.

Throughout the imperial period the Sicilians showed little interest in advancing themselves in Roman government or society. Even in the early Empire, when opportunities were numerous, hardly any Sicilians joined the legions or entered the imperial career service; no Sicilian is known to have attained the rank of Roman senator until the end of the first century. The contrast with southern Gaul, Spain, North Africa or Asia Minor is striking. And yet there are numerous outward signs of prosperity among the middle and upper classes, who expended locally such wealth and energy as they cared to devote to public affairs, on theatres, amphitheatres, aqueducts, baths and the other urban amenities which became characteristic of Roman society everywhere—in Nero's time the Roman Senate gave Syracuse permission to exceed its allotment of gladiatorial shows. Behind this urban wealth there lay, as always in antiquity, profitable exploitation of the land, which in turn created a foundation for export activity (and in Catania, at least, shipbuilding), service trades, and a variety of specialized industries. Agrigentum, furthermore, was the centre of a newly developed sulphur industry, the mining of which was apparently a monopoly of the emperor's, worked through concessions.

Precisely how large or populous the cities were in the imperial centuries, either absolutely or by comparison with earlier times, is unanswerable. When Augustus re-colonized Syracuse, according to the contemporary geographer Strabo (6.2.4), Ortygia and the immediately adjacent mainland district of Achradina were sufficient for the entire population. Perhaps the city grew subsequently and spread into other districts which had once been inhabited. A curious poem by Ausonius, called

Ordo urbium nobilium, in which he ranks the seventeen most celebrated cities, beginning with Rome, Constantinople and
Carthage, and ending with his native Bordeaux, places Catania
and Syracuse thirteenth and fourteenth, respectively. Syracuse
is called "quadruple", which could indicate considerable expansion in Ausonius' time, the late fourth century. On the
other hand, the six lines devoted to the two Sicilian cities are
restricted to two bits of traditional lore, about an act of
heroism when burning lava once flowed over Catania and
about the source of the Fountain of Arethusa in Syracuse. Too
much literal stress can therefore not be laid on this evidence.
Nevertheless, that Catania (called Catina in Latin) was now
one of the leading cities is demonstrable archaeologically; so
is the expansion of Palermo and, on the evidence of large
cemeteries from the imperial period, the populousness of
Messina and Agrigentum. But neither Himera nor Gela nor
Selinus recovered as urban centres beyond the level of squatters'
hamlets, and Morgantina in the interior seems to have been
finally abandoned at the beginning of the reign of Augustus. In
the absence of statistics, that kind of unsatisfactory catalogue
is the best one can offer.

The archaeological evidence further suggests a well-popu-
lated countryside, with clusters of villages, hamlets and larger
farm-complexes covering the island. There is nothing to indicate that Sicily began to suffer from abandonment of arable
and pasture, as did some of the traditionally most productive
regions of Italy in the later Empire, or from deforestation and
its damaging after-effects. On the contrary, there seems even
to have been an upsurge in Sicilian agriculture from the third
century on. Considerable caution is needed, however. Archaeologists have until recently tended to neglect Roman Sicily, and
their conclusions cannot always be blended satisfactorily with
the scattered literary and administrative texts. The latter, in
turn, give a one-sided picture because their sole interest in
Sicily, except when something notable took place (the Vandal
invasions or the Byzantine conquest), was in its rôle as a sup-
plier of corn to the city of Rome (and of taxes). Nothing
specific is said about the trade with North Africa, for example,
yet many pottery lamps from Africa have been found in Sicily,
over a period of several centuries, and a few wine-jars

discovered in Pompeii and in Africa are labelled *vinum Meso-potamium*, a Sicilian vintage. Similarly for the trade with Spain and Gaul: the island's harbour dues were substantial enough for Vibius Salutaris of Ephesus to head a second company, responsible for their collection, at the same time that he was buying up corn for Rome; a mid-second-century inscription found on the site of the Forum of Narbonne, honouring one of its wealthy, distinguished citizens, mentions that he had been honoured by Syracuse, Thermae and Panormus with the insignia of four municipal offices, presumably because of his rôle in the commerce between Sicily and south-western Europe, for which Narbonne was a major continental port[1]; a linen-merchant from Alexandria, possibly a factor, was buried in Panormus in 602.[2] Such data are important pointers, but no more: they cannot reveal the scale of production and trade or the conditions of labour and enterprise.

One conclusion which nevertheless emerges with certainty from all the evidence is that there was a steady concentration of holdings in land and much effort to consolidate holdings into great continuous tracts. The Vandal invasions did not disrupt the trend. On the contrary, Vandal control of North Africa seems to have put an end to corn shipments from that continent to Rome, re-establishing Sicily in its old rôle as "nurse" of the Roman populace, Cato's word echoed, perhaps deliberately, by a sixth-century historian of the Goths (Jordanes, *Getica*, ch. 60) who was explaining why Belisarius had to secure Sicily before attempting to conquer Italy. At the same time, Italian agriculture was in a bad state. When Theoderic the Goth established himself firmly on the throne in Rome in 493, he left property undisturbed in Sicily, in contrast to central and northern Italy where he confiscated perhaps as much as one third of the region in order to settle his veterans and followers. A powerful contributory factor was the emergence of the papacy as a great Sicilian landowner. From Augustus on, the emperor himself was the largest holder there. However, the popes rapidly began to match him after Christianity became recognized under Constantine. There is no evidence from which to trace the growth of the "patrimony of St. Peter", but it seems

[1] E. Espérandieu, *Inscriptions latines de Gaule Narbonnaise*, no. 573. 7193, 7195.
[2] Dessau, *Inscriptiones Latinae Selectae* 7564.

to have advanced a long way, both in substance and in administrative organization, by the time of Pope Gelasius (492–96). Imperial and private gifts and bequests were the main sources, but there were also purchases and an amount of illegal and extortionate acquisition, too. When Gregory the Great became pope in 590, the Sicilian division of the patrimony of St. Peter probably exceeded the emperor's possessions there. The chief administrator was a *rector*, a member of the lesser clergy, based on Syracuse (later replaced by two officials, the other in Panormus), whose duties also included ecclesiastical supervision and negotiations with the civil authorities responsible not to Rome but to Constantinople. There are more letters of Gregory's dealing with his Sicilian patrimony than with all the rest together, in various parts of Italy, Gaul, Dalmatia and Africa.

There were also Sicilian estates in the possession of the sees of Milan and Ravenna and of local bishoprics and monasteries. These concentrations, like those belonging to the popes (and unlike the imperial holdings), were normally not broken up. Otherwise there was a considerable movement in land-holdings, by purchase, gift, dowry and bequest, which reveals the existence of a class of large private *latifundia*, normally the property of absentee owners. In the later Empire the regular term for an estate became *fundus*, for a consolidated group of *fundi*, a *massa* (literally a 'kneaded together mass or lump'). These words were not always used consistently (and in North Africa, for example, their connotations and relationships were quite different) and they give no indication of actual size, but there are several ways to get at some notion of the extent and actual movement of property. One clue comes from the so-called Antonine Itinerary of the fourth century, based on a late second-century original, which records the distances between main stations on the highways of the Empire. In the Sicilian section, the Itinerary names districts or *latifundia* where there are no cities. One archaeologically important example is the station called Philosophiana (now securely identified with modern Sofiana between Piazza Armerina and Mazzarino), a well-watered, fertile, populous region in Roman imperial times.

On the coastal road between Syracuse and Agrigentum there are listed, among other stations, the Mesopotamian "region", the rich territory fanning out from the long abandoned city of

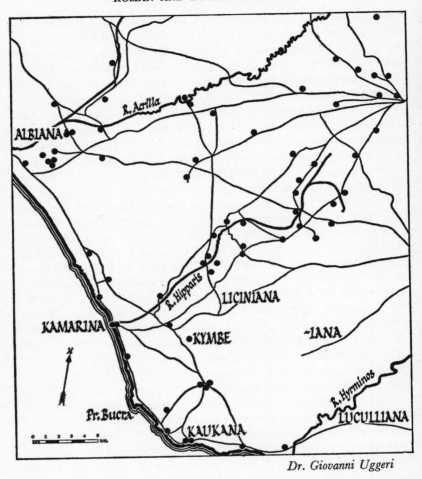

Dr. Giovanni Uggeri

Fig. 6   The Kamarina Region in Roman Times

Each dot represents a large farm-complex or settlement.

Kamarina (Figure 6), and a *massa*, the Calvisiana, presumably named after the man who first assembled the estate. One main farmstead-complex of this *massa* has recently been excavated on a low hillock at the mouth of the Gela River. It was constructed in the early third century on the ruins of a much smaller, abandoned building of the time of Augustus. Hundreds

9 a. Section of fortification-wall, Gela

COINS OF SYRACUSE (*actual size*)

9 b. Silver tetradrachm, after 305
B.C. (Agathocles)

9 c. Bronze 5-litra piece, Hiero II

9 d. Silver tetradrachm, Hiero II

10 a. Odysseus in the cave of the Cyclops

PAVEMENT MOSAICS, PIAZZA ARMERINA

10 b. The end of a chariot race

of tiles have been found, bearing the legend CAL or CALVI, and their distribution indicates that this one estate extended, on the eastern side of the Gela River, some ten miles north by east to Niscemi. None of the Calvisiana finds can be dated much later than the middle of the fourth century. There are no clues which would explain, and no way to determine whether the *massa* was then broken up, or even if it continued as a single holding for any length of time after it had been assembled. A man named Calvisianus was the *corrector* who presided over the tribunal in Catania which tried and condemned St. Euplus in 303/4, but that isolated bit of information does not help.

Two Latin papyri which happen to survive from the Ravenna archives (presumably because the property eventually found its way into the estates of the bishopric) are most instructive on the general question of property transfers.[1] The first, dated in 445 or 446, deals with the Sicilian estates of an old man named Lauricius, who had once been the Grand Chamberlain (literally 'superintendent of the sacred bedchamber') of the emperor Honorius, who died in 423. Lauricius will have been a eunuch, purchased as a young slave boy somewhere in the east, castrated, baptized and introduced into the imperial household, where he made his fortune. The Ravenna document names three *massae*, two *fundi* and part of a third, all in Sicily, the annual rents from which brought Lauricius 2100+ gold *solidi* a year (12.5 kg.' of gold). The second papyrus is a very elaborate account of the transaction whereby in 489 Odoacer rewarded a Roman senator by an outright gift of Sicilian land. The gift was assembled by carving various named *fundi* or parts of *fundi* out of the *massa Pyramitana* near Syracuse. The annual rental was 490 *solidi*.

The occasion for the Lauricius document was a change in his managerial personnel in Sicily brought about by the failure of the chief agent to bring in all the rents due in the previous three years. That takes us back almost to the first Vandal attack, in 440. Yet the defaulting agent offered no defence on that score. No doubt the Vandals were destructive enough. However, despite the fact that their activity in Africa and Sicily has given us the common word 'vandal', there is something excessive in

[1] J. O. Tjäder, *Die nichtliterarischen lateinischen Papyri Italiens* (Lund 1955), nos. 1, 10–11.

the traditional picture. In 441 the emperor remitted six-sevenths of the Sicilian taxes, specifically because of Vandal damage. That action stands alone in the documentary record, apart from brief, tendentious remarks by hagiographers, polemicists and chroniclers, and the conclusion seems justified that the Vandals caused little permanent harm, especially not in the countryside. Otherwise neither of the two Ravenna papyri would be intelligible. Nor would the heavy reliance by Odoacer, and by Theoderic after him, on Sicily to feed the Roman populace. Theoderic had some difficulties in Sicily on his accession, but they may be attributed to internal problems in the realm (he gained power by military victories over Odoacer, ending with the latter's assassination). He stationed only a few small garrisons in Sicily, and by the end of his reign he was even able to raise the tax rate because of "the great increase in wealth and population which his long and peaceful reign had brought with it" (Cassiodorus, *Variae* 9.10).

As everywhere in western Europe, the imperial era saw a change in the labour system in Sicily. Slaves continued to be numerous: Gregory's letters contain evidence enough, especially in his insistence on strict enforcement of the law prohibiting Jews and heretics from owning Christian slaves. However, on the large estates slaves were steadily being replaced, from the early Empire on, by tenant-farmers, originally free peasants (*coloni*) who by the fourth century were tied to the soil. Some absentee owners put agents in charge, like the papal *rector*, but others dispensed with this intermediary post. Either way, the normal procedure was to lease the land in larger units to entrepreneurs, and they in turn sub-let to the working peasants, the *coloni*. The owners and tenants-in-chief made large profits; the peasants seem to have been rather badly off. Not only were they required to pay both rents and taxes in gold (with perhaps some commutation in kind), but they also were subject to various perquisites (such as fines on the marriage of a son or daughter) and to unceasing attempts at extortion. In one letter (I 70) Gregory instructed his *rector* to purchase fifty pounds of gold worth of corn from outside the patrimony and, he added, buy it, don't try to screw it out of our *coloni*. That he was not being gratuitously insulting is apparent from the rest of the correspondence. A stream of imperial legislation had shackled the peasantry, and both landholders and emperors had good reason to enforce the laws to the limit. But that was far enough.

The most spectacular evidence, visible today, of wealth and luxury in Sicily is the villa (or hunting lodge) in the wooded valley at Casale, 6 km south-by-west of present-day Piazza Armerina. Erected on four levels, as required by the terrain, the villa (which replaced an earlier one that can be traced back to the first century) had nearly fifty rooms, courts, galleries, baths and corridors, arranged in four complex groupings approached by a monumental entrance (Figure 7). Little remains of the marble architectural elements, the sculpture and the murals, but the prime attraction was surely the mosaic pavements, estimated from the very extensive survivals to have covered some 400m² of floor space, far outdistancing in scale (and therefore in financial outlay) everything else of the kind known today. The individual sections range from geometric patterns through scenes of marine and animal life, of bathing, dancing, fishing, hunting, wine-pressing, musical and dramatic performances, to complicated pictorial and narrative compositions, most of them drawn from Greek mythology, such as Odysseus and the Cyclops (Plate 10a) or the labours of Heracles. Despite the variety—no composition is ever repeated—there is an over-all unity, not only of artistic conception but also in the thematic orientation. The villa was a pleasure dome, not a year-round residence, and its original owners were pagans, ostentatiously so. It was occupied until the Arab conquest and again for a time under the Normans when it was destroyed by King William the Bad late in the twelfth century. There were frequent alterations and reconstructions, yet, curiously, the pagan quality seems to have continued undisturbed. Although the date of construction is still being discussed, the early decades of the fourth century seem increasingly certain.

Nothing points conclusively to the owners except that they could only have been among the richest men in the empire, from the Roman senatorial class, possibly the owners of the nearby *massa Philosophiana*. The predominance of Greek scenes (though there is one (Plate 10b) of games which might possibly represent those in the Circus Maximus at Rome) is normal. They had become widely diffused in Italy long ago and were now com-

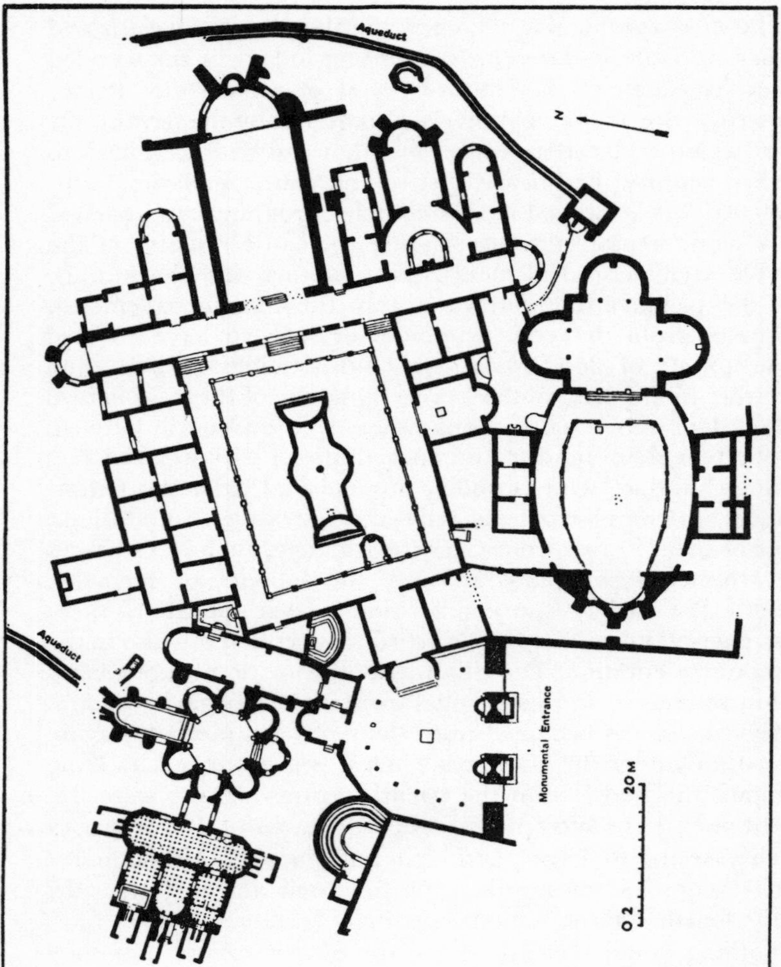

Fig. 7 Ground Plan of the Villa at Casale (Piazza Armerina)

Soprintendenza alle Antichità della Sicilia Orientale, Siracusa

mon in the western Empire, as was the popularity of Greek athletic competitions and Greek variety artists intermixed with the typically Roman spectacles of the amphitheatre and the circus. The Piazza Armerina mosaics were almost certainly the work of craftsmen imported from North Africa, but the style cannot be called anything but Roman imperial. Roman Sicily developed no identifiable culture of its own, unless at the village level about which not enough is known. The marble portrait-busts of Greek philosophers, Roman emperors or local dignitaries are exactly like the finds in Italy or Gaul. The 100-plus known marble sarcophagi, most from the third century, were imported from Italy, especially from Ostia, a centre of manufacture, and they are indistinguishable in their style and themes (whether pagan or, in a few cases, Christian) from sarcophagi discovered elsewhere, including Rome itself. Their quality ranges from mediocre to downright bad, but that does not warrant the 'provincial' label; rather, it reflects the great gap in wealth between the middle-class families who headed the social hierarchy in the Sicilian cities and the senatorial aristocrats, who did not live in the island even when they possessed large estates there.

Only with respect to language may one speak of cultural divergence, even competition. It was never part of the Roman programme to Latinize the Greek-speaking provinces, and Sicily was no exception under the Republic. The emperors, however, brought about a certain change there, indirectly rather than deliberately. The extensive colonization by Augustus introduced a concentrated Latin-speaking element into Sicily for the first time. There have recently been unearthed in Taormina two fragments of a Latin liturgical calendar (the first ever found outside Italy) which can be firmly dated to the period 36–19 B.C. Obviously the Roman colonists had taken their own cult with them and required a calendar to control the elaborate day-to-day rituals and taboos. All official inscriptions of *coloniae* were henceforth in Latin, too. And there is reason to believe that the literary language soon became Latin throughout Sicily. At least, almost every writer known to us during the Empire wrote in Latin (and left Sicily for the richer prospects in Rome). In the year 91, a famous Roman court orator of senatorial rank, L.

Valerius Licinianus, was accused of having sexual relations with a Vestal Virgin; he was banished to Sicily, where he earned his livelihood by teaching oratory and giving public declamations, surely in Latin. By the late Empire, the popes, emperors, and absentee landowners corresponded with their agents, tenants-in-chief, and quite low-ranking officials in Latin only. At the Council of Chalcedon, which met in 451, Bishop Paschasinus of Lilybaeum spoke in Latin, requiring the services of a Greek interpreter.

Yet the tenacity of Greek is not to be underestimated. It is actually impossible, in the present unsatisfactory state of research into the subject, to strike a precise balance-sheet of the two languages through this long period. The large majority of epitaphs and dedicatory plaques, pagan and Christian alike, continued to be inscribed in Greek: of those found in one section of the S. Giovanni catacomb in Syracuse, dated between 350 and 450, the proportion is nine Greek to one Latin; inscriptions from Catania show nearly five to one, from Lipari eight to one. Rural finds give the same picture. Even in Tauromenium and Messina there are enough Greek texts to raise doubts about the Latinity of many descendants of Augustus' colonists. Not even the west and northwest of the island, which had had no long Greek history, can be placed securely in the Latin camp. Nor do personal names prove anything; they had become as indiscriminately mixed as the population itself (without, it is worth adding, any Germanic names). In sum, the linguistic dividing-line has to be drawn between social classes, not geographically. The bulk of the population remained Greek-speaking, while the administrative and educated classes were Latin-speaking, or, more correctly, bilingual. It is the latter whom the anonymous author of the fourth-century *Expositio totius mundi et gentium*, a pagan from the eastern half of the Empire writing in Latin, had in mind when he said (ch. 65) that Sicily "has men of wealth and of learning in all studies, Greek as well as Latin".

Chapter 13

CHRISTIANITY[1]

The religion of Roman Sicily was syncretic, like that of the rest of the late Greek or Hellenistic world. The worship of such eastern divinities as the Syrian Atargatis (once patroness of the slave leader Eunus) or Cybele or Isis and Serapis from Egypt had been adopted and harmonized with traditional Greek beliefs and practices. The more Romanized Sicilians joined in readily; in this respect there was probably no real dividing-line between lower and upper classes. There was a temple of Isis in Tauromenium, for example, and a certain C. Marcius Zoilus paid his respects to Syracusan Athena under her Latin name, Minerva, by dedicating at her shrine a marble lamp inscribed in Latin. In Messina, despite its Roman immigration, there was an overwhelming preference, in the early Empire, for the Greek practice of inhumation, to which the Romans were just returning in the second century A.D. after a very long period in which they cremated their dead. There was even place for Punic survivals, as on a group of pagan funeral monuments in terracotta from Lilybaeum, dating from the late Republic and early Empire, and ranging in form from stelae to conventionalized temples. The most complex of them (Plate 11) is highly eclectic in its architectural details and decorations: the funeral banquet scene has a brief Greek inscription, whereas the pediment and columns bear such Punic symbols as the sun, a half-moon and a caduceus. This example of syncretism was also purely local, restricted to the once Punic sector of Sicily.

The other side of the island produced its characteristic group of documents, too, though later in date. These are magical texts, crudely inscribed on amulets, medallions and plaques, invoking Christ, Michael, Gabriel, and other angels, and various demons with mysterious names, and then adding, for good measure, magical symbols including the cross-monogram. So far they have been found almost exclusively in the rural districts of the southeast, and most commonly they seek to protect vineyards (one remembers the *vinum Mesopotamium*).

[1] The source references for this chapter are given in the Bibliography.

Although the number is too small for statistical reliability, and we may therefore be the victims of archaeological accident, it is hard to avoid the conclusion that we are faced with a specific, localized development among the uneducated rural population of this area. Sometimes Jewish elements, such as the 'seal of Solomon', were added. Not even funeral monuments were always immune: a poorly engraved Christian one in Latin (a rarity in the country districts) swears to "God and the *Inferos*" (lords of the underworld) seeking protection for the tomb of "the virgin Zoe, aged five".

The most curious of the magical amulets is a golden one, 5×8 cm., on which are inscribed thirteen lines of Hebrew in letters which may be of the third century. The text makes no sense in any language; apparently the writer knew no Hebrew and copied the characters mechanically. But from where? Hardly a scrap of Hebrew of this period has been found in Sicily. Greek, not Hebrew, was the language of the Jews of the Diaspora. Even in Rome, three quarters of the inscriptions in the Jewish catacombs are in Greek, the rest in Latin save for three in Hebrew and one in Aramaic. Jews began to migrate to Rome and other Italian communities before the Christian era, and one might assume Greek Sicily to have been at least as attractive to them. Certainly by the time of Gregory the Great at the end of the sixth century, there were established Jewish communities in Sicily, not only in such larger centres as Messina, Palermo and Agrigentum, but also in villages and *massae* of the interior. Gregory urged his *rector* to try to convert his Jewish *coloni* by offering them reductions in their rents and dues; he demanded enforcement of the law prohibiting Jewish ownership of Christian slaves; on petition of the Jews of Rome, he ordered Bishop Victor of Palermo to replace the synagogues which the latter had wrongfully seized and consecrated as churches, and to restore the books and ornaments removed from them.

Although the subsequent history of these communities can be followed through the Arab and Norman periods, the centuries before Gregory are an almost complete blank. A Byzantine lexicon claims, perhaps correctly, that Caecilius of Caleacte, an important rhetorician and literary scholar in Rome early in the reign of Augustus, was originally a

Jewish slave named Archagathus; there are brief references (of dubious authenticity) to Jews in late hagiographies of the third-century Sicilian saints, Marcianus of Syracuse and Euplus of Catania; and that about exhausts the literary evidence. Tombstones add something to our knowledge, but not very much. Such epitaphs as "Attinis the Elder" (from Sofiana) can be identified as Jewish solely from the seven-branched candelabra engraved on the stone. Another, from Catania, lacks the symbol but can be identified from a phrase: "Jason the Elder, *never having broken the Commandment*, bought this grave for himself and his children." These seem to be late stones, not before the fifth century (though the suggested dating of such rough inscriptions is generally insecure), and their number is surprisingly small for that period. Some have probably escaped us altogether when neither the candelabrum nor the Commandment-formula is present. Although names like Jason had become common among Diaspora Jews, they were also retained by Greeks. Biblical names are relatively rare, even in their Greek translation, as Eirene for Salome. Nor do there seem to have been segregated Jewish burial-places in Sicily, as there were in Rome. One text stands out from all the others, beginning with the fact that it is on expensive marble, not on the usual local stone. It has an opening line in Hebrew, "Peace (*shalom*) to Israel, Amen, Amen, Peace to Samuel," followed by thirteen lines of Latin, mostly threatening penalties on anyone who introduces other bodies into the grave of Aurelius Samoil and his wife Lasiferi. At the bottom there are two candelabra, and there is a precise date, October 21, 383. At least that is fixed, giving us the earliest dated document pertaining to the Jews in Sicily. Otherwise we know almost nothing about their history there during the Empire.

It follows that the common view that Christianity first took root among the Jewish communities in the eastern cities of Sicily, though plausible, must remain purely speculative. The early centuries of Sicilian Christianity are also sparsely documented. In time, Sicily produced hagiographies and martyrologies enough, but they have been called "among the most imaginative in the world",[1] and that judgment is generally

---

[1] C. Courtois, *Les Vandales et l'Afrique* (Paris 1955), p. 191.

ROMAN AND BYZANTINE SICILY

accepted. In the seventh century, claims were put forward, in competition with Ravenna, that the Sicilian church was Apostolic, but these are certainly false: Gregory the Great, for one, had never heard of them (St. Paul's three-day sojourn in Syracuse, where the ship on which he was a passenger stopped on its way from Malta to Rhegium, is irrelevant). The earliest Christian burials cannot be dated much before 200, and there are no authentic Christian personalities before the two martyrs of the mid-third-century, St. Marcianus of Syracuse (if he really was martyred) and St. Agatha of Catania, and then two in the Diocletianic persecution soon after 300, Santa Lucia in Syracuse and St. Euplus in Catania. Their early veneration can be documented (unlike that of St. Pancratius of Tauromenium). A quite elaborate Greek epitaph from the S. Giovanni catacomb in Syracuse, which is datable to about 400, memorializes a 25-year-old girl named Euskia who died "on the feast-day of my lady Lucia". In 384, Bishop Urso of Ravenna, a Sicilian in origin, dedicated a church to her in that city and donated his Sicilian property to it. Still earlier and more important, if somewhat tantalizing, is the evidence of a marble stone from Catania, dating from the 320s, no more than a decade or so after Constantine's Edict of Milan had ended the illegality of the Christian religion. There are some difficulties with the Latin text, but, on a probable reading, it says that a few days after the death of the infant Julia Florentina, her parents received a divine command in the night to cease their lamenting and to transfer the body for burial "before the Church of the Martyrs". That this church, a new one, commemorated Agatha and Euplus seems plausible enough, and also that it implies the presence of a Christian community of some size and with something of a past.

Once Constantine lifted the prohibition, Christianity advanced with rapid acceleration, more slowly in the countryside than in the cities. Recent excavations in Sofiana, for example, have been unable to find evidence of Christians before about the end of the fourth century, and the same seems to have been true of the immediate hinterland of Gela. In regions further inland (not adequately excavated), the progress may have been even slower. In general, however, as the emperors themselves quickly moved from tolerance to adoption of Christianity and then to prohibition and persecution of paganism, the only issue (apart from heresies), in Sicily as throughout the empire, became the survival power of paganism. Actually we cannot trace its demise. It might help if, for example, we had a more precise idea of the dates when pagan temples (and public baths) were converted into churches. The practice, which originated in Jerusalem, became common everywhere. In Sicily it is attested in Agrigentum, Segesta, Himera, Tauromenium (where a temple of Isis was turned into the church of St. Pancratius), in rural districts, and, of course, in Syracuse. There the temple of Athena went through at least two transformations in ancient times (not to mention its later history), first into a church and later into the cathedral (Plate 5), replacing S. Giovanni. Yet even in that instance, the one in which the transformations are most clearly and completely evident, we are unable to say more than that it was first consecrated before 600, and that it became the cathedral in the seventh century. About 600, the bishop of Tyndaris complained to Gregory that the local nobility were interfering with his efforts to stamp out pagan cults, and there was still concern about lapsed priests. But by then, these were isolated, if tenacious, pockets in an otherwise Christian world.

Church organization seems to have kept pace with conversion, as did church property. The eighth-century 'encomium' of Marcianus says that he was bishop of Syracuse. This may or may not be accurate, but there can be no doubt about Bishop Chrestus of that city, the one Sicilian representative at the Council of Arles held in 314, the year following the Edict of Toleration. In 447 Pope Leo I addressed a letter to the bishops of Sicily, mentioning by name Paschasinus of Lilybaeum (a see which can be documented as early as 417 or 418) but giving no number. By the time of Gregory the Great there were at least twelve, not only in the main cities but also in Lipari, in the unidentified Triocala which had once been the fortress-base of the second slave revolt, and in Carini, on the site of the Sican town Hyccara destroyed by the Athenians in 415 B.C. Other bishoprics are recorded for the first time in Thermae and Mylae in the seventh century, in Drepana, Halaesa and Cefalù in the eighth.

The growth tempo is dramatically demonstrated by the

catacombs, cemeteries and private burial-grounds. Sicily has been called "the classic land of early Christian funerary architecture". In quantity, scale, and, eventually, in richness of layout and embellishment, the most grandiose of the catacombs in Syracuse outstrip those of Rome. The oldest, known as S. Lucia—all the names are modern, taken from the churches or other landmarks with which the catacombs are geographically associated—was in continuous use for at least a century during the period of illegality, before Constantine. We must abandon traditional romantic ideas about catacombs: it is out of the question that S. Lucia was a secret burial-place, located as it was in the inhabited district of Achradina (Figure 1). Systematic quarrying went on year after year, in order to extend the narrow winding corridor which served as the catacomb's axis, to build galleries from the axis, and to cut numerous cubby-hole 'tombs' into the high side-walls. What pre-Constantinian S. Lucia does show, however, is the modesty of the community: there is little attempt at elegance or decoration, there are no marble epitaphs, only an occasional name painted or carved on the walls.

Then came the Edict of Toleration, and, instead of abandoning their underground cemeteries, the Christians of Syracuse enlarged them, established new ones, and introduced new architectonic elements, in order to meet the needs of a community which was exploding numerically and also becoming affluent. S. Lucia itself was greatly extended, to become the largest of the catacombs (not the smallest as was thought before the excavations of the 1950s). New ones were opened less than half a mile farther out from the centre, known as Vigna Cassia and S. Maria del Gesù, and a third beyond them, S. Giovanni. The latter had as its axis a wide central corridor along the bed of a disused aqueduct, from which the galleries proliferated in greater density and complexity than in S. Lucia (Figure 8 and Plate 12b). There was also much more variation; class distinctions were catered for, not only through more carefully cut cubicles with arched 'entrances' but also by the creation of 'rotundas' in which sculpted sarcophagi could be placed in groups. The one fine marble sarcophagus found in Sicily comes from this catacomb. Covered with carvings of scenes from both the Old and the New Testament, it carries a Latin

After Führer-Schultze

Scale 1:500

25 metres

Fig. 8   Ground Plan of the S. Giovanni Catacomb, Syracuse

epitaph of Adelfia, a *clarissima femina*, a member of the senatorial class whose husband was probably a *comes*, an official in the emperor's service (Plate 12a). Stylistic analysis suggests that this sarcophagus goes back to 350, possibly 340, while the last epitaph from S. Giovanni actually to carry a date gives the year 492, indicating use as a regular burial-place at least into the sixth century.

The catacombs were presumably managed and owned by the community or the church. The 'graves' were then purchased by individuals, as the epitaphs occasionally state, sometimes even quoting the price: "Acquisition of Felix the doctor for one *solidus*, the witnesses being Peter and Marcianus and Methius" (from S. Giovanni). Sizeable catacombs also existed in the environs of Syracuse, in the regions of Akrai, Ispica and Modica, in the west in Agrigentum, Lilybaeum, Carini and Palermo, all probably post-Constantinian. The distribution eliminates as a possible explanation of this Sicilian institution either the needs of a crowded urban centre or the geology of Syracuse with its limestone outcroppings. Elsewhere there were small subterranean burial-grounds, in old quarries, aqueducts or cisterns; pagan cemeteries were taken over, sometimes only in one sector at first (as at Sofiana), or new ones were built, with tombstones and other memorials above ground; and there was a wide scattering of private burials. The difficulty of precise dating, as of fixing a chronology for the little "rustic chapels and troglodytic sanctuaries",[1] the ruins of which keep turning up everywhere, reduces their value as a guide to the development of Christianity in Sicily. But at least they attest the populousness of the Christian communities in all parts of the island by the fifth century.

There is nothing in these inadequate records to indicate what the relations were between Greek-oriented and Latin-oriented Sicilians. One pointer is that, on the rare occasions when higher social or official rank is indicated in the epitaphs, it is almost always in the Latin ones, an observation which confirms the general conclusion reached earlier about the linguistic pattern. After 535, a new situation was created by Justinian's conquest and conversion of Sicily into a Byzantine province ruled by officials appointed, and often sent out, from

[1] G. Agnello, *Le arti figurative nella Sicilia bizantina* (Palermo 1962), p. 13.

Constantinople. For the next two centuries, the Sicilian church was still allowed to remain under the direct jurisdiction of the popes. Gregory's Sicilian letters refer more frequently to matters of ecclesiastical administration and jurisdiction than to the patrimony, instructing, exhorting, reprimanding bishops and abbots, or seeking to conciliate among them. Like the more able and energetic of his predecessors, such as Gelasius I, he did what he could to Romanize the church, in liturgy and doctrine as in organization. At the same time, it was essential to maintain a *modus vivendi* with the Byzantine provincial administration, a task made more difficult by the inevitable involvement of the church in secular matters after the effective disappearance of the old community organs. Within six months of his election to the papacy, Gregory sent instructions that the bishops were not to meddle in secular litigation except in defence of the poor.

There was also papal concern with heresies, as distinct from the division between Rome and Constantinople, but in a low key. In the fundamental controversy over the nature of the Trinity that divided Christendom, politically as well as doctrinally, Sicily remained firmly in the Athanasian camp, against the followers of Arius. In 366 a provincial synod formally approved the Nicene creed, that God the Son was "begotten, not made, of one substance with the Father". Presumably there were some Arians in the Sicilian communities, but it is to be doubted that they were as numerous, or as vicious, as later chroniclers make out. In these works, the Sicilian Arians are alleged to have taken advantage of the arrival of the Vandals to massacre many faithful Catholics. The intransigent Arianism of the Vandals seems at least as responsible as their raiding and looting for their persistent ill-fame in later centuries. There were also Manichaeans in Sicily, and other heretical sects. But violent disturbances arising out of such doctrinal disputes, common in certain other provinces, were apparently not a factor in Sicilian Christianity before the final Byzantine take-over.

If there are no signs, meantime, that the emperors in Constantinople, beset with far greater troubles, were much concerned about Roman influence and authority over the Sicilian churches, it does not necessarily follow that there were no strong feelings on that score among the people of Sicily themselves. The question is perplexing and controversial. On balance, the answer seems to be that the persistence of the Greek language was a symptom of a closer affinity with the culture of the Eastern empire in general. There are indications in the religious history of the period. Leo I's letter of 447 to the Sicilian bishops was directed against the Eastern practice of baptism at Epiphany, which in the West was a feast-day commemorating the Adoration of the Magi. Half a century later Gelasius was compelled to raise the question with Sicily again. Gregory was much exercised over the reluctance of the island's lesser clergy to accept the rule of celibacy (rejected by the Eastern church), and his letters leave no doubt that he was contending with a general resistance, not with individual backsliders.[1] Monasticism, of course, was brought from the East, where the practice originated. The first certain reference records the arrival of the noted anchorite Hilarion in the fourth century, with a single disciple. He stayed only long enough to win converts to monasticism, which then spread, especially in the rural areas. The popes tried hard to bring the hermits and monks under discipline; Gregory himself founded six monasteries in Sicily. And again the evidence is of an Eastern orientation: the isolated location of many of the monasteries, the appointment about 680 of abbot Theophanes of S. Pietro ad Baias in Syracuse to be Patriarch of Antioch, the absence of Benedictine monasteries before the Norman period, all argue that way.

One could have more confidence in the conclusion if one knew more about urban church architecture, sculpture and painting in the centuries after Constantine. Of monumental religious buildings we are left with not very much more than the marble columns, capitals and other decorative elements now exhibited in the Museo Bellomo in Syracuse. The destruction, not all of it caused by earthquakes or Moslems, and the

---

[1] Ironically, an earlier pope, Pelagius I, agreed to consecrate a married man with children in Syracuse at the time when the emperor Justinian was taking a strong stand against such a practice at the level of bishops. The pope demanded a bond of the candidate that he would not give or bequeath to his family any church land or any property he might acquire after his consecration.

11 Terracotta *heroön*, Lilybaeum, 91.5 cm. high

12 a. Sarcophagus of Adelfia, Syracuse, *c.* A.D. 350

12 b. S. Giovanni catacomb, Syracuse

radical reconstructions in later times have combined to leave nothing more substantial to examine. Down to the sixth century most churches in the empire were basilical in their plan: a rectangular nave, with or without aisles, ending in one or more semi-circular apses. Then the Eastern provinces began to favour the centralized church, in one variation or another of the Greek cross. A few of these were erected in Sicily, too, but the basilica remained much the most common form. To that extent Sicily was Western. However, the surviving architectural fragments in marble begin to reveal a marked transformation from about the middle of the sixth century, away from the old Graeco-Roman styles towards the early Byzantine (with a complete disappearance of human figures from their sculptural embellishments). Direct importation from Eastern centres, in Greece and Asia Minor, is now proven: late in 1960 a wreck was discovered off the coast of Marzamemi at the southern end of the Gulf of Noto, containing enough fully carved marble columns and capitals almost to warrant the label, "a prefabricated Byzantine basilica", which has been attached to the find. As for fresco painting, hardly any has survived from this period at all. The most important, severely damaged, is the group covering the walls and ceiling of an oratory built in the catacomb of S. Lucia. The style and spirit are indubitably Byzantine, but no more precise dating is possible than 'pre-Arab', more likely the eighth century than earlier.

It is also notable that the only Sicilian to achieve distinction in the intense theological and philosophical debates of the age was Gregory of Agrigentum, who belonged wholly to the Eastern camp. There was also, to be sure, Firmicus Maternus, a member of the senatorial class, who in about 335 wrote in Latin the longest, though not the ablest, work on astrology to have come down from antiquity, then became converted to Christianity and produced, by 350, a biting polemic, *On the Error of the Profane Religions*. But his career was almost certainly made in Italy, not Sicily, whereas Gregory, born near Agrigentum, went to Carthage, became a monk in Jerusalem, went on to study in Constantinople, joined the Greek monastery of S. Saba in Rome, and then obtained the see of Agrigentum, still young enough to have met with opposition on that score.

He spent the remainder of his life in that post; among his works is a commentary on Ecclesiastes in ten books, which displays much erudition not only in Christian doctrine and writings but also in the works of Aristotle. His fame in the East, where he was venerated, was long-lasting enough to entitle him to a full-length portrait among the celebrated, late eleventh-century mosaics in the church at Daphni outside Athens.

Unfortunately there is no certainty about this Gregory's dates. The surfeit of Gregories has produced inextricable confusion in the one biography of him we possess, and modern opinions range from the early sixth century to the late seventh. What matters, however, is that he was the Gregory who represented the victorious side, not Gregory the Great. However one interprets the earlier situation, the popes lost in the end. By the second half of the seventh century the Sicilian church was Eastern in every important respect, including the liturgy and the ceremonies, other than its administrative attachment for a while longer to Rome. There is no need to seek, in explanation, a new Hellenic infusion through migrations, which has been suggested from time to time without foundation. Greek speakers were always the majority in the Sicilian population. All they needed was the onset of a new phase in the perennial political and military struggle between Rome and Constantinople (to which Lombards, Persians, Slavs and Islam also contributed). So complete was the Eastern triumph in Sicily then, that even the educated and politically influential minority abandoned the Latin language and returned to Greek.

Chapter 14

BYZANTINE RULE:
THE END OF ANCIENT SICILY

When the Byzantine general Belisarius sailed west in 533 to recapture North Africa from the Vandals, he stopped in Sicily on the way to obtain supplies and horses. The Ostrogoth rulers of Rome were cooperative, having no reason to divine the extravagant dreams of the new Eastern ruler, Justinian. The latter had come to the throne in 527, full of schemes to reestablish the old unified Roman Empire and a united Church. The circumstances were hardly propitious. Sclavenes, Bulgars and Avars were flooding into the Danube Valley and the Balkans (in 540 the Bulgars actually reached the walls of Constantinople). There was chronic fighting, at times on a large scale, with the strong Sassanid dynasty in Persia. In the west some of the Germanic peoples were settling into relatively formidable military powers; those who were not, always threatened a conquering migration into the more attractive regions. Religious controversy between Rome and Constantinople was exacerbated by a long-standing quarrel, concentrated in the east, over the nature of Christ as God and Man, which much exercised the population at large. Egypt was rather solidly monophysite; the doctrine also had strong support in Syria and Palestine, and some in Constantinople itself. As always in this period, such differences had serious political consequences, both within the ecclesiastical hierarchies and in the government.

Nevertheless Justinian acted quickly and with determination. Three years after his accession he negotiated an 'Eternal Peace' with the Persians (which lasted seven or eight years), and he risked a revolt at home by taking a firm stand against the monophysites in order to win papal support. He also embarked on an ideological campaign to revive the old Roman spirit, as in his great codification of Roman law, the *Corpus Iuris Civilis*, completed rapidly (528–34) and issued in Latin. However deeply attached Justinian may have been to the old traditions, on the other hand, he had no intention of allowing

179

sentimental archaism to interfere with practical requirements; his subsequent legislation, correcting and supplementing the *Corpus Iuris*, was very detailed and extensive. And so, too, with his administrative measures. When he took Sicily, he gave the provincial governor the title of praetor, "after the manner of antiquity". But the title (and the retention of Syracuse as his capital) was all the antiquity there was about the office; the praetor's powers and duties were not those of a Verres but of an imperial Byzantine official of the sixth century. Nor did he need a Greek interpreter to enable him to communicate with his subordinates and subjects.

Sicily fell to Belisarius in 535 with the greatest of ease. Only the small Gothic garrisons in the larger cities resisted; Palermo had to be besieged. Fifteen years later the Ostrogoth ruler of Rome, Totila, who had temporarily regained the upper hand in Italy, took revenge on the Sicilians for their capitulation— "just as the most faithless slaves would have behaved" (Procopius, *Gothic War* 7.16.15). Modern historians have tended to see in the Sicilian passivity a desperate hope that rule from Constantinople would be less oppressive than rule by Rome. That may be, and some allowance must also be made for the fact that Sicily, like the Eastern Empire, was Greek, not Latin. However, it is worth recalling that the civilian population of the Roman Empire had no tradition of taking up arms against invaders; that was solely the army's responsibility. Details about the Byzantine administration in Sicily, including the tax system, are so slight that one cannot say whether, in terms of relief, the island did or did not gain from the change in masters. Property relations (including church property) were unchanged; so was the social structure. What the Sicilians did win they could not have anticipated. Justinian's moves were followed by more than a century of constant warfare in Italy and North Africa, overflowing into Spain and also involving the Franks of Gaul. Only Sicily was spared, apart from Totila's brief intervention, when he pillaged the island thoroughly, removing horses, cattle, corn and treasure to Italy. Peace was a gain of no small consequence: much of Italy and North Africa was ruined, and for Sicily to have escaped was a rare experience in her long history at the crossroads.

From Africa and Sicily, Belisarius moved on to Italy. The

ruling Ostrogoth dynasty had taken to quarrelling after the death of Theoderic, and was in a weakened state. An excuse for intervention, if one was needed, came with the assassination in 535 of the queen-regent, Amalasuntha, technically an ally of Justinian's. Success was rapid. Then a Gothic revival under Totila regained almost the whole of the peninsula between 541 and 550, whereupon a new Byzantine effort, with somewhat larger forces, soon won back much of the lost ground and brought peace to Italy for a few years. The very small size of the field forces, to be counted in the tens of thousands, is significant. By comparison with the armies of Augustus and Sextus Pompey, not to mention the earlier wars with the Carthaginians, these are paltry numbers. And they had to be made up to a considerable extent by expediencies: in the army which defeated Totila in Italy in 552 there were 5500 Lombards, supplied from their then homeland in the Austrian mountains, and 3000 recruited from another Germanic people, the Heruls. Although the Byzantine state was reasonably solvent, it had to expend most of its available resources on the armies defending the long and dangerous frontiers in the east. Once the Eternal Peace had been broken by the Persians, who invaded Syria, Justinian fought a two-front war, and he had no choice but to give priority to meeting the eastern threat. On this score, his western conquests were probably a liability. Belisarius brought much booty back from Africa, as well as several thousand Vandal prisoners who were promptly enrolled in the eastern forces. But that was a windfall, not repeatable. Taxes from Africa and Sicily, rents from the royal estates taken over in both provinces, and the spasmodic income from Italy were unlikely to have exceeded local administrative costs and the requirements of the western armies, if they actually managed to cover them fully, which we cannot tell. They surely made little contribution to the general budget of the Empire or to the private fortune of the emperor.

Imperial self-glorification, in short, lacked the resources with which to achieve its aims. When Justinian died in 565, he left an empire which was financially and economically in ruins, though it had returned to Europe and Africa. His successors were unable, and probably unwilling, to cut their losses, and by 568 they had a new menace to contend with. The Lombards decided to leave their poorish lands, crossed the Alps in a typical military migration, and within two years controlled Venetia and Liguria (including Milan). Constantinople tried to stem them by inducing the Franks to engage in war with them, and other pressures were momentarily relieved by another short-lived peace with Persia and by subsidies to the Avars and others. To little avail: soon the Lombards were in possession of all Italy except for the Ravenna district, the city of Rome and the southernmost section of the peninsula. Meanwhile the Moors were creating difficulties in North Africa and the Visigoths began their ultimately successful campaign to win back southern Spain. Sicily alone was untouched, and when the emperor Maurice (582–602) tried a new administrative system in his western outposts, setting up strict military organizations, known as exarchies, he based them on Ravenna and Carthage. Sicily was not a suitable centre under the existing conditions, nor did it require military control for internal reasons. However, the time was to come soon enough, in the middle of the seventh century, when the exarch of Ravenna was twice compelled to send troops to Sicily.

In this situation the popes and emperors needed each other's assistance. Hence the care with which Gregory the Great dealt with matters impinging on the imperial interest, and the freedom with which he was allowed to administer his Sicilian possessions. Soon, however, theological disagreements brought about conflicts again, and then violence. The emperor Heraclius (610–41) sought to win back the still troublesome monophysite dissenters in eastern provinces by supporting a compromise doctrine, known as monotheletism, which held that, although Christ had two natures in his one person, they worked with a single will or 'energy'. Despite the support of Patriarch Sergius of Constantinople and other Eastern church dignitaries, the compromise created more trouble than it quelled in the East, and it roused the popes to active opposition. Heraclius' successor, Constans II, therefore abandoned monotheletism for yet another, fine-spun compromise. The newly elected pope, Martin I, resisted this, too, and a hastily summoned synod in 649 backed him with a firm declaration of the duality of Christ's nature (approved by the Sicilian bishops who participated). Constans ordered Olympius, the exarch of Ravenna, to arrest the pope, but he refused. The precise situation in Rome and Ravenna in the next year or two is unclear, and then a new factor came into play. In 651 or 652, the Arabs, already in control of Syria and Egypt less than twenty years after Mohammed's death, dispatched a fleet from the eastern Mediterranean to raid Sicily. An urgent appeal to Rome brought the exarch with his army. The Arab invaders were not numerous enough to fight a war; after a few skirmishes, they withdrew with their booty. Olympius, however, died in an epidemic before he could return to Italy, and his successor carried out the emperor's orders. Pope Martin was arrested and sent to Constantinople to be tried for high treason: he and Olympius, it was charged, had planned to use Sicily as the base for a rebellion. He was convicted and banished to the Crimea, where he died within a few months.

For Constans this was a triumph without any gain. The Italian clergy remained hostile and venerated the martyred pope; the latter's successors firmly upheld the Lateran synod against monotheletism. Meanwhile Constans was preoccupied with growing difficulties at home, and in 660 he took the unexpected decision to move the capital back to the west after more than three hundred years in Constantinople. The hostility to Constans in the sources makes it difficult to judge his actions. They describe his departure from Constantinople rather as an expulsion, the result of popular discontent which reached its climax following the murder of his brother, but it may have been a mad idea to carry on from a central base Justinian's dream of a revived Roman Empire. Whatever the truth, he moved slowly, spending a considerable time in Athens and Thessalonica before reaching Tarentum in 663. Some minor military successes against the Lombards were followed by brief sojourns in Naples and Rome, and then he settled permanently in Syracuse, with his court and an army.

For the next five years Syracuse was the capital of the Byzantine Empire (or, as its rulers preferred to call it, the Roman Empire). If the Sicilians had a momentary vision of glory and material benefits, they were quickly disillusioned. The financial burden of harbouring the emperor and his retinue proved to be intolerable, as did Constans' tyrannical behaviour. In 668 he was assassinated in his bath by his chamberlain, the agent in a plot in which Byzantine nobles were implicated and which quickly turned into a secessionist rebellion. The soldiers named a young Armenian aristocrat as emperor, to popular acclaim in Sicily and with applause from the clergy. But when the murdered emperor's son, Constantine IV, who had been left in command in Constantinople, arrived early the following year at the head of an army supplied for the most part by the western exarchies, the revolt collapsed, and Constantinople was restored as the capital. Later in the same year the Arabs attacked Sicily again, and it is hard to believe in a mere coincidence. This time the base was Alexandria: a fleet of 200 descended on the island, plundered it and sailed away.

The Arabs, advancing with a speed unprecedented since the exploits of Alexander the Great, were now the most dynamic factor in the struggle for the Mediterranean world. While Constans II was stationed in Syracuse, the Arabs raided Asia Minor annually. From 673 to 678 they kept Constantinople under blockade. In Africa they advanced westward from Egypt, to Tripoli, to their new Holy City of Kairouan in Tunisia, and then to Carthage, which they captured in 689. Soon they would proceed to Spain. In about 700 they captured the island of Pantelleria lying midway between Sicily and Tunisia, and for the next fifty years Sicily was subjected to repeated raids. Then came a half-century of immunity, while the Arabs of Africa were kept busy with troubles on that continent. Indeed, were it not for the disunity and clashes which had already developed within Islam, it is possible that neither the Eastern Empire nor the Western would have survived at all.

Interesting consequences also followed for the ecclesiastical hierarchies. Of the four patriarchates which had stood more or less equal, whatever the claims of Constantinople, three—Antioch, Jerusalem and Alexandria—were now in Islamic territory, finding contact with Constantinople difficult and also plagued with heresy. In the west, there was a lull in theological quarrels, but a watchful eye had to be kept on Constantinople on this score. The Roman clergy were intellectually ill-equipped for the purpose, those in the Germanic lands even more so, and North Africa was lost. Monks and other churchmen who had found asylum in Rome when they fled from Arabs or Bulgars made a contribution, but the burden fell primarily on those Greek "nations" (as they are called in the compilation known as the *Liber pontificalis*) which were loyal, or at least friendly, to the papacy: Syria, Greece proper, and Sicily. The elevation of the Syracusan abbot, Theophanes, to the patriarchate of Antioch in about 680 is a case in point. Even more dramatic is the reversal among the popes themselves. Of the fourteen successors to Gregory the Great (between 604 and 678), only two were non-Italians, John IV from Dalmatia and Theodore from Greece. But in the next period, down to the Lombard capture of Ravenna in 751, two popes were Roman in origin, the rest were 'Greeks'. Of the latter, four—Agatho (678–82), Leo II (682–3), Conon (686–7) and Sergius I (687–701)—were Sicilians either by birth or by upbringing. This has no narrow national significance. In the *Liber pontificalis*, Sergius is identified as belonging to the "Syrian nation". Yet he was born in Palermo of an Antiochene family which had migrated to Sicily; he moved to Rome as a youngster to become an acolyte, and he made his career there. The real significance of these 'Sicilian' popes is as testimony to the complete cultural identification of the island with the East. Circumstances now enabled Sicily to make a new contribution to the welfare of the papacy, in addition to the long-standing contribution from the papal possessions there.

It must be stressed that the temporary 'Hellenization' of the papacy was not brought about by direct pressure from Constantinople. The Empire was too weak in this period to play that game. The exarch of Ravenna was notified of each new papal election and ratified it, but that was an empty formality, since he never refused, not even if he had himself supported another candidate, as happened when the young and vigorous Sergius was chosen. Besides, exarchs often found it in their own interest to make common cause with the Roman clergy and nobility. Nor were the Greek popes notably subservient to Constantinople. One of Constantine IV's gestures of reconciliation following his father's assassination was a formal abandonment of monotheletism; when a usurper tried to reestablish the doctrine in 711, the pope, a Syrian, led the unanimous and violent opposition of the West. In 685 or 686 John V, another Syrian, won from Justinian II tax concessions for the papal estates in Calabria and Sicily. And in 692 Sergius led the successful resistance against an attempt by the same emperor to remove certain Latin rites from the ceremonial. Orders were sent to Ravenna to arrest the pope, but popular resistance blocked the effort and no more was heard of it.

That fiasco may have been the incident which finally induced the emperor to make an important administrative change in Sicily. Earlier in the century Heraclius I had reversed the whole Roman imperial tradition and militarized those easternmost provinces which were under constant enemy attack. The name given to the new kind of province was "theme", from the Byzantine Greek word for an army corps, *thema*. No effort was made at the time to extend the system to the west, where it seemed less suitable. But at a date which can be pinpointed between 687 and 695, Justinian II established the theme of Sicily (and in 695 of Hellas). The suggestion is attractive that it was the rebelliousness of Ravenna in 692 which decided the emperor to post another military force in the west, to serve as a check on the exarchs and to help meet Saracen pressure from Africa. Sicily remained a theme so long as Constantinople controlled the island, for a time including Calabria and Naples. A local fleet was organized, considerable fortification-work was carried out, and the strong points were garrisoned in some force.

After little more than a generation, the new military set-up was put to the test inside Sicily itself. In 726 the emperor Leo III began his campaign against the veneration of religious images, thereby launching a fateful conflict (and earning for himself the sobriquet of 'the Iconoclast'). Resistance in Italy was solid, not only in the regions under papal authority but also in the Lombard territories. Pope Gregory II at once condemned the imperial decrees as heretical, although, it is important to add, he equally resisted popular demands for an outright political revolt. The two succeeding popes, Gregory III and Zacharias, both Syrians, also stood firm. Leo had promptly retaliated by confiscating the papal patrimony in

Sicily and Calabria, which was never restored. Yet Sicily seems to have remained quiet for a long time, not because there was much support for iconoclasm but, presumably, because of the presence of a military force which remained loyal to the emperor. Nor do the records reveal active opposition when, after the fall of Ravenna to the Lombards in 751, Leo's even more doctrinaire son, Constantine V, transferred the Sicilian church (and also the Calabrian and Illyrian) from papal jurisdiction to the patriarchate of Constantinople. Externally this step was a response to the open negotiations now undertaken by the pope with the Franks, leading to alliances (climaxed on Christmas Day 800 when, in St. Peter's, the pope crowned Charlemagne as Roman Emperor). Internally it meant direct control of the Sicilian church from Constantinople. Metropolitan (or archepiscopal) status, formerly held by the popes themselves, was now assigned to the bishop of Syracuse.

The passivity in Sicily, it is only fair to add, is a conclusion drawn from very little information. At the beginning of the reign of Leo III, while Constantinople was under Arab siege and before the iconoclast decrees had been promulgated, the governor of Sicily rebelled and nominated another emperor. He was dealt with effortlessly, having no visible backing in Sicily. There was no reason why Sicilians should have involved themselves in this particular struggle for the throne. Nearly half a century later, in August 766, at the peak of the iconoclast persecution by Constantine V, nineteen high imperial officials were executed in the Hippodrome in Constantinople for their opposition, one of them the Sicilian governor. Nothing is known of his activity. The next incident came in 781, in the midst of another dynastic struggle: the governor Elpidius rebelled in favour of one of the contenders and this time his soldiers and the populace blocked efforts to arrest him. However, when an army arrived from Constantinople the following year, Elpidius fled to Africa, where the Arabs welcomed him and even made the empty gesture of recognizing him as the emperor. Iconoclasm seems not to have been at issue, and anyway that conflict was coming to an end (though there was a weak renewal a generation later). At a council held in Nicaea in 787, summoned by Empress Irene, iconoclasm was condemned as a heresy. Those bishops who had been guilty of it were let off lightly; they were merely required to abjure the heresy before the assembly. Not one of the Sicilian bishops in attendance found himself in this position.

With reserve, we may generalize that Sicily was solidly committed to the images (and provided a few martyrs in their defence); that the governors varied in their loyalty to Constantinople, were increasingly compelled to act autonomously, and, like the Ravenna exarchs, were not always loath to try open rebellion when the circumstances seemed favourable; that the people of Sicily had no love for Byzantine rule, but were unable and, on the whole, unwilling to put up any resistance. How could they have? On all sides were powers only too happy to step in and replace Constantinople by another foreign sovereign and by either Latin Christianity or Mohammedanism. How much the Sicilians feared the Arabs in particular is not easy to judge. The damaging piratical raids of the first half of the eighth century had ceased. An uneasy truce prevailed; in 805 the governor of Sicily signed a treaty with the Aghlabid rulers of Tunisia (probably without consulting Constantinople), and there was another in 813 which included an agreement to examine mutual trading interests; Arab merchants were living in Sicily.

The position in 800 was reminiscent of the old days of Carthaginian power. So was the incident which changed everything. In 827, the emperor ordered the arrest of the admiral Euphemius, who had once successfully raided Africa from Sicily. Euphemius organized a popular revolt, defeated the governor and executed him, captured Syracuse, declared himself emperor, and set up his own government on the island. One of his deputies promptly rebelled in turn, and Euphemius appealed to the Aghlabid emir, offering Sicily as a tribute-paying province on condition that he be appointed governor with the title of emperor. The response came immediately. An élite army of more than 10,000 men—Arabs and Berbers from Africa, other Moslems from Spain—landed at Mazara, and the conquest of Sicily had begun. All previous assaults were piratical raids; now the Arabs set out to take the island and colonize it. The task proved to be very difficult. Constantinople, despite its internal weakness and its many enemies, fought hard for its last western outpost.

The war went on for fifty years, pitiless, eating up the island's men and resources, bringing famine and plague, probably worse than the two Punic Wars of the third century B.C. Palermo fell in 831 and after twenty years the Arabs were in control of the western half of the island. Fortresses such as Enna and Cefalù were fought over, year in and year out, before they were finally lost, burned out wrecks, Enna in 859 by treachery, Cefalù the year before. Neither Christian Europe nor the Moslem East gave much help to their co-religionists; Naples even joined the Arabs in the siege and capture of Messina in 843.

As in the past, Syracuse was the key. The invaders tried repeatedly, and they at last succeeded in 878. Although Taormina held out until 902, and Rometta in the mountains west of Messina until 965, the fall of Syracuse marks the end of ancient Sicily. Its population was massacred, and, if the monk Theodosius, one of the few survivors, is to be believed, the booty taken out was fabulous. For 1500 years Syracuse had been the first city of Sicily, for a time the richest and most powerful in all Europe. Its preeminence in Sicily had survived Roman and Byzantine conquest, as it had survived the conversion to Christianity. But it was now compelled to give way to Palermo, as Christianity gave way to Mohammedanism, the Greek language to Arabic. When the island was next conquered, by the Normans in the eleventh century, a new society was created, new in language, religion and culture, in the economy and the social system, in the political structure. There are still survivals of the pre-Arab civilization, symbolized by the Duomo of Syracuse. But the better symbol is the Sicilian dialect, which in its rare uniformity reveals that Italian was an immigrant language, without a long Latin tradition behind it inside Sicily itself. The dividing-line in Sicily between the ancient and the medieval was perhaps the sharpest in Europe.

NOTES ON THE PLATES

1. Late Palaeolithic drawings from a small cave, the Grotto dell' Addaura, in the north flank of Monte Pellegrino, Palermo. This group of deeply incised figures is, as a composition, unique among Palaeolithic cave finds so far.

Reproduced by courtesy of the Soprintendenza alle Antichità, Palermo.

2. *a*. Museo Nazionale Archeologico, Siracusa. A rough-grained marble *kouros* (male nude) from a necropolis in Megara Hyblaea, 1.19 m. tall (originally published by L. Bernabò Brea and G. Pugliese Carratelli in *Annuario della Scuola archeologica italiana di Atene*, vol. 24/26, 1946–8, pp. 59–68), reproduced G. M. A. Richter, *Kouroi* (3rd ed., London 1970), no. 134. Dated stylistically to the middle of the sixth century B.C., this is the earliest *kouros* found in Sicily. The inscription running down the right thigh reads: "Som(b)rotidas the physician, son of Mandrokles."

Reproduced by courtesy of the Soprintendenza alle Antichità, Siracusa.

b. Silver drachma, Zancle, about 500 B.C., twice actual size. Only the obverse is shown: dolphin in sickle-shaped harbour; legend, Dankle. The city (later called Messana) is said to have taken its name from the Sicel word *danklon*, meaning a sickle, because of the shape of the harbour.

c. Silver didrachm, Gela, twice actual size. This represents one of the earliest coin series of Gela, minted under Hippocrates or Gelon before 485 B.C. Obverse: naked galloping horseman wearing conical helmet and brandishing a spear. Reverse: the river-god Gelas as a bull with human face; legend, Gela.

Coins reproduced by courtesy of the Fitzwilliam Museum, Cambridge.

3. *a*. Museo Nazionale Archeologico, Palermo. Two of the four surviving metopes from the frieze of a little temple on the Acropolis of Selinus, probably of the second quarter of the sixth century B.C. They represent the oldest temple sculpture from Selinus, still under strong mainland influence in style, specifically from the Peloponnese. The material is local tufa. The metope at left above depicts a winged sphinx. The metope below right depicts Zeus, in the guise of a white bull, carrying Europa off from Tyre by sea (hence the

two dolphins beneath the bull) to Crete, where she bore him two sons, Minos and Rhadamanthus.

Anderson photographs, reproduced by courtesy of The Mansell Collection.

b. Lion's head, serving as a rain spout, from the north side of the so-called temple of Nike (Victory) at Himera. This Doric temple was erected to commemorate the victory over the Carthaginians in 480 B.C., and was destroyed by the latter in 409. Fifty-six heads have been found, most of them in the excavations of 1929–30; the best, including this one, are on display in the Museo Nazionale Archeologico in Palermo. See P. Marconi, "Griechische Löwenköpfe aus Sizilien", *Die Antike* 6 (1930) 179–201.

Reproduced by courtesy of the Soprintendenza alle Antichità, Palermo.

4. *a*. One panel of a pavement mosaic from a private house on Motya. Although this type of mosaic, made of white and black river pebbles, is otherwise unknown in Sicily, there are parallels from contemporary Greece. Dating is difficult and controversial: contrast C. M. Robertson in *Journal of Hellenic Studies* 85 (1965) 72–89 and V. Tusa in *Studi semitici* 24 (1967) 85–95.

Reproduced by courtesy of the Soprintendenza alle Antichità, Palermo.

b. A section of the *tophet* (sacrificial burial-ground), Motya, excavated in 1965. The urns and stelae of this *tophet*, on the north shore of the island, are typically Punic. Inside the urns few identifiable bones survived the incineration, the majority of animals, a few of children. The *tophet*, discovered in 1919, is now known to have been in continuous use from at least the sixth century B.C. to the destruction of Motya by Dionysius I in 397 B.C., and again from perhaps the middle of the fourth century to the middle of the third. This recent evidence provides proof of a modest reoccupation of Motya after 397, usually denied in histories of Sicily.

Reproduced by courtesy of the Soprintendenza alle Antichità, Palermo.

5. Cathedral, Syracuse: view of the south aisle with the colonnade of the original Doric temple of Athena incorporated in the cathedral wall. The pavement and iron gateways date from the Renaissance.

Photograph Hirmer Fotoarchiv München, reproduced by courtesy of Thames & Hudson Ltd.

6. **The Citadel, Eryx.** Virtually no trace remains of the temple of

Aphrodite; the stone was used for the mediaeval fortifications, the ruins of which can be seen in the photograph.

Photograph Publifoto Palermo, reproduced by courtesy of the Soprintendenza alle Antichità, Palermo.

7. Silver coins, all actual size, Fitzwilliam Museum, Cambridge. The most common denomination was the tetradrachm, followed by the drachma and didrachm. Larger coins were rare, usually minted as special commemorative issues.

Reproduced by courtesy of the Fitzwilliam Museum, Cambridge.

a. Akragas, tetradrachm, before the middle of the fifth century B.C. Obverse: eagle with folded wings; legend (reading clockwise), Akragas. Reverse: crab.

b. Himera, didrachm, about 480–470 B.C. Obverse: cock; legend, Himera. Reverse: crab (replacing a hen after Himera fell to Akragas).

c. Syracuse, decadrachm, period of Dionysius I. Obverse: Victory flying to crown a female driver; below, shield and armour. Reverse: head of the nymph Arethusa, dolphins, a cockle-shell to the right. This specimen lacks the signature of Euaenetus, and the die may not have been engraved by him personally.

d. Panormus, tetradrachm, about 400 B.C. Obverse: Victory flying to crown a charioteer; legend (in Punic letters), Ziz. Reverse: head of Arethusa with dolphins. The Syracusan model for this coinage is obvious from a comparison with the preceding coin. The legend is the basis for the guess that Ziz may have been the Punic name for Panormus.

e. "Siculo-Punic" tetradrachm, about 350 B.C. Obverse: head of Arethusa with dolphins. Reverse: horse's head and date-palm; legend (in Punic letters), people of the camp. These coins were struck in a number of mints in western Sicily, in order to pay mercenaries. The Greek for "date-palm" is *phoinix*, and the pun on the word "Phoenician" was presumably the reason for the tree's inclusion, to help Greek speakers identify the coin.

8. *a.* British Museum, no. 1823-6-10-1. This almost spherical bronze helmet, 8″ high, was dedicated to Zeus at Olympia by Hiero, tyrant of Syracuse, from the booty taken following a famous victory in the Bay of Naples in 474 B.C. The metrical inscription reads: "Hiero son of Deinomenes and the Syracusans (dedicated) to Zeus Etruscan (spoils) from Cumae."

Reproduced by courtesy of the British Museum.

b. Small copper coin (2½ times actual size) minted at Enna by

Eunus, leader of the first slave revolt, after he became King Antiochus. Obverse: veiled head of Demeter wearing corn wreath. Reverse: ear of corn; legend (in two lines reading down), Basi(leus) (= King) Anti(ochus). The photo was taken from a cast in order to bring out the detail of this badly worn coin a little better. Only one other specimen is known, in Syracuse. The coin was identified by E. S. G. Robinson in *Numismatic Chronicle*, 4th ser., 20 (1920) 175–6. All the coin-types from Enna were connected with Demeter, and the slaves maintained the tradition.

Reproduced from a cast supplied by the British Museum.

c. The site of Kale Akte from the air. This city, on a platform in the heavily wooded, mountainous zone behind modern Caronia on the coast, was founded by the Sicel leader Ducetius soon after the middle of the fifth century B.C. (an earlier settlement scheme by Samian refugees had been abandoned). Four centuries later it was visited by Cicero in preparing the prosecution of Verres, and it is known to have continued in existence into the early Empire; a distinguished scholar-rhetorician in Rome in the time of Augustus, Caecilius of Caleacte, was a Jewish freedman who also wrote a history, of which nothing survives, of the Sicilian slave revolts.

Aerial photograph reproduced by courtesy of the Aerofototeca of the Gabinetto Fotografico Nazionale, Roma.

9. *a.* A section of the fortification-wall at Capo Soprano, the western end of Gela. The lower courses are of stone blocks, the upper of coarse brick. (The studs visible in the picture hold in place the transparent covering now protecting the brick.) The thickness is uniformly 2.70 m.; the height of the surviving sections varies, with a maximum of 8 m. The original construction dates to the time of (or soon after) Timoleon, with subsequent improvements and reinforcements under Agathocles. The section now recovered had been buried under the sand soon after the destruction of Gela in 282 B.C.; whatever had remained above ground was employed as a quarry when Frederick II built Terranova in A.D. 1230. For a convenient summary, see D. Adamesteanu in *Revue archéologique*, 6th ser., 49 (1957) 32–43.

Reproduced by courtesy of the Soprintendenza alle Antichità, Agrigento.

b. Silver tetradrachm of Agathocles, after 305 B.C. Obverse: head of Persephone wreathed in barley; legend, Koras (= Maiden in the genitive). Reverse: winged Victory about to nail a helmet as a trophy; at right, a *triskeles*; legend, Agathocles.

c. Bronze 5-litra coin of Hiero II. Obverse: head of Hiero wearing diadem. Reverse: armed warrior on prancing horse; legend, Hiero.

d. Silver tetradrachm of Hiero II. Obverse: head of Hiero's wife, Philistis, wearing diadem and veil. Reverse: winged Victory driving four-horse chariot; legend, Queen Philistis.

Coins reproduced by courtesy of the Fitzwilliam Museum, Cambridge.

10. Pavement mosaics from the villa at Casale (Piazza Armerina). Alinari photographs, reproduced by courtesy of The Mansell Collection.

a. Odysseus in the cave of the Cyclops, serving wine in an attempt to intoxicate the one-eyed monster. This large mosaic (most of which is shown in the picture), more than 5 m. square, occupied the entire floor of the room (off the long corridor) immediately to the north of the great basilical hall at the eastern end of the villa (Figure 7).

b. One section of an elaborate composition depicting a chariot race (possibly at the Circus Maximus in Rome), which filled the long room, more than 20 m., with an apse at either end, which one reached by walking almost straight on from the monumental entrance (Figure 7). An official is about to offer the palm of victory to the winning charioteer while the trumpeter plays. The obelisk in the lower left-hand corner of the composition is one of several statues and altars worked into the mosaic representing the central rectangular "enclosure" of the race-course. The columns at the back supported the roof-vaulting of the chamber.

11. Museo Nazionale Archeologico, Palermo. Terracotta funeral monument in the form of a *heroön* (shrine of a hero), Lilybaeum, 91.5 cm high. This is the best preserved of these syncretic monuments, discussed at the beginning of chapter 13. A name had been inscribed above the banquet scene; only a few letters remain (not visible in the reproduction), and it appears possible that the name was deliberately obliterated.

Reproduced by courtesy of the Soprintendenza alle Antichità, Palermo.

12. *a.* Museo Nazionale Archeologico, Siracusa, no. 864. Marble sarcophagus found in the S. Giovanni catacomb in 1872; 2.07 × 0.84 m., height 0.71 m., lid 0.20 m.; probably to be dated A.D. 340–350. Much the finest sarcophagus found in Syracuse, it is covered with scenes from the Old and New Testaments, most of them easily

identifiable. The epitaph inscribed on the lid reads: IC ADELFIA CF / POSITA CONPAR / BALERI COMITIS. "Here rests Adelfia, a *clarissima femina* (woman of senatorial rank), wife of Count Valerius." (*Comes*, literally "companion", was a title recently created by Constantine.) See V. Tusa, *I sarcofagi romani in Sicilia* (Palermo 1957) pp. 173–81.

Reproduced by courtesy of the Soprintendenza alle Antichità, Siracusa.

b. A section of the vast S. Giovanni catacomb in Syracuse (Figure 8).

Alinari photograph, reproduced by courtesy of The Mansell Collection.

BIBLIOGRAPHY

GENERAL

The Evidence

The nearest we have to a continuous history of ancient Sicily, down to the late Roman Republic, will be found in the surviving books of the *Universal History* of Diodorus (for which there is now an admirable index by R. M. Geer in the *Loeb Classical Library* edition, vol. 12, 1967). For shorter periods or episodes, there are Thucydides, books VI–VII, on the Athenian invasion of 415–413 B.C.; Polybius, book I, and Livy, books XXI–XXX (based largely on portions of Polybius now lost) on the Punic Wars, in which Sicily was heavily involved; Cicero's Verrine orations on the administration of Sicily in the Roman Republic; Plutarch's lives of Nicias, Alcibiades, Dion and Timoleon; Appian, *Civil Wars*, books IV–V, on Sextus Pompey; and numerous letters of Gregory the Great, pope from 590 to 604. The miscellaneous references scattered in these and other ancient writers and the inferior derivative works, such as the short biographies by Nepos or the historical epitome by Justin, cannot be itemized.

For an account and evaluation of the literary sources, see B. Pace, *Arte e civiltà della Sicilia antica* (4 vols., Rome and Naples 1936–49; 2nd ed. of vol. I, 1958) III 139–72; the notes in the relevant sections of F. Jacoby, ed., *Die Fragmente der griechischen Historiker* (unfinished); G. De Sanctis, *Ricerche sulla storiografia siceliota* (Palermo 1958); T. S. Brown, *Timaeus of Tauromenium* (Berkeley and Los Angeles 1958); A. Momigliano, "Atene nel III secolo a.C. e la scoperta di Roma nelle storia di Timeo di Tauromenio", *Rivista storica italiana* 71 (1959) 529–56, reprinted in his *Terzo contributo alla storia degli studi classici e del mondo antico* (Rome 1966) I 23–53; F. W. Walbank, "The Historians of Greek Sicily", *Kokalos* 14/15 (1968–69) 476–98.

The epigraphical material has been less rewarding than for other regions of the ancient world. Greek inscriptions found *in* Sicily (which are not always the most important for the history of Sicily) were published in *Inscriptiones Graecae*, vol. XIV (1890). Later finds are published in a great variety of journals, many of them reprinted in the annual *Supplementum epigraphicum graecum* (suspended for several years but now about to resume publication); for comments see the annual "Bulletin épigraphique" of J. and L. Robert in the *Revue des études grecques*. Latin inscriptions are published in the

Corpus Inscriptionum Latinarum, vol. X 2 (1883), and thereafter in *L'année épigraphique.*

Archaeological publications are numerous and widely scattered. Mention should be made of the journal *Kokalos,* published in Palermo since 1955; of R. Stillwell, ed., *The Princeton Encyclopaedia of Classical Sites* (Princeton 1976); and of a few longer or very recent studies: J. A. de Waele, *Acragas Graeca,* vol. 1 so far published (*Archeologische Studiën van het Nederlands Historisch Instituut te Rome* III, 1971); L. Bernabò Brea, *Akrai* (Catania 1956); B. Pace, *Cumarina* (Catania 1927); A. Holm, *Catania antica* (Catania 1925); G. Libertini, *Centuripe* (Catania 1926); M. T. Currò *et al.,* "Eloro", *Monumenti antichi* 47 (1966) 203–340; V. Giustolisi, *Hikkara* (Palermo 1973); Istituto d'Archeologia, Università di Palermo, *Himera* I–II (Rome 1970–76); J. D. Evans, *The Prehistoric Antiquities of the Maltese Islands: A Survey* (London 1971); G. Vallet and F. Villard, *Mégara Hyblaea* (in progress), and on the cemeteries, the articles by M. Cébeillac-Gervasoni and M. Gras in *Kokalos* 21 (1975) 3–53; *Mozia,* in *Studi semitici,* published at irregular intervals since 1964 by the Centro di studi semitici, Università di Roma; B. S. J. Isserlin and Joan du Plat Taylor, *Motya* I (Leiden 1974); *Kokalos* 21 (1975) on Selinus; E. Gàbrici, "Studi archeologici selinunti", *Monumenti antichi* 43 (1956) 205–407; V. Giustolisi, *Cronia-Paropo-Solunto* (Palermo 1972), H.–P. Drögemuller, *Syrakus, Zur Topographie und Geschichte einer griechischen Stadt* (*Gymnasium,* Beiheft 6, 1969).

On roads, see G. P. Verbrugghe, *Sicilia* (*Itinera Romana* II, Bern 1976); on harbours, the best account, based on aerial photography but unfortunately restricted to the Phoenician ones, is G. Schmiedt, in *L'Universo* 45 (1965) 258–72.

The temples at Syracuse, Selinus, Akragas and Segesta are described and illustrated in H. Berve, G. Gruben and M. Hirmer, *Greek Temples, Theatres and Shrines* (London 1963), pp. 416–43. The basic study remains R. Koldewey and O. Puchstein, *Die griechischen Tempel in Unteritalien und Sicilien* (2 vols., Berlin 1899).

A technical analysis, with illustrations, of the theatres at Segesta, Tyndaris, Syracuse, Akrai and Taormina will be found in H. Bulle, *Untersuchungen an griechischen Theatern* (Bayerische Akademie d. Wiss., phil.-hist. Klasse, *Abhandlungen* 33, 1928). See also R. Stillwell, "The Theater of Morgantina", *Kokalos* 10/11 (1964–5) 579–88; E. Di Miro, "Il teatro di Heraclea Minoa" (Accademia nazionale dei Lincei, *Rendiconti della Classe di scienze morali* . . . , 8th ser., 21 (1966) 151–68).

On coins, C. M. Kraay, *Archaic and Classical Greek Coins* (London 1976), ch. 10, must be the starting-point. Despite all the advance which has been made in the study of the strictly numismatic aspects of Sicilian coinage and of the artistic side, the interpretation of the coins for economic and political history is still full of uncertainties— see C. M. Kraay, *Greek Coins and History* (London 1969), pp. 19–42, 51–63; K. Christ, "Historische Probleme der griechisch-sizilischen Numismatik", *Historia* 3 (1954–5) 385–95—and reference will therefore be limited to G. E. Rizzo, *Monete greche della Sicilia* (2 vols., Rome 1946), an excellent descriptive and photographic record; E. Gàbrici, *La monetazione del bronzo nella Sicilia antica* (Palermo 1927), though the actual collection is now somewhat antiquated; G. K. Jenkins, *The Coinage of Gela* (Berlin 1970); L. Lacroix, *Monnaies et colonisation dans l'Occident grec* (Acad. royale de Belgique, Classe des lettres . . . , *Mémoires* LIX 2, 1965), a group of studies primarily on the religious symbols and their implications for the early colonies in their relations with their mother-cities; Istituto italiano di numismatica, *La circolazione della monetà ateniese in Sicilia e in Magna Grecia* (Rome 1969); A. Tusa Cutroni, "Aspetti e problemi della monetazione arcaica di Selinunte (inizi—480 a.C.)", *Kokalos* 21 (1975) 154–73.

Modern Works

(*Note:* None of the titles in this section or in the preceding one on archaeology will be repeated under the chronological sections of this bibliography.)

The three fundamental large-scale works on ancient Sicily are that by Pace (to the Arab conquest), already mentioned, which must be given priority; E. A. Freeman's unfinished *History of Sicily* (4 vols., Oxford 1891–4), to 289 B.C.; A. Holm, *Geschichte Siciliens im Altertum* (3 vols., Leipzig 1870–98). Freeman also wrote a popular one-volume *Sicily* (London 1892), to the end of the Roman period; cf. L. Pareti, *Sicilia antica* (Palermo 1959), to the Roman conquest.

Many relevant articles, uneven in value, appear under personal and geographical names in *Paulys Realencyclopädie der classischen Altertumswissenschaft*, begun in 1894 and at last approaching completion. Much valuable discussion will be found in two classic works, K. J. Beloch, *Griechische Geschichte* (2nd ed., 4 vols. in 8, Strassburg, then Leipzig and Berlin 1912–27), and G. De Sanctis, *Storia dei Romani*, the first volume of which was published in Turin in 1907, now being reissued in Florence (4 volumes in 8), with some revisions of the earlier volumes; among recent histories, in Ed. Will, *Histoire politique du monde hellénistique (323–30 av. J.-C.)* (2 vols., Nancy 1966–7). For Sicilian history from the point of view of Magna

Graecia, see the relevant chapters (at times too 'patriotic') in E. Ciaceri, *Storia della Magna Grecia* (3 vols., Milan 1924–32).

The most complete guide-book is the remarkable one published by the Touring Club Italiano (5th ed., Milan 1968); in English, M. Guido, *Sicily. An Archaeological Guide.* (rev. ed., London 1977).

On population: J. Beloch, *Die Bevölkerung der griechisch-römischen Welt* (Leipzig 1886), ch. VII; D. Asheri, "La popolazione di Imera nel V. secolo a.C", *Rivista di filologia classica* 101 (1973) 457–65.

On Sicily and Carthage, see generally B. H. Warmington, *Carthage* (Penguin ed. 1964); V. Merante, "La Sicilia e Cartagine dal V secolo alla conquista romana", *Kokalos* 18/19 (1972–3) 77–103; C. R. Whittaker, "Carthaginian Imperialism", in *Imperialism in the Ancient World* ed. by C. R. Whittaker and Peter Garnsey (Cambridge 1978), chap. 3. Special studies are listed in the appropriate sections below.

Olympic victors are listed and discussed by L. Moretti, "Olympionikai, i vincitori negli antichi agoni olimpici" (Accademia nazionale dei Lincei, *Memorie della Classe di scienze morali* ...., 8th ser., 8 (1959) 55–198), with supplements in *Klio* 52 (1970) 295–303. See generally M. I. Finley and H. W. Pleket: *The Olympic Games. The First 1000 Years* (Chatto 1976).

PART 1

PREHISTORIC AND ARCHAIC SICILY

Prehistoric

The basic book on prehistoric Sicily is L. Bernabò Brea, *Sicily before the Greeks*, translated by C. M. Preston and L. Guido (London 1957; 4th Italian ed., Milan 1966).

Special studies: P. Graziosi, *Levanzo* (Florence 1962); Lord William Taylour, *Mycenaean Pottery in Italy* (Cambridge 1958); S. Tinè, "L'origine delle tombe a forno della Sicilia", *Kokalos* 9 (1963) 93–128.

Archaic

The fundamental study (to 480 B.C.) is T. J. Dunbabin, *The Western Greeks* (Oxford 1948), though his general views on the economic side and on Greek-Carthaginian relations are not accepted in this book. A. Schenk von Stauffenberg, *Trinakria. Sizilien und Gross griechenland im archaischer und frühklassischer Zeit* (Munich and

Vienna 1963), is a paean, in the footsteps of Pindar, to the first tyrants, "who blasphemously founded a new order and liberated the Greeks of the West from a mortal embracing menace."

On Greek colonization: J. Bérard, *La colonisation grecque* (2nd ed., Paris 1957); John Boardman, *The Greeks Overseas* (2nd ed., Penguin 1973); G. Vallet, *Rhégion et Zancle* (*Bibliothèque des Écoles françaises d'Athènes et de Rome*, no. 189, Paris 1958), "La colonisation chalcidienne et l'hellénisation de la Sicile orientale", *Kokalos* 8, (1962) 30–51, and, with F. Villard, "Mégara Hyblaea, IX: Les problèmes de l'Agora et de la cité archaique", *Mélanges d'archéologie et d'historie* 81 (1969) 7–35; G. Rizza, "Siculi e greci sui colli di Leontini", *Cronache di archeologia e di storia dell' arte* (1962) 3–27, with more archaeological detail in his report in *Notizie degli scavi* (1955) 281–376; articles by S. Mazzarino and G. Vallet on relations between colony and mother-city in *Metropoli e colonie di Magna Grecia* (*Atti del terzo Convegno di studi sulla Magna Grecia*, Naples 1964); P. Orlandini, "L'espansione di Gela nella Sicilia centromeridionale", *Kokalos* 8 1962) 69–121; R. Van Compernolle, *Etude de chronologie et d'historiographie siciliotes* (Brussels and Rome 1959); G. Vallet and F. Villard, "La date de fondation de Sélinonte", *Bulletin de correspondance hellénique* 82 (1958) 16–26; E. Lepore, "Classi e ordini in Magna Grecia", in *Recherches sur les structures sociales dans l'antiquité classique*, Caen 25–26 April 1969 (Paris 1970), pp. 43–62.

On the Phoenicians in the west in general, and in Sicily in particular; V. Tusa, "La civiltà punica", in *Popoli e civiltà dell' Italia antica*, vol. 3 (Rome 1974), pp. 9–142, heavily illustrated; C. R. Whittaker, "The Western Phoenicians: Colonization and Assimilation", *Proceedings of the Cambridge Philological Society*, n.s. 20 (1974) 58–79; *Studi semitici*, no. 36 (1970), no. 38 (1971); V. Merante, "Sui rapporti greco-punici nel Mediterraneo occidentale nel VI sec. a.C.", *Kokalos* 16 (1970) 267–74; S. Moscati, "La penetrazione fenicia e punica in Sardegna" (Accademia nazionale dei Lincei, *Memorie della Classe di scienze morali . . . .*, 8th ser., 12 (1966) 215–50; S. Luria, "Zum Problem der griechisch-karthagischen Beziehungen", *Acta Antiqua* 12 (1964) 53–75; Ph. Gauthier, "Grecs et Phéniciens en Sicile pendant la période archaique", *Revue historique* 224 (1960) 257–74.

On the survival of pre-Greek religion, the viewpoint here adopted is that of A. Brelich, "La religione greca a Sicilia", *Kokalos* 10/11 (1964–5) 35–54; contrast E. Manni, *Sicilia pagana* (Palermo 1963). For the view that there is genuine history beneath the legends of Daedalus and Heracles in Sicily, see E. Manni, "Minosse ed Eracle nella Sicilia dell' età del bronzo", *Kokalos* 8 (1962) 6–29. Contrast

BIBLIOGRAPHY

L. Pearson, "Myth and *archaeologia* in Italy and Sicily—Timaeus and his Predecessors", *Yale Classical Studies* 24 (1975) 171–95. Special studies: J. H. Croon, "The Palici", *Mnemosyne*, 4th ser., 5 (1952) 116–29; R. J. Buck, "Communalism in the Lipari Islands", *Classical Philology* 54 (1959) 35–39; D. Ahrens, "Stufen der Verbildlichung in der Terakottenkunst von Selinus, Akragas und Gela", *Jahreshefte des österreichischen archäologischen Instituts* 46 (1961–3), Beibl. 95–144; H. Riemann, "Die Planung der ältesten sizilischen Ringhallentempel", *Mitteilungen des deutschen archäologischen Instituts. Römische Abteilung* 71 (1964) 19–59; E. Sjöqvist, "Perche Morgantina?" (Accademia nazionale dei Lincei, *Rendiconti della Classe di scienze morali* . . . . , 8th ser., 15 (1961) 291–300); R. Van Compernolle, "Ségeste et l'Hellénisme", *Phoibus* 5 (1950–1) 183–228.

PART 2

THE GREEK TYRANTS

H. Berve, *Die Tyrannis bei den Griechen* (2 vols., Munich 1967), with a complete listing of the literary sources (less adequate on the archaeological and numismatic evidence), does not replace his preliminary studies, which are cited, with occasional comments, in the appropriate sections below.

W. Hüttl, *Verfassungsgeschichts von Syrakus* (Prague 1929), the only work of its kind, is not reliable. H. Wentker, *Sizilien und Athen* (Heidelberg 1956) is perverse and wrong-headed; see the review by P. A. Brunt, in *Classical Review*, n.s. 7 (1957) 243–5. F. P. Rizzo, *La Repubblica di Siracusa nel momento di Ducezio* (Palermo 1970), ranges more widely than the title indicates.

Van Compernolle, *Etudes* (already mentioned), defends the traditional dates for the early tyrants, adopted in this book, against L. Pareti, *Studi siciliani ed italioti* (Florence 1920).

On special fifth-century topics: E. Lo Cascio, "Le trattative fra Gelone e i confederati e la data della battaglia d'Imera", *Helikon* 13/14 (1973–4) 210–55; Ph. Gauthier, "Le parallèle Himère-Salamine au Ve et au IVe siècle av. J.-C.", *Revue des études anciennes* 68 (1966) 5–32; D. Adamesteanu, "L'ellenizzazione della Sicilia e il momento di Ducezio", *Kokalos* 8 (1962) 167–98, with important topographical discussion; G. V. Gentili, "Cinturone enea con dedica da Paliké", *Mitteilungen des deutschen archäologischen Instituts. Römische Abteilung* 69 (1962) 14–20; P. R. Franke, "Leontinishce *phygades* in Chalkis?", *Archäologischer Anzeiger* (1966) 395–407;

A. Burford, "Temple Building at Segesta", *Classical Quarterly*, n.s.
11 (1961) 87–93; U. Laffi, "La spedizione ateniese in Sicilia del
415 a.C.", *Rivista storica italiana* 82 (1970) 277–307; H. D. Westlake,
"Hermocrates the Syracusan", *Bulletin of the John Rylands Library*
41 (1958/9) 239–68; F. Grosso, "Ermocrate di Siracusa", *Kokalos* 12
(1966) 102–43, which is as much about Thucydides as about
Hermocrates; K. F. Stroheker, "Die Karthagergesandtschaft in
Athen 406 v. Chr.", *Historia* 3 (1954/5) 163–71.

Dionysius I and II

K. F. Stroheker, *Dionysius* I (Wiesbaden 1958), is standard,
though too idealized and 'psychological'. See also F. Sartori, "Sulla
dynasteia di Dionisio il Vecchio nell' opera diodorea", *Critica storica* 5
(1966) 3–61; G. Woodhead, "The 'Adriatic Empire' of Dionysius I
of Syracuse", *Klio* 52 (1970) 503–12; Y. Garlan, *Recherches de
poliorcétique grecque* (*Bibliothèque des Ecoles françaises d'Athènes et de
Rome* 123, Paris 1974), pp. 155–69; L. Maurin, "Himilcon le
Magonide. Crises et mutations à Carthage au début du IVe
siècle avant J.-C.", *Semitica* 12 (1962) 5–43.

The fullest study of Dion is H. Berve, *Dion* (Akad. d. Wiss. u.
der Literatur, Mainz, *Abhandlungen der geistes- u. sozialwiss. Klasse*,
1956, no. 10), which accepts the Platonic saga in essence. See also
J. Christien, "Mercénaires et partis politiques à Syracuse de 357 à
354", *Revue des études anciennes* 77 (1975) 63–73; A. Fuks, "Redistribution of Land and Houses in Syracuse in 356 B.C. . .", *Classical
Quarterly*, n.s. 18 (1968) 207–23.

On the Platonic letters, *pro:* G. R. Morrow, *Plato's Epistles*
(Indianapolis and New York 1962), with a translation; Kurt von
Fritz, *Platon in Sizilien* (Berlin 1968), more than 150 pages of special
pleading and circular argument; *con:* L. Edelstein, *Plato's Seventh
Letter* (Leiden 1966), with an important review by G. Muller in
Göttingische Gelehrte Anzeiger 221 (1968) 187–211; N. Gulley, in
Pseudepigraphica I (*Entretiens* of the Fondation Hardt 18, 1972), pp.
105–30.

Timoleon

R. J. Talbert, *Timoleon and the Revival of Greek Sicily, 344–317* B.C.
(Cambridge 1974), replaces previous books and provides a full
bibliography. See also J. Seibert, *Metropolis und Apoikie* (diss.
Würzburg 1963), ch. IX, XI; and the brief but important analysis
by C. Mossé, *La fin de la démocratie athénienne* (Paris 1962), pp.
340–7.

Vol. 4 of *Kokalos* summarizes the archaeological evidence for the recovery begun under Timoleon; see also P. Orlandini, "Tipologia e cronologia del materiale archaeologico di Gela dalla nuova fondazione di Timoleonte all' età di Ierone II", *Archeologia classica* 9 (1957) 44–75, 153–73; A. D. Trendall, *The Red-figured Vases of Lucania, Campania and Sicily* (2 vols., Oxford 1967), bk. III, with supplements in the *Bulletin of the London Institute of Classical Studies*, Supp. 26 (1970).

Agathocles

The fullest narrative remains that of H. J. W. Tillyard, *Agathocles* (Cambridge 1908), which accepts uncritically the Timaean moralizing tradition; see the sounder and more sophisticated account by G. De Sanctis in his *Scritti minori*, ed. S. Accame, I (Rome 1966) ch. XVI. H. Berve, *Die Herrschaft des Agathokles* (*Sitzungsberichte der Bayerischen Akad. d. Wissenschaften* 1952, Heft 5), is obsessed with constitutional-law formulations; see H.-J. Diesner, "Agathokles-Probleme: Der Putsch vom Jahre 316", *Wiss. Zeitschrift der . . . Univ. Halle-Wittenberg*, Ges.-Sprachw. VII/4 (1958) 931–8, and the incisive comments by Ed. Will, *Histoire politique* (already cited), I 94–103.

Special studies: C. Dolce, "Diodoro e la storia di Agatocle", *Kokalos* 6 (1960) 124–66; Martin Müller, *Der Feldzug des Agathokles in Afrika* (diss. Leipzig 1928); R. Van Compernolle, "La clause territoriale du traité de 306/5 conclue entre Agathokles de Syracuse et Carthage", *Revue belge de philologie et d'histoire* 32 (1954) 395–421; A. Di Vita, "L'elemente punico a Selinunte nel IV e III secolo a.C.", *Archeologia classica* 5 (1953) 39–47; D. White, "The Post-Classical Cult of Malophorus at Selinus", *American Journal of Archaeology* 71 (1967) 335–52; G. Schmiedt, "Contributo della fotografia aerea alla ricostruzione della topografia antica di Lilibeo", *Kokalos* 9 (1963) 49–72.

PART 3

ROMAN AND BYZANTINE SICILY

No systematic account of Roman Sicily is available. Vol. 2 of I. Scaturro, *Storia di Sicilia* (Rome 1950), which goes down to the ninth century (no more was published), is uncritical and takes a romantic view of history. V. M. Scramuzza, "Roman Sicily", in

An Economic Survey of Ancient Rome, ed. T. Frank, III (Baltimore 1937), pp. 225–377, is primarily a useful collection of materials.

The Roman Conquest

The basic work on Pyrrhus, P. Lévêque, *Pyrrhos* (*Bibliothèque des Écoles françaises d'Athènes et de Rome*, no. 185, Paris 1957), presents too idealistic a view of his Sicilian phase, whereas G. Nenci, *Pirro. Aspirazioni egemoniche ed equilibrio mediterraneo* (Univ. di Torino, *Pubblicazioni della Facoltà di lettere* . . . , V 2, 1953), assumes too complex a motivation in international relations; see Will, *Histoire politique* (already mentioned) I 104–11.

Special topics: H. Berve, "Das Königtum des Pyrrhos in Sizilien", in *Neue Beiträge zur klassischen Altertumswissenschaft*, ed. R. Lullies (Stuttgart 1954), pp. 272–7; A. Vallone, "I Mamertini in Sicilia", *Kokalos* 1 (1955) 22–61; H. Berve, *König Hieron II* (Bayerische Akad. d. Wiss., phil.-hist. Klasse, *Abhandlungen*, n.F. 47, 1959), replacing all previous work on Hiero; P. R. Franke, "Historisch-numismatische Probleme der Zeits Hierons II von Syrakus", *Jahrbuch für Numismatik und Geldgeschichte* 9 (1958) 57–85; D. Roussel, *Les Siciliens entre les Romains et les Carthaginois . . . 276 à 241* (Paris 1970).

On aspects of the Punic Wars: F. Hampl, "Zur Vorgeschichte des ersten und zweiten Punischen Krieges", in *Aufstieg und Niedergang der romischen Welt*, ed. H. Temporini, I 1 (1972), pp. 412–41; A. Heuss, "Der Erste Punische Krieg und das Problem des römischen Imperialismus", *Historische Zeitschrift* 169 (1949) 457–513; W. Hoffman, "Hannibal und Sizilien", *Hermes* 89 (1961) 478–94; on the naval side, at great length and with many digressions, J. H. Thiel, *A History of Roman Sea-Power before the Second Punic War* (Amsterdam 1954) and *Studies on the History of Roman Sea-Power in Republican Times* (Amsterdam 1964), ch. II; for an ingenious attempt to impose a pattern of development in rather formal juristic terms on the relations first between Carthage and Syracuse and then with Rome, S. Mazzarino, *Introduzione alle guerre puniche* (Catania 1947).

Sicily under the Roman Republic

Modern accounts have been much under the sway of the inventive reconstruction by J. Carcopino, "La Sicile agricole au dernier siècle de la République", *Viertaljahrschrift für Sozial- und Wirtschaftsgeschichte* 4 (1906) 128–85, and *La loi d'Hiéron et les Romains* (Paris 1914), from which there is a considerable divergence in the present volume. For a summary of the problems as seen today from an approach closer to Carcopino's, see S. Calderone, "Problemi dell' organizzazione della *provincia* di Sicilia", *Kokalos* 10/11 (1964–5) 63–98, and "Il problema delle città censorie e la storia agraria della Sicilia romana", *Kokalos* 6 (1960) 3–25. The four articles published by R. T. Pritchard in successive volumes of *Historia* (1969–72) are a retrograde step in every respect. The fullest straightforward, balanced account of Verres' governorship and trial remains the book by E. Ciccotti, *Il processo di Verre. Un capitolo di storia romana* (Milan 1895); cf. N. Marinone, *Quaestiones Verrinae* (Univ. di Torino, *Pubblicazioni della Facoltà di lettere* . . . , II 3, 1950), on the chronology and on Cicero's tour of inquiry in Sicily.

Special topics: E. Gabba, "Sui Senati delle città siciliane nell' età di Verre", *Athenaeum*, n.s. 37 (1959) 304–20; U. Kahrstedt, "Die Gemeinden Siziliens in der Romerzeit", *Klio* 35 (1942) 246–67; Jola Marconi-Bovio, "Inconsistenza di una Selinunte romana", *Kokalos* 3 (1957) 70–8; G. Manganaro, "Città di Sicilia e santuari panellenici nel III e II sec. a.C.", *Historia* 13 (1964) 414–39, with inferences about city autonomy which are not persuasive; F. Sartori, "Le dodici tribù di Lilibeo", *Kokalos* 3 (1957) 38–60; for what little is known about Roman immigration, A. J. N. Wilson, *Emigration from Italy in the Republican Age of Rome* (Manchester 1966).

Venus at Eryx: R. Schilling, *La religion romaine de Vénus* (*Bibliothèque des Écoles françaises d'Athènes et de Rome*, no. 178, Paris 1954), pp. 233–66, more briefly in his "La place de la Sicile dans la religion romaine", *Kokalos* 10/11 (1964–5) 259–83, but cf. for some important corrections, tied to dubious generalizations, D. Kienast, "Rom und die Venus vom Eryx", *Hermes* 93 (1965) 478–89; G. Cultrera, "Il 'temenos' di Afrodite Ericina e gli scavi del 1930 e del 1931", *Notizie degli scavi* (1935) 294–328.

Slave revolts: J. Vogt, *Ancient Slavery and the Ideal of Man*, translated by T. Wiedemann (Oxford 1974) ch. 3, with important criticisms by F. Bömer, *Untersuchungen über die Religion der Sklaven in Griechenland und in Rom* III (Akad . . . Mainz, *Abhandlungen* . . . , 1961, no. 4), pp. 84–5, 96–102; P. Oliva, "Die charakteristischen Züge der grossen Sklavenaufstände zur Zeit der römischen Republik", in *Neue Beiträge zur Geschichte der alten Welt*, ed. E. C. Welskopf, II (Berlin 1965), pp. 75–88; J.-P. Brisson, *Spartacus* (Paris 1959), ch. V, VII, IX, XIII, with review by M. Capozza in *Paideia* 16 (1961) 179–87; L. Pareti, "I supposti 'sdoppiamenti' delle guerre servili in Sicilia", *Rivista di filologia classica*, n.s. 5 (1927) 44–67, reprinted in his *Studi minori di storia antica* III (Rome 1965), pp. 73–92.

Sicily under the Roman Emperors

On Sextus Pompey and Augustus: M. Hadas, *Sextus Pompey* (New York 1930), ch. VI-VIII: F. Vittinghoff, *Römische Kolonisation und Bürgerrechtspolitik unter Caesar und Augustus* (Akad. d. Wiss. u. d. Literatur, Mainz, *Abhandlungen d. geistes- u. sozialwiss. Klasse*, 1951, no. 14).

For a view of the Vandals chiefly as 'vandals' and persecutors of the faithful, with good bibliography, see F. Giunta "Genserico e la Sicilia", *Kokalos* 2 (1956) 104–41.

The best account of the land regime in the late western Empire generally is that of A. H. M. Jones, *The Later Roman Empire 284–602* (3 vols., Oxford 1964), ch. XX. On the literary evidence, see K. Hannestad, *L'évolution des ressources agricoles à l'Italie* (K. Danske Videnskabernes Selskab, *Historisk-filosofiske Meddelelser*, 40 no. 1, 1962); on the *massa* Calvisiana, D. Adamesteanu, "Due problemi topografici del retroterro gelese" (Accademia nazionale dei Lincei, *Rendiconti della Classe di scienze morali* . . . , 8th ser., 10 (1955) 198–210); P. Orlandini, "Lo scavo del thesmophorion di Bitalemi e il culto delle divinità ctonie a Gela", *Kokalos* 12 (1966) 8–35.

I have followed the analysis and chronology of the villa at Casale (Piazza Armerina) originally proposed by A. Carandini, *Ricerche sulle stile e la cronologia dei mosaici della villa di Piazza Armerina* (Rome 1964), elaborated and slightly modified by Carandini and others, "La villa del Casale a Piazza Armerina. Problemi, saggi stratigrafici ed altre ricerche", *Mélanges de l'École française de Rome: Antiquité* 83 (1971) 141–281.

On aspects of culture: N. Bonacasa, *Ritratti greci e romani della Sicilia* (Palermo 1964), with review by J. and J. Ch. Balty in *L'Antiquité classique* 35 (1966) 529–47; V. Tusa, *I sarcofagi romani in Sicilia* (*Atti dell' Accademia di scienze, lettere e arti di Palermo*, Supp. no. 5, 1957); I. R. Arnold, "Agonistic festivals in Italy and Sicily", *American Journal of Archaeology* 64 (1960) 245–51; G. Sfameni Gasparro, *I Culti orientali in Sicilia* (Leiden 1973), uncritical but valuable for the catalogue of objects and monuments; L. Robert, "Epitaphe d'un comédien à Messine", *Hellenica* 11/12 (1960) 330–42; S. Lagona, "L'acquedotto romano di Catania", *Cronache di archeologia e di storia dell' arte* 3 (1964) 69–86.

On language: O. Parlangèli, "Contributi allo studio della grecità siciliana", *Kokalos* 5 (1959) 62–106 (but see the comment in the next section of this bibliography); G. Manganaro, "Tauromenitana", *Archeologia classica* 15 (1963) 13–31, and "Iscrizioni latine e greche del nuovo edificio termale di Taormina", *Cronache di archeologia e di storia dell' arte* 3 (1964) 38–68.

Christianity

S. L. Agnello, *Silloge di iscrizioni paleocristiane della Sicilia* (Rome 1953), offers a selection of 85 Greek and 21 Latin epitaphs, nearly all from Syracuse and Catania, with translation and commentary. New finds are reported in the *Rivista di archeologia cristiana*, though not as fully as the archaeological material. A systematic summary of the letters of Gregory the Great is given by Holm, *Geschichte Siciliens* (already cited under general works) III 286–312.

On the documents and finds discussed in the text: P. Orsi, "Messana. La necropoli romana di S. Placido", *Monumenti antichi* 24 (1916) 121–218, and, on the burial practices generally, A. D. Nock, "Cremation and Burial in the Roman Empire", *Harvard Theological Review* 25 (1932) 321–59; A. M. Bisi, "Influenze italiote e siceliote sull' arte tardo-punica: Le stele funerarie di Lilibeo", *Archeologia classica* 22 (1970) 92–130; G. Manganaro "Nuovi documenti magici della Sicilia orientale" (Accademia nazionale dei Lincei, *Rendiconti della Classe di scienze morali* . . . , 8th ser., 18 (1963) 57–74), and "Iscrizioni latine e greche di Catania tardo imperiale", *Archivio storico per la Sicilia orientale*, 11/12 (1958–9) 5–30, on the epitaph of Julia Florentina; A. Di Vita, "Una nuova testimonianza di latino 'volgare' della Sicilia sudorientale: l'epitaffio di Zoe", *Kokalos* 7 (1961) 199–215; S. Calderone, "Per la storia dell' elemento giudaico nelle Sicilia imperiale" (Accademia nazionale dei Lincei, *Rendiconti della Classe di scienze morali* . . . , 8th ser., 10 (1955) 489–502); G. Libertini, "Epigrafe giudaico-latine rinvenuta a Catania", *Atti della Accademia delle Scienze di Torino, Classe di scienze morali* . . . , 64 (1928–9) 185–95.

On the predominance of Greek, the point of view here adopted is that of S. Borsari, *Il monachesimo bizantino nella Sicilia e nell' Italia meridionale prenormanne* (Naples 1963), pp. 7–38, rather than that of Parlengèli and Di Vita already cited, or of the otherwise fundamental work of F. Lanzoni, *Le origini della diocesi antiche d'Italia* (Rome 1923), pp. 370–400.

The basic book on the catacombs remains J. Führer and V. Schultze, *Die altchristliche Grabstätten Siziliens* (*Jahrbuch des deutschen archäologischen Instituts*, Ergänzungsheft VII, 1907), despite weaknesses in the general historical analysis. On newer excavations: S. L. Agnello, "Recenti esplorazioni nelle catacomba siracusana di S. Lucia", *Rivista di archeologia cristiana* 30 (1954) 7–60, 31 (1955) 7–50; L. Bonomi, "Cimiteri paleocristiani di Sofiana (Retroterra di Gela)", *Rivista di archeologia cristiana* 40 (1964) 169–220; D. Adamesteanu, "Nuovi documenti paleocristiani nella Sicilia centro-meridionale", *Bolletino d'arte* 48 (1963) 259–74.

Modern study of art and architecture is dominated by a series of fully illustrated publications by Giuseppe Agnello, including, among others, several shorter synoptic books, *I monumenti bizantini della Sicilia* (Florence 1951), primarily an account of 5th-7th century churches; *La pittura paleocristiana della Sicilia* (Vatican City 1952); *Palermo bizantina* (Amsterdam 1969); and a longer study of individual monuments and fragments, *Le arti figurativi nella Sicilia bizantina* (Palermo 1962); cf. his "Il ritrovamento subacqueo di una basilica bizantina prefabbricata", *Byzantion* 33 (1963) 1–9.

Byzantine Rule

There appears to be no satisfactory modern account of Byzantine Sicily. The chapter in vol. 4 of Pace's *Arte e civiltà* (cited early in this bibliography) is surprisingly scrappy and unreliable, while the standard histories of Byzantium deal with Sicily only incidentally.

Special studies: J. Gay, "Quelques remarques sur les papes grecs et syriens avant la querelle des iconoclastes (678–715)", in *Mélanges offerts à M. Gustave Schlumberger* (Paris 1924), pp. 40–54; V. Grumel, "L'annexion d'Illyricum oriental, de la Sicile et de la Calabrie au Patriarcat de Constantinople", *Recherches de science religieuse* 40 (1951–2) 191–200; S. Borsari, "L'amministrazione del tema di Sicilia", *Rivista storica italiana* 66 (1954) 133–58; N. Oikonomides, "Une liste arabe des stratèges byzantins du VIIe siècle et les origines des thèmes de Sicile", *Rivista di studi bizantini*, n.s. 1 (1964) 121–30; P. J. Alexander, "Les débuts des conquêtes arabes en Sicile et la tradition apocalyptique byzantinoslave", *Bulletino del Centro di studi . . . siciliani* 13 (1973) 5–35; G. Rohlfs, *Scavi linguistici nella Magna Grecia* (Rome 1933).

The great pioneering work of M. Amari, *Storia dei Musulmanni di Sicilia*, remains fundamental but it is organized in a complicated way and it sometimes suffers from an excess of imagination; the edition to consult is the 2nd, republished under the editorship of G. Levi della Vida and C. A. Nallino (3 vols. in 5, Catania 1930–9). Amari also published an Italian version of the Arabic sources for the period: *Biblioteca Arabo-Sicula* (Turin 1880). The best short account (only to 867) will be found in A. A. Vasiliev, *Byzance et les Arabes*, French ed. by H. Grégoire *et al.*, vol. 1 (Brussels 1935).

INDEX

213